RUSSIA SINCE

1917

J. N. Westwood

RUSSIA SINCE 1917

ST. MARTIN'S PRESS
New York

ISBN 0-312-69607-8

Library of Congress Cataloging in Publication Data

Westwood, J. N.
  Russia since 1917.

  Previous ed. (1966) published under title: Russia, 1917–1964.
  Includes index.
  1. Russia—Politics and government—1917–
I. Title.
DK266.W47 1980   947.084   79-27598
ISBN 0-312-69607-8   FE 12'82

084839

Preface

The preface to the previous edition of this book regretted that in a short account things which go wrong tend to receive more attention than those which go right. If this book sometimes reads like a chronology of trial and error, even of trials and terror, it is not because the author is unaware that, for example, the six decades of Soviet power have given new opportunities and inspiration to millions. It is simply that the deeper meanings of the Soviet experience are better left to a more discursive book.

In any case there is much to be said for an account that lays some emphasis on the problems and difficulties encountered by an authoritarian but well-intentioned regime struggling against six centuries of distorted development. The Soviet experience does have relevance outside the USSR. While western-style democracy may have leaned too far towards individual liberty at the expense of the collective good, Soviet-style democracy lies at the other extreme, and both can usefully learn from the other's self-generated difficulties.

The Soviet regime has an unusual respect for the truth, regarding it as too important to be left open to access by unauthorised persons. This means that key information is sometimes secreted away. However, this volume probably provides more factual information than other books of similar length; enough, it is hoped, to enable readers to develop their own conclusions.

J. N. WESTWOOD

Contents

CONTENTS

UNION OF SOVIET SOCIALIST REPUBLICS, 1950

SPITSBERGEN

ARCTIC OCE

NORWEGIAN   SEA

NORWAY

SWEDEN

Gulf of Bothnia

BALTIC SEA

BARENTS   SEA

ZEMLYA

NOVAYA
ZEMLYA

FINLAND

KARELIA

Murmansk

POLAND

Warsaw

ESTONIA
LATVIA
LITHUANIA

Leningrad
(Petrograd)

Archangel

ARCTIC   CIRCLE

WHITE
RUSSIA

UKRAINE

MOLDAVIA

Kiev

Moscow

Dnepr

Don

Kazan

Volga

URAL   MOUNTAINS

Ob

RUSSIAN   SOVI

SOCIALIS

Sverdlovsk
(Ekaterinburg)

BLACK

SEA

CAUCASUS

CAUCASUS   MTS

GEORGIA

ARMENIA
AZER
BAIJAN

Stalingrad
(Tsaritsyn)

Astrakhan

CASPIAN

SEA

Omsk

Kuzne
Basi

TURKEY

Baku

IRAQ

IRAN
(PERSIA)

ARAL
SEA

KAZAKHSTAN

Lake Balkhash

UZBEKISTAN

TURKMENISTAN

Bokhara

KIRGIZIA

Alma-Ata

TADZHIKISTAN

AFGHANISTAN

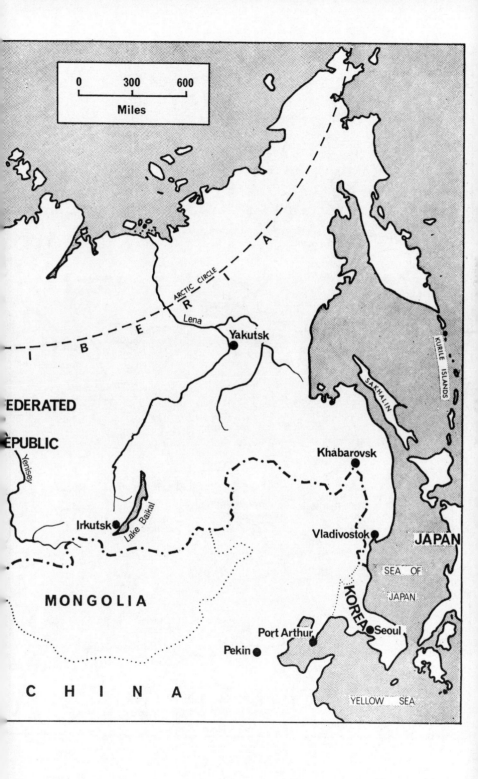

EUROPEAN RUSSIA, 1950

(1939 Boundary — — —)   0   200
                         Miles

I

The Revolutions

Tsarist Russia

IN 1914, for the second time in ten years, the Russia of Nicholas II was at war. In 1904 Russian ambitions in the Far East had led to the Russo-Japanese war, which saw the annihilation of the Russian fleet at Tsushima and the humiliation of the Russian army in Manchuria. Although the Japanese leaders carefully ascribed their victories to the benign influence of the spirits of their Emperor's ancestors, and Nicholas wondered why God had not favoured his cause, in reality the Russians were defeated because a willingness to sacrifice masses of stolid soldiers and sailors was not enough to compensate for poor leadership, poor equipment and poor training. The defeats of the war against Japan were followed by strikes inside Russia, the mutiny of troops returning home on the new Trans-Siberian Railway, and unorganised but armed rebellion in many cities. This rebellion, which passed into history as the 1905 Revolution, was savagely quelled, but the Tsar was forced to make some concessions.

Among the concessions was a partial abandonment of autocracy. Hitherto the will of the Tsar had been absolute. He chose his own ministers and approved or refused to approve their proposals, while the ministers, who tended to owe their positions more to favouritism than to competence, carried out their administration through a network of officials. The latter collectively formed what was at that time the world's most inefficient, petrifying, abusive, corrupt, clumsy and unenterprising bureaucracy. After 1905 the Tsar agreed to allow an elected body, the Duma, to help rule the country. Although the ministers remained answerable to the Tsar and not to the Duma, those Russians who put their faith in the Duma envisaged that sooner or later it would develop into a Russian House of Commons, and that tsarism would evolve into constitutional monarchy. Nicholas and his favourites, however, had other ideas, and as the Tsar's position became stronger he began to limit rather than enhance the role of the Duma. Nevertheless, in the half-decade preceding the First World War there was significant social and economic improvement: local governments were able to improve the situation in education, health and roads, while the national economy which had already experienced a railway boom in the nineties began to develop at a fast rate. It is true that there were some serious strikes, but nevertheless life seemed to be getting better and Russian backwardness might have disappeared, given a few decades of peace, and a willingness on the part of the Tsar, the aristocracy and the bureaucracy to share their privileges and responsibilities with their fellow-citizens. But autocracy, aristocracy and bureaucracy did not weaken, and in 1914 came war.

It is arguable that Russian backwardness had its roots in the tenth century, when the ruler of Kievan Russia adopted the Greek Orthodox rendering of Christianity as the state religion. This choice of state religion isolated Russia from Roman Catholic Europe: there was no Renaissance for Russia. For ten centuries the Russian Orthodox Church was to persuade the people that their suffering under the tsars was good for the soul, and thereby dampened the urge for improvement.

Three centuries after the adoption of Orthodox Christianity another misfortune overtook Russia. The Tartars under Genghis Khan's successors advanced from Central Asia and easily conquered and colonised Russia. For over two centuries the country was under Tartar overlords, who employed trusted Russian princes as their bailiffs for the collection of tribute and the denouncing of enemies. This interposing of middlemen between ruler and ruled is possibly the origin of that Russian archetype, the official who cringes before superiors but bullies those who have less power than he: certainly the conditions under the Tartars and later under the tsars allowed this kind of person to flourish. The practice of denunciation was also fostered by the Tartar occupation. More than one Russian prince discovered that the easiest way to eliminate his rivals was to tell the khan that they were conspiring against the Tartars.

The Tartars were eventually driven out by the princes of Moscow, who later styled themselves 'Tsar' (i.e. Caesar), and established Muscovite Russia. From Moscow the boundaries of this state were forced out until, by 1914, Russia bordered Turkey, China, the Pacific and the Arctic, while Poland and Finland were subject territories. From the time of the early Moscow princes until the beginning of the nineteenth century there was a succession of entirely unlovable rulers, most of whom were eccentric and many bordering on insanity. While the comparatively harmless eccentricities are best remembered—Elizabeth's 4,000 dresses, Catherine the Great's innumerable lovers, Peter the Great's beard-cutting—these were cruel times, with the people impoverished and finding only in God and vodka comfort from famine, plague, rebellion, bureaucratic terrorism and, most important, serfdom.

Whereas Western Europe tended to give more and more freedom to its slave labour (serfs) so that eventually a more or less free peasantry developed, in Russia the process was reversed. In time the Russian peasant became a serf belonging absolutely to his owner. He could be exploited, beaten, starved, bought, sold, even given away to pay his master's gambling debts, and could only escape by attempting against all the odds to flee to the borderlands of Russia. He was obliged to work on the land of his owner and in return was allowed to scrape a meagre living from his own little plot.

In the nineteenth century there were tsars, like Alexander I and Alexander II, who realised that changes were necessary, and that in particular serfdom should be abolished. But because the landowners, the most influential class, had a vested interest in the serf system, the reforming wishes of the tsars were usually circumvented. Nevertheless in 1861 the serfs were at last formally freed, but because of the resistance of the landowners what they obtained was only personal freedom on hire-purchase terms (the government compensated the serf-owners, and in turn the new free peasants reimbursed the government over a period of years). The redemption payments, the fact that the landowners still kept their land for themselves, and the general ignorance and inability of the peasants to look after themselves after centuries of dependence meant that most began to feel that they were worse off than before. Later there were some reforms to answer this dissatisfaction and on the eve of the First World War there was emerging a prosperous group of successful peasant farmers owning their own land. But the majority of peasants were dissatisfied with their role as landless hired labourers, faced with the choice of working for the minority of well-off peasants or of migrating to the growing industries of the towns.

But progress was slow and this, together with the impatience of a small but growing educated class which was denied political power, led to the emergence of groups believing that only the overthrow of tsarism would enable Russia to overcome its backwardness. The

13

revolutionary activities of these groups caused even the most reformist tsars to adopt repressive policies, and this in turn drove ever-increasing numbers of educated Russians into the ranks of the revolutionaries.

The Revolutionaries

There was a succession of peasant rebellions throughout the tsarist period of Russian history. Most were small and local, typically involving the murder of a landowner by his resentful serfs, or the burning of his farmstead. Only a few rebellions, like those of Stenka Razin and Pugachov, attracted large-scale support and seemed to threaten the autocracy, before they were cruelly suppressed. Besides these, the tsars lived in fear of palace revolts; a suspicious—paranoid even— nature was the best guarantee of survival. Ivan the Terrible surrounded himself with devoted thugs as protection against real and imagined enemies; Peter the Great killed his own son, when he suspected that he might become a threat to his own rule. Paul I despite his suspicions did not escape his murderers, who had the acquiescence of his son the future Alexander I.

But in the nineteenth century the threat came from a new quarter, from the educated. After Napoleon had been defeated in Russia in 1812, the Tsar's troops occupied Paris and returned home to spread the news that, compared to Western Europe, Russia was dead, drab, repressed and backward. The first open manifestation of the army officers' desire for change came in 1825 in the so-called Decembrist Revolt. When Alexander I died, his two brothers, Nicholas in Russia and Constantine in Poland, each thinking that the other was the new Tsar, swore allegiance to each other. The St Petersburg officers took advantage of the resulting confusion to stage a revolt against autocracy. But this failed and the plotters were executed or sent to Siberia.

For some time after, those of the gentry whose consciences were troubled by the plight of the peasants and of the poor contented themselves with clandestine meetings at which were discussed new ideas contained in books smuggled from abroad. The government meanwhile improved its secret police (the 'Third Section'), with its spy and informer network. Occasional arrests and deportations were made, and many intellectuals went to live abroad where they could openly develop their revolutionary philosophies. Some of the émigrés printed their own Russian-language periodicals and pamphlets, which they contrived to smuggle in to their sympathisers at home.

The chaos of the Crimean War and the petering out of Alexander II's reforming zeal raised new recruits for the revolutionary groups, especially among students. There were many different tendencies among these. Although all regarded tsarism as the enemy, some merely wished to reform it while others hoped to destroy it. Some trusted that time and education would lead to a slow but peaceful change, while others held that only a revolution would solve Russia's problems. In the seventies the Populist movement became strong. This sent young enthusiasts into the villages as revolutionary missionaries. But their ignorance of village life and customs, their failure to realise that the peasants were not capable of grasping abstract revolutionary ideas, and the peasants' loyalty to the Tsar, caused these missions to be a miserable failure: many of the Populists were denounced to the police by the peasants themselves. However, they did learn that to achieve success they had to vulgarise their lofty principles into simple slogans which even the most thick-headed peasant could grasp and approve.

From the Populists developed the 'Land and Liberty' movement, again mainly interested in the peasantry: it proposed that the landowners' estates should be handed over to the peasants, and that there should be a popularly-elected government. Unlike its predecessors, it gave much attention to organisation: it had its own printing press, employed full-time paid revolutionary activists, and placed its own spies in the Third Section. This movement gradually came under the control of those with a leaning towards terrorism. Some spectacular successes were achieved, including the murder not only of several local police chiefs but also the head of the Third Section himself. But the members became obsessed by a desire to kill the Tsar, and after many attempts succeeded in 1881 in exploding a bomb under him. In so doing they killed a number of innocent bystanders, spoiled their own chances because the peasants whose interests they claimed to be advancing were incensed by the murder of Alexander, and moreover prevented changes which they themselves had demanded because the Tsar had been on the point of approving a set of new reforms.

In the following two decades these revolutionaries, whose roots were in Populism and who put their faith in the peasantry, developed into the Social Revolutionary Party. Together with a violent past, they inherited the policy of confiscating the big estates and dividing the land among the peasants. This policy naturally gained them increasing support among the peasantry. Meanwhile, however, rival revolutionary groups were devoting themselves to the town workers, Russia's small but growing proletariat.

The Marxists

Karl Marx was born in Germany in 1818, but was soon obliged to emigrate, and spent the most productive part of his life in London, where he associated with another like-minded intellectual, Engels. Among other things, these two were notable for being the first influential economists to treat unemployment as an evil which is predictable and avoidable. They are more celebrated, however, for their writings on the relationships between economics, politics and society —of which the best-known are their *Communist Manifesto* and *Capital* —in which they postulated that society, like the physical world, depends on certain fixed laws and can therefore be studied scientifically.

What became known as Marxism is an enormous body of detail from which is derived a number of salient 'laws' of social development. Different Marxists have tended to adopt different, sometimes conflicting, interpretations of the philosophy. The aspects of Marxism which have had most significance for subsequent Russian history are dialectical materialism and historical materialism.

The former asserts that change is not so much the replacement of the old by the new, but a struggle between old and new from which emerges something combining the features of both. Any situation (the 'thesis') is matched by a directly opposing situation ('antithesis'), and between them is an 'inherent contradiction'. From the inevitable struggle between thesis and antithesis there is born the 'synthesis', which combines and replaces both. Marx used this approach in his analysis of society, and detected various relationships between different social groups. Historical materialism is the all-embracing system and pattern which he described, and which seemed to account for all the social phenomena he had observed.

Historical materialism claims that it is the nature of the means of production (tools and techniques) which determines the shape of society. This is because the means of production in use at a given time require a certain type of organisation of production and of trade; steam power, for example, could not be utilised by cottage industry and hence the factory system developed. In turn, the way production is organised determines the structure of society and its division into certain classes; there were no shepherds when man lived by hunting, no factory-owners before factory production appeared. Although each class makes use of (exploits) the others, there is always one particular small class which contributes little but over-exploits the rest of society because it has control over the means of production: slave-owners in one era, landowners in another, capital-owners in Marx's time. Finally, the structure of society determines the nature of its political institutions. The latter, which organise and administer society, also mitigate the contradictions between various classes. When these contradictions become unmanageable, when for example the class which owns the old means of production refuses to hand over political power to the class owning the new means of production (as when a land-owning aristocracy refuses to concede power to an emerging merchant and capital-owning class), equilibrium is achieved by revolution.

Marx noted that in primitive communal society, where the production process was simple, there was no division of labour and hence no classes. Each individual made his contribution to the common effort and received his due share of what was produced. According to Marx, mankind's task was to return to this 'communist' organisation of society, while retaining the modern prolific means and methods of production. He believed that the time was ripe for the 'historically inevitable' revolution which would introduce a new society, in which for the first time since the disappearance of the primitive communes there would be no struggle between classes. He had observed that social structure depends on who owns the means of production and that when industry and trade developed those who controlled these new productive forces—the capitalists—had wrested political power from the monarchy and aristocracy. Moreover, wrote Marx, under capitalism production was embarked upon not directly for use, but for profit. Thus the capitalist entrepreneur was superfluous: he was working for profit, not for society. Marx concluded from all this that in western society (France, Germany, England) the capitalists would continue to use their political power progressively to impoverish and exploit the proletariat (i.e. the town wage-earners) for their own profit, until one day the latter would rise and become the new ruling class, owning the most important and only permanent means of production —their own labour. This proletarian revolution would eventually produce a classless society, where there would be no exploitation of man by man, where the conventional controls of government could be dispensed with, and each person would contribute according to his ability and receive according to his needs.

Marxist thinkers, armed with this doctrine, produced many novel, breathtaking even, insights into modern society. Undoubtedly their way of looking at society enabled them to see things which had hitherto been unnoticed. It is true also that the Marxist technique was sometimes abused, and quite untenable conclusions reached. But a hundred years after Marx his approach is still a valuable and incisive analytical tool; even those who deny this are often unconsciously influenced by it. Certainly Marx's interpretation of human history in terms of economics (that is, man's struggle against, and exploitation of, his environment) is more useful than the concept of history as a succession of kings and battles.

On the other hand it may also be admitted that some of the common criticisms of Marxism cannot be lightly dismissed. It is perhaps true that Marx undervalued non-economic forces (tradition, patterns of culture, human foibles, etc.), although such factors were more important in static societies than in rapidly changing Europe. Another criticism has been that Marxists, believing in the inevitable revolution resulting from the inherent contradictions of capitalism, have opposed any mitigation of those contradictions (that is, they have opposed reform) because it would slow down the revolutionary process. A third criticism has been that, while Marx's analysis of social history may have been invaluable, the blueprint he provided for what would happen after the proletarian revolution was vague and unhelpful.

Despite criticisms, the philosophy was welcomed by many who were disturbed by the sub-human situation of the workers and who were glad to be shown that this would be remedied by a historically inevitable process. It provided an intellectual backing for those who advocated revolution; they now not only felt, but knew, that the ruling class should be overthrown. Moreover, the Marxist way of looking at society did seem to provide a guide to what should happen after the revolution. The philosophy had a special allure in Russia, and in 1898 the Russian Social Democratic Party was formed to promote Marxist ideas. But Marxism was difficult to apply in Russia, because that country was still primarily peasant, not proletarian, and had yet to experience the capitalist or 'bourgeois' revolution which had long since occurred in Western Europe and which according to Marx had to precede the final, workers', revolution. The ruling class was still the monarchy and its bureaucracy, not the bourgeoisie. Thus some Russian Marxists, unable to envisage an immediate proletarian revolution, devoted themselves to priming the prerequisite bourgeois revolution, while others totally abandoned the idea of revolutionary changes and occupied themselves with agitating for better treatment of the workers and encouraging trade unionism. Marxism in Russia could not provide ideological backing for a party which wished to be dynamic and revolutionary. At least, not until the doctrine had been Russianised by Lenin.

Lenin and the Bolsheviks

Vladimir Ilyitch Ulyanov was born in 1870. His father was a school inspector of moderately liberal views. When Vladimir Ilyitch was 17 his elder brother was executed for plotting a murder attempt on the Tsar, and he himself was expelled from Kazan University. He soon became a leading St Petersburg Marxist and was duly imprisoned and then sentenced to a quite comfortable exile in Siberia. In exile he married a fellow-revolutionary, Krupskaya, and in 1900 he joined the Russian émigrés, spending most of his time up to 1917 in England and Switzerland, where he organised his supporters, and played the leading part in producing the illegal newspaper *Iskra*, which was smuggled into Russia together with copies of other revolutionary books and pamphlets. In 1901 he adopted his final pseudonym, Lenin, derived from the River Lena in Siberia.*

Lenin was energetic, single-minded, and strong-willed. He also had a useful unscrupulousness in dealing with those who opposed him. This was not because he was ruthless and dishonest by nature, but because he was so certain of his own rightness that any means of assuring the victory of his ideas seemed justified, and in any case he had rejected much of conventional morality. (This ruthlessness subsequently became a hallmark of successful Communist leaders, including some who possessed few other qualities to excuse it.)

What Lenin brought to the Russian Marxists was a modification of doctrine to make Marxism more suitable for Russian conditions, and the concept of a select and professionalised party, single-minded and able, if necessary, to act decisively without the support of public opinion. He incorporated into Marxist doctrine the possibility of one social class making not one, but two, revolutions. This concept at once enabled Marxists to expect a workers' revolution in their own lifetime. It also gave a place to Russia's dominant social class, the peasantry; for in the first—bourgeois—revolution envisaged by Lenin

---

* Revolutionary pseudonyms became common among the Marxists; Stalin means 'man of steel', Molotov is derived from the word 'hammer'. Another Marxist, Bronstein, chose the name Trotsky, probably derived from the German word for 'resistance'. Trotsky's brother-in-law Rosenfeld called himself Kamenev—'stone'.

the bourgeois attack on the monarchy was to be stimulated and largely executed by the proletariat acting in alliance with the peasants. In the second revolution the proletariat would overthrow the bourgeoisie, again with the help of the peasantry.

Lenin realised that neither the workers nor the peasants were really interested in Marxism or in revolution; they simply wanted to improve their own material situation. Lenin's devoted élite party would therefore become the 'vanguard of the working class' and would strive to teach the workers that their true interest lay in revolution, not just in wage increases and better working conditions.

The party which Lenin created was highly professionalised, with its officials receiving a salary from party funds. There was inflexible discipline and unquestioned obedience to the centre: that is, to Lenin. At a congress of the Russian Social Democratic Party held in London in 1902 Lenin caused a split and the movement divided into two factions, Lenin's 'Bolshevik' Party and the 'Menshevik' Party, whose adherents would not accept Lenin's unscrupulousness and his demand for tight control over members. The next two years witnessed constant squabbles between the two factions, especially among the émigrés, and this was one reason why the Marxists were ineffective during the 1905 Revolution. In this competition the Mensheviks had more support (especially among the workers) but this was balanced by the greater decisiveness of the Bolsheviks.

The pre-war decade was a lean time for the revolutionaries. With their leaders abroad and engaged in pamphlet quarrels, and various reforms and improvements taking place inside Russia, it seemed that peaceful and constitutional evolution promised more than revolution. Support for the Marxists, and especially for the Bolshevik wing, further diminished in the first years of the First World War, when a genuine if misguided patriotism inspired all parties—except, that is, Lenin's, who openly hoped for a Russian defeat which would pave the way for revolution.

The Russian Revolution

After some successes it soon became clear that Russia had again embarked on a war for which she was ill-prepared. The soldiers lacked munitions, equipment and clothing, and the railways were failing. Readiness to throw into battle masses of poorly trained and poorly equipped infantry was of little avail, and by the third winter of the war Russians of all classes saw the need for a change of government. The upper classes were repelled by the intrigues at St Petersburg (now renamed Petrograd, which sounded less Teutonic). In the Tsar's absence, the Empress under the influence of Rasputin—a politically ignorant holy man—interfered in government and planted incompetent favourites in key positions. The townspeople were hard-hit by rising prices and by transport breakdowns which caused food shortages. The peasants were the main suppliers both of infantry and horses and were beginning to realise that both were being uselessly sacrificed.

In December 1916 Prince Yusupov and his associates filled Rasputin with cyanide and bullets and dumped the body in the River Neva; so strong was approval of this deed that the assassins were merely exiled to their country estates. In March 1917 bread rationing was introduced in the capital, and badly organised. There were strikes and then street demonstrations, followed by riots and bigger strikes and demonstrations. Many of the garrison troops who were ordered to suppress the disturbances showed sympathy towards the demonstrators, and some joined in. A few officials and ministers were roughly handled, prisoners were released, and the courts burned. In all there were about a thousand serious casualties in March in Petrograd, but little blood was shed elsewhere.

Meanwhile, the few revolutionary leaders still in Petrograd organised a council ('soviet') of workers' and soldiers' representatives, elected by factories and by regiments. This Soviet held its sessions next to the Duma. Then, in mid-March, Nicholas was persuaded by his generals and the Duma leaders to abdicate. The Grand Duke Michael, whom he appointed as his successor, refused the title: Russia was without a Tsar.

What was left to fill the power vacuum was the Soviet of Workers and Soldiers, which had an executive representing various left-wing parties and factions (including the Bolsheviks), and the Duma, which formed a Provisional Government composed of liberal and conservative leaders (and one Social Revolutionary). The Duma suspected that the Soviet was deliberately fostering violence and chaos, while the Soviet feared that the Duma (which after all was a legal and properly-elected body) would use troops to suppress it. Both the Duma and the Soviet were afraid that monarchist army officers would mobilise forces to restore the old regime. Largely to forestall this the Soviet issued its famous Order No. 1, which called on soldiers to ignore their officers and elect their own regimental committees.

The Soviet and the Duma agreed to maintain Provisional Government consisting chiefly of Duma members and to arrange country-wide elections for a Constituent Assembly, which would decide how the new Russia should be ruled. Meanwhile the German government, anxious to promote chaos in Russia so that it would be forced out of the war, arranged the shipment of about 30 revolutionary émigrés (including Lenin and other Bolsheviks) from Switzerland to Petrograd.

The Bolshevik Revolution

Lenin arrived in Petrograd in mid-April and immediately criticised the local Bolsheviks for co-operating so willingly with the other left-wing groups in the Soviet. He declared that the Provisional Government should receive no support that the land should be given to the peasants and that the war against Germany should stop. Although many Bolsheviks at first opposed him they changed their minds when they realised that slogans like 'All land to the Peasants' and 'No More War' were gaining support for the Party. In May, anti-government demonstrations were staged, resulting in six left-wing ministers joining the Provisional Government and Kerensky, a Social Revolutionary and a member of the Soviet, becoming Minister of War.

Kerensky, partly in response to western pleas, partly to create a wave of patriotism which would carry the Government forward, launched a big offensive in July which after initial advances degenerated into a retreat. This defeat, together with Bolshevik agitation,* set off further demonstrations and the slogan 'All Power to the Soviets' was put forward. Revolutionary sailors from the Kronstadt naval base were brought to the capital by the Bolsheviks, who hoped to unseat the Government.

But this first attempt to dislodge the Provisional Government failed to win enough popular support and, when it was reported that the Bolsheviks had received money from the German government, opinion in the streets turned against them. Lenin was forced into hiding in Finland. Kerensky became Prime Minister and the remaining Bolsheviks contented themselves with propaganda work, especially in the army, and with the creation of their own illegal armed force. This was the Red Guard, consisting of factory workers equipped with rifles purloined from the army.

---

* 'Agitation' in Bolshevik usage means 'stirring up', and usually refers to verbal, grass-roots, propaganda activity.

In September a combination of mistrust and misunderstanding caused the Commander-in-Chief, Kornilov, to march against Petrograd. His advance fizzled out, defeated more by the Petrograd Soviet than by Kerensky; Kornilov's soldiers, confronted by armed workers from the capital and influenced by Bolshevik agitation in their ranks, refused to fight. The Bolshevik members of the Soviet had a leading part in these events and could henceforth claim to have 'saved the Revolution'. Trotsky, a former Menshevik turned Bolshevik, and a brilliant orator and organiser, was released from prison; Bolsheviks began to muster majorities in the Petrograd Soviet and the subsequently formed Moscow Soviet.

At the same time those who wished to see the restoration of law and order lost confidence in the Provisional Government. Under the sway of the liberal minister Milyukov, it had certainly achieved some needed reforms—freedom of the press, equal rights for Jews, abolition of the death penalty, real autonomy for Poland and Finland —but it could only act with the acquiescence of the Soviet. It had responsibility but lacked authority. A politically mature middle class on which it might have leaned had never developed under tsarist autocracy. The weakness induced by the two-headed leadership (with the Soviet constantly gaining public support at the expense of the government and Duma) was paralleled by the growing ineffectiveness of the Social Revolutionaries, who were numerically strong in both the Soviet and the Duma. They were split into various factions and moreover were hampered by their desire, or need, to coalesce with the liberal Cadet Party. The latter opposed determined action (including at one stage determined action against the Bolsheviks) and succeeded in postponing the convening of the promised Constituent Assembly. The Provisional Government lost much support among the peasants by postponing land reform so that it might be discussed by the Constituent Assembly. Also, its continuation of the war hampered its action in other fields and was an enormous burden; but peace with Germany was possible only at a very high territorial price which few Russians would accept.

In October the Petrograd Soviet appointed a 'Military Revolutionary Committee' to prevent another Kornilov-type threat, and under the leadership of Trotsky the Bolshevik members of this soon dominated its proceedings. Trotsky succeeded in obtaining rifles for thousands more of the Red Guard, agitators continued their work, street demonstrations were organised. By this time the Provisional Government could muster few reliable forces; the old and unpopular police force had been disbanded and most army units were paralysed by Bolshevik agitation. On 6 November Lenin appeared in disguise at the Bolshevik headquarters and that night the Red Guards occupied key points in the capital—railway stations, telephone exchanges, banks, printing presses. Kerensky slipped out of the Winter Palace, where his ministers were conferring, to seek loyal troops. In his absence the Palace was occupied by Red Guards and sailors, and the ministers were arrested. Kerensky was unable to assemble a reliable army to restore the situation; at one point he only escaped capture by disguising himself as a sailor. He took no further part in events, settling down to a long and comparatively quiet life in the USA.

In Petrograd the Bolshevik takeover had been almost bloodless, but in Moscow and some other towns there was protracted fighting as the Bolsheviks took power with their armed workers, soldiers and sailors. And except in a few solidly 'Red' localities, like Kronstadt, there was a possibility of counter-insurrection. Moreover, having used the support of other left-wing parties, the Bolsheviks were faced with the possibility of a coalition government, a prospect which Lenin did not relish. At the Congress of Soviets, which met immediately after the Bolshevik coup and contained representatives of workers' and peasants' soviets from many Russian towns, the Bolsheviks and their temporary ally, the Left Social Revolutionary Party, had a majority. But they were faced with strong opposition from orthodox Social Revolutionaries and Mensheviks. However, taking advantage of a protest walk-out by their opponents, they passed resolutions establishing the Congress as the supreme ruling body, appointing a Council of People's Commissars (all Bolsheviks) to be a ruling cabinet, confiscating the landowners' estates, and proposing an end to the war with Germany.

Thus the Bolsheviks—even though they lacked the support of a majority of Russians—were in power.

II

War Communism

The Civil War

HAVING ACHIEVED POWER, its retention was the main preoccupation of the Bolsheviks for the next four years. In 1917 there seemed little reason to suppose that the Bolshevik Party—soon renamed the *Communist Party of the Soviet Union (Bolsheviks)*, or CPSU (B)—would hold power any longer than its predecessor. After all, it was numerically small, its policies had hitherto been disruptive rather than constructive, and it was not popular. Yet in fact the Communists did consolidate their position and by 1921 other political groups had been destroyed.

The period from the October Revolution* to the summer of 1921 is dominated by the Russian Civil War and by the savage and austere internal policy known as War Communism. Although by the end of 1917 the Bolsheviks controlled Petrograd, Moscow and most of the key cities, they had less influence in the countryside and none at all in many outlying areas. It was not difficult therefore for their opponents to assemble and organise anti-Red (i.e. White) armies. These opponents were initially army officers who had seen their units dissolve under the influence of Red agitation, and who believed the Bolsheviks to be in alliance with the Germans against Holy Russia.

The assembly of White forces, the advance of German armies, and the declarations of independence by former Russian dominions (the Ukraine, Poland, Finland, the Baltic Provinces, the Caucasus and Central Asia), together with pressure and intervention from Russia's former allies (notably England and France), all added up to a threat which seemed certain to sweep the Bolsheviks from power. Lenin's policy in these circumstances was to suffer temporary humiliation by

---

* Which took place in November 1917, according to the western Gregorian Calendar, introduced in Russia in 1918.

making peace with Germany and accepting the dismemberment of the old Russian Empire, thus gaining the freedom to concentrate his forces against the Whites. In the meantime he temporarily cultivated the friendship or at least the acquiescence of political parties of the left, so long as this did not involve compromise, and supported revolutionary movements abroad.

Intervention by the West was half-hearted and muddled, and was hardly directed against the Bolsheviks as such, even though the Whites did receive much material and technical help. Although there were times when the fate of the Reds hung in the balance, the inability of the Whites to agree among themselves threw away their chances of victory. The Reds were better disciplined, and with their internal lines of communication could switch their forces from one front to another as the military situation changed. Local populations had little affection for either Reds or Whites, but the former handled them more successfully and were less troubled with rebellions in their rear. Moreover, the Whites were associated with the former ruling and property-owning classes, and nowhere in the world was the gulf between the under-privileged and the well-endowed so great and so skilfully exploited. At the end of 1920 the last White army was forced to evacuate the Crimea, and the Civil War was over.

The Party

One reason why so many observers underrated the Bolsheviks was their failure to realise that this was a political party of an entirely new kind. Other Russian parties were characterised by a lack of realism and an inability to reach agreement either by compromise or by coercion. This was why they so frequently split into ineffective splinter groups. With the Bolsheviks it was different: they were disciplined and dedicated, and were led by men who knew what they wanted and were sufficiently ruthless and intelligent to choose the best means of getting it.

They were disciplined largely because they were carefully chosen. Not everyone could become a Party member. Despite its belief in the historic role of the masses, the Party had no intention of becoming a mass party. Rather was it conceived as a kind of élite which, though rooted in the masses, would yet lead them. In its early years this theoretical concept was adhered to in practice: even though its leaders were educated men and usually of bourgeois origin the rank and file was drawn principally from workers, students and soldiers. From its beginnings in tsarist times up to the end of the Civil War a Party member was usually a man of courage and dedication; the tsarist police were not gentle in their treatment of Bolsheviks, and capture by the Whites in the Civil War meant certain execution. Yet despite its losses during the Civil War there were rarely lacking new recruits to maintain the Party's strength.

Not all depletions were at the hands of the enemy. Because Communists were expected to set an example of restrained and up-right behaviour they were always liable to expulsion from the Party should they fail to satisfy its standards. Execution was also a distinct possibility. An army commissar found drunk on duty, or suspected of cowardice, might well be shot. (The White Army, in contrast, seemed to take no action against its own drunken officers.)

Probably the most decisive feature of the Party was, and remains, the obedience of members to its orders. No matter what task or policy was laid down it was the duty of the individual member to carry it out irrespective of any personal fear or misgivings. At meetings proposals could be discussed, disputed and rejected, but once a proposal was accepted it became a decision and an unquestionable obligation. Those who had voted against were expected to pursue it as enthusiastically as those who had voted for. This could mean that a Party member might deliver a speech one day in direct contradiction to what he had said the day before, and this gave opponents a chance to deride the Bolsheviks. On the other hand, at times of crisis the speed with which the Communists moved into action was limited only by the speed with which decisions were taken. There was no need to waste time persuading recalcitrant members to conform.

The organisation of the Communist Party was based on 'Democratic Centralism', with the emphasis more and more on centralism. This term meant that while the centre, or top leadership, was in unquestioned command the lower ranks had a chance to influence policy. The basic group was the cell, which consisted of a handful of members who happened to be employed in a given army unit, institution or factory (at this time about one factory worker in every 20 was a Party member). The cell would elect a representative to the next higher body, the town committee, which in turn would be represented on the provincial body, and so on, the supreme national Party organ being the Party Congress. As this Congress met only annually, it elected a Central Committee consisting of less than one-tenth of its members to carry on its day-to-day work. A fraction of the members of the Central Committee made up the Political Bureau, which decided matters needing prompt action. In the Civil War period this Politburo usually consisted of five members, of whom two were always Lenin and Trotsky. The Central Committee also had an Organisation Bureau which was responsible for allocating duties among the members.

While this pyramid of authority seemed to permit lower bodies to choose the members of the higher organisations, usually the former voted into office persons approved by the leaders. In the conditions under which the Party worked there was less place for the democratic process than had been hoped. Obedience was the main ingredient of success and implied among other things voting for persons recommended by the leadership. Usually this was done quite willingly, for there was a great difference of intellect and knowledge between the leaders and the ordinary members. The Party was in some ways a military-style organisation, with the majority of its members ready and conditioned to do or die under the trusted guidance of its high command.

In practice the Central Committee rarely questioned the decisions of its Politburo, nor did the annual Congress have a decisive influence, although on certain issues it was able to modify Party policy. In reality, therefore, Russia was ruled by a handful of men. Lenin of course was the undisputed leader, but his proposals were always open to criticism and when such criticism was strong he was usually prepared to compromise. However, his political sense was so acute and his analysis of situations so unerring that his colleagues were usually content to follow his lead. On the most important occasion when Lenin's recommendation (for an immediate peace with Germany) was not accepted, later events proved him right. Although Lenin at times showed no hesitation in dismissing the incompetent, and even though he occasionally arranged suitably distant assignments for colleagues who were opposed to him, he never excluded from political life Communists of proven ability, even though they might criticise his policies and even himself. This was a key difference between Lenin and his successors.

At this time Lenin's main colleagues were Trotsky, Kamenev, Zinoviev, Dzerzhinsky, Sverdlov, Chicherin, Bukharin, Rykov, Stalin and Krassin. If Lenin was the grand strategist of the Civil War, Trotsky was its hero. Without his work, particularly his virtual creation of the Red Army, the Bolsheviks would certainly have been defeated. At times his individualistic behaviour made him difficult to work with, he was prone to order disciplinary executions with a song in his heart, and on occasions he was brilliantly wrong, but there is little doubt that his intelligence, energy and oratory made a contribution to the Bolshevik cause second only to Lenin's. Kamenev and Zinoviev were old associates of Lenin and were responsible for Moscow and Petrograd respectively. Dzerzhinsky was a Polish Communist with a blend of fanaticism, idealism and ruthlessness which made him an ideal choice as head of the Cheka, the terroristic counter-revolutionary militia. Sverdlov and Stalin were good organisers. The former as president of the Soviet Executive Committee (i.e. head of the 'government') and Lenin as head of the Party settled many administrative matters between themselves. Bukharin was an effective orator and specialist in Communist ideology. Rykov was another veteran Communist and was responsible for industry, in which he was assisted by Krassin, an engineer with useful industrial and commercial experience. Chicherin, unlike his colleagues, was neither bourgeois nor proletarian. He was of an old aristocratic family, highly cultured and somewhat eccentric—qualities which suited him for his position as People's Commissar* for Foreign Affairs.

Party membership fluctuated wildly in this period between the Revolution and the end of the Civil War. When things were going well for the Bolsheviks, membership tended to increase as the Party attracted careerists eager to jump on the bandwagon. To counter this there was a purge in 1919, when the credentials of all members were examined and many of those suspected of being 'radishes' (i.e. red outside, white inside) were expelled. Thus by the end of 1919 membership stood at around 150,000, compared to about double that number before the purge. However, this reduction was followed by a deterioration in the military situation and a consequent Party recruiting drive. It was assumed that at this time of doubt only the most dedicated would venture to join, but as the Whites retreated membership again inflated and by the spring of 1921 there were nearly three-quarters of a million members.

Agitation and leadership were the functions of the Party member. By setting an example of upright behaviour and friendliness he or she could gain the confidence of workmates and colleagues, quietly convincing them of the virtues of the Bolshevik cause. As the member's position became stronger he could organise meetings which would pass resolutions in line with Party policy, agreeing to work harder or fight more bravely, and to expose enemies or slackers.

* Between 1917 and 1946 the term 'People's Commissar' replaced 'Minister'.

Voting at such meetings was by a show of hands, which meant that pressure could be brought on the unenthusiastic. It was Communists who organised the 'Communist Saturday' on the Moscow–Kazan Railway, on which members voluntarily worked on their holiday. This idea spread and it was not long before non-Party workers also were working on holidays all over Russia. In areas occupied by the Whites the Party cells which survived went underground, spreading anti-White propaganda and preparing the ground for revolts and disturbances. In these ways the Party member justified his description as 'vanguard of the working class', enabling the Politburo to communicate with and mobilise not only the Party but also much of the working population.

Although the Bolsheviks had a solidarity lacking in other parties, serious disagreements did appear from time to time. The so-called Left Communists were jealous of what they considered the original purity of the Party, and opposed on principle the humiliating peace with Germany, and the use of tsarist officers in the Red Army. Later there developed the Workers' Opposition, consisting of Party members who still retained ties with the workers, in contrast to those who had become part of the bureaucracy or the Red Army. They retained the visions of 1917, when the workers believed that they were fighting to take possession of the factories for themselves. Although Lenin was not prepared to hand industry to its workers, this opposition did prompt him to appoint more workers to the higher posts. A milder opposition was voiced by the Group of Democratic Centralism, which condemned the ever-spreading bureaucracy and urged a return to true democratic processes inside the Party.

The Political Situation

The second, Bolshevik-dominated, all-Russian Congress of Soviets had as its executive organ the Soviet of People's Commissars, which consisted entirely of Bolsheviks and was headed by Lenin. Apart from this the Congress elected from its members a Central Executive Committee which had a Bolshevik majority. In the days following the Revolution the question facing the Party was whether, and with whom, it should form a coalition in order to strengthen its position. The Bolsheviks were only a minority socialist party; the Social Revolutionaries had the support of the peasantry while the Mensheviks were particularly strong in the trade unions. Lenin was against a coalition but wished to prevent an anti-Bolshevik grouping of all the other socialist parties. Inside the Bolshevik Party there was a strong undercurrent in favour of coalition; many members saw that without such an alliance civil war was probable. However, by skilfully playing for time Lenin ensured that negotiations between the Bolsheviks and Social Revolutionaries broke down, while an alliance with the small Left Social Revolutionary group was achieved, thus perpetuating the split between the opposing wings of the Social Revolutionary Party and enabling the Bolsheviks to claim that they had peasant support. Among the 'moderates', who temporarily resigned from the Party in protest at Lenin's decision to avoid coalition and hence impose minority rule, were Kamenev, Zinoviev and Rykov.

Linked with the question of coalition was press freedom. When in opposition, freedom of the press was one of the most powerful slogans of the Bolsheviks, and their own printing presses played a great role in their own success. The Bolsheviks had promised that after their assumption of power each political party would be guaranteed the right and the facilities to produce its own newspaper. However, having achieved power Lenin was unwilling to allow opposing parties to print their own, probably anti-Bolshevik, propaganda, and one of his first actions was to close down not only right-wing but also socialist papers. To formalise this repression the Central Executive Committee passed an appropriately-worded decree as early as 17 November, but only at the cost of a temporary revolt in the Party. Several of Lenin's supporters could not accept so drastic a reversal of the Party's earlier ideals.

In the last resort, the basic and inflexible purpose of the Bolshevik leaders was to retain real power. They realised that any compromise or sacrifice of principle made to retain this power could be retracted when their situation was less vulnerable. The first major political threat which they faced was the approaching Constituent Assembly. In the period before the October Revolution the election of a Constituent Assembly had been one of the major demands of the Bolsheviks. Knowing that the country wanted such a body they lost no occasion to embarrass the Provisional Government by accusing it of unwillingness to put its popularity to the test in free elections. At the time the Bolsheviks seized power, elections to this Assembly had been scheduled for 25 November, and Lenin wished to postpone them. But under pressure from Trotsky and others, who held that a failure to keep earlier Bolshevik promises of an immediate Constituent

Assembly would lose the Party much support, Lenin agreed to hold the elections as scheduled.

This was the first and last multi-party general election held under the auspices of the Soviet Government. Although some of the right-wing parties suffered from the restrictions imposed on their press and some of their leaders were arrested, in general the various left-wing and liberal groups were free to put their case to the people, and votes were counted more or less honestly. Almost 36 million votes were cast, and nine million of these (mainly in the towns) were for the Bolsheviks. Thus of the 707 seats the Bolsheviks won 175 (and their allies the Left Social Revolutionaries another 40), the Cadets 17 and the Mensheviks 16. The Social Revolutionaries' total of 370 seats gave them an absolute majority in the Assembly. In effect Russia had voted for socialism but not for Bolshevism. The few liberal Cadets who were elected were never allowed to take their seats.

Between the election and convening of the Assembly on 18 January 1918 the Social Revolutionaries spent their energies devising policies and programmes, and planning the conduct of the forthcoming debates. The Bolsheviks and the Left Social Revolutionaries on the other hand allocated all their resources to agitation among the proletariat and garrison of Petrograd, endeavouring to kindle massive support for the Soviets and disenchantment with the idea of a Constituent Assembly. As this agitation was not entirely successful (workers and soldiers preferring to wait and see how the situation would develop), Lenin brought a wholly reliable Latvian light infantry division to the capital.

When the Constituent Assembly opened it was surrounded by troops loyal to the Bolsheviks, but placed there ostensibly to protect the members. An unarmed public demonstration welcoming the Assembly was dispersed by bullets, with some casualties, and the Bolshevik and Left Social Revolutionary members walked out of the debate when outvoted on a resolution to transfer all government power to the Soviets. After their departure resolutions ending private land ownership and proposing a socialist peace conference were passed, and Russia was declared a federal democratic republic.

When members arrived for the second sitting the troops barred their way, and the Soviet of People's Commissars at the same time ordered the dissolution of the Assembly. Two leaders of the Cadet Party were murdered in hospital by Red sailors, and henceforth members of the non-Soviet parties were treated as potential enemies of the regime. A new Constitution confirmed the supremacy of the

Soviet. The violent end of the Constituent Assembly was accepted quite quietly in the country as a whole; Lenin once again was proved tactically right. But by branding the other parties as 'counter-revolutionary' he had made civil strife almost inevitable.

In the Civil War, even though the Menshevik and Social Revolutionary leaders were accused by the Bolsheviks of seeking to restore the old regime, in fact they were entirely hostile to the Whites, and urged their supporters to resist them. Perhaps for this reason the Bolsheviks took no final measures against them while the Civil War was still raging: they were expelled from the local Soviets in mid-1918, they had little freedom to propagandise their cause, some were arrested, but they continued to exist. And towards the end of the Civil War more and more of the workers turned towards the Mensheviks and against the Bolsheviks, while the Social Revolutionaries' support among the peasantry did not diminish. In these circumstances, with the Bolsheviks having a monopoly of power and the rival socialist parties having the popular support, the elimination of the latter seemed the only alternative to a new anti-Bolshevik revolt.

Hence after about 1920 the prisons began to fill with Social Revolutionaries and Mensheviks, and the Communist Party was left without any serious rivals. The erstwhile allies of the Bolsheviks, the Left Social Revolutionaries, had been suppressed in a blaze of violence in mid-1918. They had soon realised that Bolshevik policy was far removed from their own idealistic ambitions. The Bolshevik failure to observe the new law against capital punishment and the decision to accept the German peace conditions were the final straw. The Bolsheviks were not sorry to lose their former allies, having little further need of them. But they did not seem to foresee that a party like the Left Social Revolutionaries, which had a tradition of terroristic political activity behind it, would not remain quiet. In July 1918 the recently-appointed German ambassador was assassinated by members of this party, apparently in order to wreck the peace treaty with Germany. Popular risings were engineered in Moscow, Petrograd and other cities. These revolts were suppressed, although the Yaroslavl rising lasted two weeks. Numerous and often arbitrary executions were carried out by the Bolsheviks, and Lenin ordered a massive Red Terror in the Penza area. However, resistance continued sporadically: Bolshevik leaders were assassinated and in August Lenin himself was seriously wounded by a female gunman. But this was the last major coup of the resistance; few of the new terrorists escaped the Cheka's policy of execution on mere suspicion.

The Cheka

While he was still in Switzerland Lenin envisaged a 'Red Terror' in the months following a successful revolution. This would have the effect both of weeding out the new regime's enemies and deterring any fresh enemies from raising their heads. In the first weeks after the October Revolution Red Guards were the main means of keeping order, but they were inadequate for this task and had little time to spread terror among the bourgeoisie.

For this reason, in December 1917 was established the All-Russian Extraordinary Commission against Counter-Revolution, Sabotage and Speculation (usually abbreviated as 'Cheka'). In charge was Felix Dzerzhinsky, a stern and incorruptible revolutionary who had spent many years of his life in prison. His headquarters were in the former offices of an insurance company on Lubyanka Street, which subsequently became Moscow's best-known prison and interrogation centre, the Lubyanka. Local Cheka organisations affiliated to this central co-ordinating body were set up in towns under Communist control. Until the summer of 1918 the Cheka tended to execute individuals rather than groups, although spontaneous acts of terrorism and violence directed by other elements against the bourgeoisie or political opponents did occur. In February, for example, sailors pillaged Sevastopol, killing hundreds of persons suspected of bourgeois origin. But the Cheka's terrorism was different in that it had the full backing of the government, and was organised.

The July revolt of the Left Social Revolutionaries (some of whom had in fact participated in the Cheka), together with the attempted assassination of Lenin, was the signal for the Cheka to begin its campaign. The execution of 400 suspected and actual Left Social Revolutionaries in Yaroslavl was perhaps the opening move. About 500 people, including tsarist ex-ministers, were shot in Petrograd in revenge for the attack on Lenin. All over the country the local Cheka executed, sometimes after torture, anyone suspected of counter-revolutionary activity. There was no preliminary investigation or trial; landlords, army officers, priests, scholars, former police officers, in fact anybody whose social class or occupation was one from which anti-Bolshevik opposition could be expected, were at the mercy of the Cheka detachments with their house searches and punitive expeditions. Nor were workers immune: a denunciation, however implausible, from a suspicious or unfriendly fellow-worker could lead to imprisonment or execution. In the provinces even loyal Communists occasionally became victims.

At its peak the Cheka had more than 30,000 workers and its local branches maintained their own small private armies for suppressing minor revolts. Although Dzerzhinsky was himself a man of integrity, though ruthless, the same could not be said of all of his subordinates. Into the ranks of the Cheka were absorbed not only men imbued with class hatred but also thugs who in tsarist days had whetted their taste for violence in the anti-Jewish pogroms, and bloodthirsty individuals who did not particularly care who their victims were. Then there were those who were simply out to plunder, who had found that murder of any persons of property and the looting of their possessions had become an honoured, if feared, profession.

It is not surprising therefore that the Cheka often came into conflict with the local soviets. But although in August 1918 Dzerzhinsky ordered his men to maintain good relations with the soviets the latter were not granted any right to interfere in the work of the Cheka.

When in July 1918 Czech forces advanced towards Ekaterinburg, where the Royal Family was detained, the local Cheka with imprecise authorisation from Moscow prepared the execution of Nicholas. The Tsar and his family, as well as his doctor, cook, valet and maidservant, were ordered to take shelter in the cellar of their house. Here they were all shot and the bodies taken to a disused mine several miles away. They were then dropped down the shaft and burned with benzine and sulphuric acid. Having thus ensured that the victims were not merely dead, but very dead, the remains were again transported and strewn in a swamp (presumably so that no bones would ever be found, to become objects of veneration). To avoid public revulsion at the killing of women and children the official announcement of the Tsar's execution added that the Empress and her children had been 'despatched to a safe place'.

After 1918 the rate of executions slackened, and there were times when it seemed that the Terror was about to be lifted. But whenever the regime was seriously threatened, the Cheka intensified its efforts and it remained in existence until 1922, when it was transformed into the OGPU (a section of the NKVD, the Ministry of the Interior).

The Cheka could never be termed an intelligence service, for most of its operatives were unintelligent, and frequently illiterate. But by killing or imprisoning every possible suspect it did ensure that among each hundred innocent victims would be one or two genuine and dangerous enemies of the regime. For this reason it can be said

35

to have been successful in its main aim. The White Terror, the somewhat similar but anti-Communist, and in practice anti-socialist, movement in areas held by the Whites, was just as violent and undiscriminating, and it is impossible to know just how many Russians were killed by these Red and White 'security' organisations. But probably their victims outnumbered the deaths from actual fighting between the Civil War armies.

But, as Lenin pointed out, the world had just witnessed a Great War in which millions had been killed in aid of no real cause. Compared with this, 50,000 or so deaths to make the Revolution safe did not seem unreasonable.

Foreign Policy

Probably the biggest factor contributing to the fall both of the monarchy and of the Provisional Government was the war against Germany and Austria. If the Provisional Government could have ended the war it had inherited it might well have gained the strength to consolidate its position. The Bolsheviks, on the other hand, had gained some popular support by promising to end the war. Lenin was not displeased at the spectacle of Europe tearing itself to pieces, knowing that the greater the damage the easier it would be to cultivate revolution in Central and Western Europe. At the same time Lenin had every reason—national and Party interest, personal conviction, past promises—to withdraw Russia from the conflict. In fact, having engineered the disintegration of army discipline as a step towards taking power, there was little alternative.

Propaganda efforts (like the 'Decree on Peace') did not persuade the European proletariat to force their governments to end the war, so the only course was to make a separate peace with the Central Powers (Germany, Austria-Hungary, Bulgaria, Turkey). No doubt realising the weakness of the Bolsheviks the Central Powers demanded harsh terms, including the sacrifice of Russian territories in Poland and the Baltic States. Moreover the separatist Ukrainian government, which had just taken the Ukraine out of Russian control, was to be recognised by Germany and would naturally become a satellite supplying the Central Powers with its agricultural and heavy industrial products.

These conditions would have robbed Russia of about a quarter of its population and three-quarters of its coal and iron production.

Against Lenin's advice, the Bolsheviks rejected the proposed treaty, and Trotsky, who was the Russian negotiator, made an imposing but futile 'declaration of neither peace nor war'. This did not have any moral effect and German troops advanced deep into Russia, compelling the Soviet government to reverse its stand. The resulting Treaty of Brest-Litovsk (March 1918) was even harsher than the earlier, rejected, treaty. Turkey gained Russian territory (including Kars and Batum) in the south Caucasus, and German troops installed a puppet regime in the Ukraine.

Lenin had no intention of honouring this treaty longer than he needed, nor did he expect the Germans to. This was one reason why the capital was transferred to Moscow at this time; Petrograd was perilously near the German advanced units. In fact the Central Powers did in the main observe the agreements, which the Soviet government abrogated as soon as the Western Allies forced Germany to accept the Armistice.

The Soviet government had begun its peace negotiations with Germany in December 1917, and even before this the Russian situa-had alarmed England and France. The situation on the Western Front and in Italy was grim, and could only become dangerously worse if final Russian withdrawal from the war enabled Germany to bring up its eastern armies—about two million men. Worse still, it was not impossible that Germany might occupy much of Russia and make use of its food and industrial resources to nullify the naval blockade. For this reason the Allies, particularly France and Britain, did all they could to keep Russia in the war. They hoped at first to persuade the Bolsheviks to continue the war, then, when this seemed hopeless, to permit Allied troops to land in Russia. When efforts with the Bolsheviks proved unfruitful, secret negotiations with the Whites were started.

In 1918 all the signs pointed to the establishment of diplomatic relations between Germany and Russia, and the case for western military intervention grew stronger. With Bolshevik acquiescence, but not formal agreement, a few Allied units had been in Murmansk and Archangel since early 1918 to protect the vast stocks of munitions and material which had accumulated there ever since the Allies began their support of the tsarist armies. Minor British detachments also occupied Transcaucasia (to prevent the Turks capturing its oilfields) and parts of Central Asia (with an eye to the defence of India). However, mainly because President Wilson did not favour intervention, it was not until August 1918 that large-scale landings were made.

Earlier, in April 1918, Japan anticipated events by landing troops at Vladivostok with the intention not of proceeding through Asiatic and European Russia to fight the Germans (as the Allies at one time fondly hoped) but simply of extending Japanese power and influence in the Far East.

In August 1918 additional British, French and American troops landed in Murmansk and Archangel, while American, British, Japanese, French and Italian troops entered Vladivostok. The Americans were still reluctant to act against the Bolsheviks and their presence in the Far East had the aim of preventing this part of the Russian Empire falling into the hands of the Japanese. At the same time an American railway mission did much to improve the operation of the Trans-Siberian Railway. United States intervention in the far north was more to avoid recrimination from the French and British than to pursure any positive policy. At this stage, too, the other Allied forces took little action and on a local level there was often toleration and even co-operation between them and the Bolsheviks.

After the Armistice the avowed purpose of the intervention dissolved, but at the same time influential voices were raised urging direct action against the Bolsheviks. Among these voices those of Churchill, Lord Milner and Marshal Foch were prominent. They warned that Bolshevism was a dangerous threat to world society and should be crushed while it was still weak. Meanwhile the Soviet government had made new enemies in the West by its renunciation of pre-war Russian debts, nationalisation without compensation of foreign investments, the murder of the Tsar, and support of revolutionary agitation in Central and Western Europe. But America with its revolutionary tradition was still unwilling to act against a new revolution, Lloyd George was unenthusiastic (perhaps fearing opposition by British workers), and even in France, where dislike of the Bolsheviks was strongest, suspicion of the Napoleonic postures of Marshal Foch discouraged the government from wholeheartedly following his advice.

In practice, therefore, the intervention was no anti-Bolshevik crusade, but a half-hearted muddle with uncertain aims and little enthusiasm. Except in the Black Sea area where sizeable French forces were in action, there was no large-scale fighting against the Bolsheviks. British troops sent to North Russia were largely in the C. 3 medical group, and those that were not were unreliable; having survived the horrors of the Western Front they were unwilling to die now the war was over. Mutiny not only occurred among the British troops but also among the French Black Sea sailors, and, after one French crew had hoisted a red flag on its ship, Paris ordered the fleet home. When the decision was finally taken to recall the interventionist forces, the withdrawal took place just as the Whites seemed poised for victory. Only the Japanese were unwilling to leave, but they evacuated in response to American pressure. In anticipation of territorial gains they had already introduced Japanese-speaking railwaymen on the eastern end of the Trans-Siberian Railway.

Although the Whites were disappointed in their hopes of substantial armed support from the West, they did benefit considerably from technical help and munitions received from the Allies. This help prolonged the Civil War, so the advocates of intervention could claim that it had not been wholly in vain. In 1918 war-wracked Central Europe was in a revolutionary mood. The Russian Bolsheviks counted on immediate Communist revolutions in other countries, and did what they could to encourage them. During the winter of 1918–19 a communistic government gained temporary power in Bavaria, and Bela Kun's Communist government in Hungary enjoyed a brief life. In January 1919 the Bolshevik Karl Radek did much to bring about the German so-called Spartacist revolt. This, however, was crushed and its leaders Karl Liebknecht and Rosa Luxemburg murdered. Those who had supported western intervention had some grounds for claiming that, if the Bolsheviks had not been pre-occupied with their own prolonged Civil War, they would have been able to give more conclusive aid to revolutionary movements abroad.

On the other hand opponents of intervention could claim that it solidified the Communist belief that the capitalist world would seek to stifle the first Communist state, and gave it an excuse in subsequent years to plead foreign threats in justification of internal repression. Moreover, even if the intervention had been pressed vigorously and the Bolsheviks defeated, there would still have remained a Russian problem.

The Red and White Armies

The All-Russian Collegium for the Organisation of the Workers' and Peasants' Red Army was established in 1917, but 1918 is a more realistic year of birth for the Red Army. After the poor showing of the Bolshevik troops preceding the loss of Kazan, Trotsky arrived at the front as Commissar for War, entrusted with creating a real fighting organisation. His train, so heavy that two engines were always assigned to it, carried a printing press, emergency supplies and munitions, staff accommodation, and an automobile in which the Commissar could visit off-line units. With a generous number of executions for cowardice (sometimes general and arbitrary, like shooting every tenth man of a unit which fled the battlefield), conferences to allocate and telegrams to obtain supplies, and a series of new decrees, Trotsky not only made the Red Army fight but also laid the foundations of the future armed forces.

Notable among the decrees of this time were those establishing conscription, appointing as officers NCOs of the old army, defining the role of political commissars, and reintroducing capital punishment for desertion. These reflect some of the principal worries of the War Commissariat at this time: shortage of soldiers, shortage of officers, lack of fighting spirit and discipline.

The Bolshevik armed forces after the Revolution consisted mainly of soldiers from the old tsarist army belonging to units which had thrown in their lot with the Reds, supplemented by armed workers and by sailors. The latter were real fighters, but their contempt for ordinary soldiers and their indiscipline were a constant worry. There was a lack of volunteers from the villages and this fact, that the burden of self-sacrifice was borne by the urban proletariat while the predominating social class stood aside, was one of the reasons for conscription.

This conscription caused an immediate influx of infantry. As there was no intention of putting arms into the hands of hostile individuals, conscripts who were considered 'bourgeois' were organised into labour battalions for service in the rear. Thus the more educated recruits were unavailable for training in gunnery and engineering. So, although conscription produced numbers (there were about three million men under arms by 1920), it did not produce the much-needed specialists. There was similar difficulty in finding enough officers. The officers of the old army were either fighting for the Whites, or were passively opposed to the Reds, and those that did make themselves available were treated badly.

To remedy this situation two general policies were adopted: promotion from the ranks was encouraged, and an effort was made to reinstall former tsarist officers. A decree giving officers' commissions to former NCOs of the tsarist army was one of the first measures, and this really did give the ordinary soldier the prospect of a field-marshal's baton (few in fact did climb so high: Marshal Budyenny is the example most often mentioned). Officer training schools were opened, giving courses at three levels, with selected commissars providing political instruction. But the output of these schools was variable, partly because the trainees recommended by their units were often by no means the best available; commanders did not wish to send away their most useful men. An instruction was subsequently issued establishing minimum requirements for officer candidates: ability to read and write, and to multiply, subtract, divide and add.

The position of the old regular officers was not happy. The Revolution had begun with the killing and degrading of officers, and it had become a revolutionary tradition that the tsarist officer was a principal foe. Anybody who had held officer's rank before 1917 was automatically suspect. Thus the re-establishment of the old officers was almost impossible. But Trotsky achieved it, appointing old officers as military 'specialists', with a commissar attached to each as protection against betrayal.

At the higher levels these experienced officers played an important, even indispensable, role. On a lower level they were more of a mixed blessing: they lacked the confidence of the men, and temptations to desert to the Whites were many. Even the higher officers sometimes deserted, and their support of the Red cause was usually lukewarm, although this was partly due to the way they were treated. For example, Frunze treated his adviser ex-General Novitsky with courtesy, and was well served by the latter. On the other hand, at Tsaritsyn, of the three military specialists one was executed for treason, and one deserted to the enemy. But all three had been subjected to the crude discourtesies of the local Bolshevik commander, Voroshilov, and the local commissar (Stalin) made no secret of his dislike of Trotsky's policies and appointees.

Political commissars had been introduced by Kerensky before the Revolution. They served as the political representatives of the government and had the task of restoring military efficiency and fostering the loyalty of officers and men. They played a part in thwarting the Kornilov coup. The commissars of the Red Army had similar aims, although pride of place was given to their work as watchdogs over the loyalty of the troops. The decree of April 1918 stated that military commissars were to ensure that the Red Army did not grow apart from the Soviet system, and that the various military establishments did not become focal points of conspiracies against the workers and peasants (i.e. against the government). An insult to a commissar was equivalent to an insult against the Soviet state. Only orders counter-signed by a commissar were valid, but the commanding officer was responsible for the content of purely operational orders. There was thus some scope for friction between the commander and the com-missar of a unit, for by withholding his signature the latter could block any order of the former. Also, as time passed the functions of the commissar tended to grow, and many developed a taste for purely military command, fancying themselves as tacticians and heroes and neglecting their political work. Some began to issue their own orders without the participation of commanding officers.

Opinions differ as to the value of the commissars during the Civil War. Undoubtedly they were a link with the central Party authorities, a link both for control and for information. Their effect on morale is less certain; there seemed to be a very wide gap between the best and the worst of them. The ordinary Party members fighting in the ranks as soldiers probably did much more to strengthen the fighting spirit of the army.

Because the peasant conscripts had little enthusiasm, Red com-manders valued their regiments according to the proportion of workers included in them. In the army as a whole perhaps 15 or 20 per cent of the soldiers were of urban origin. Units with less than five per cent worker-content were more or less ineffective, while those with more than 20 per cent were regarded almost as shock troops. In few of the foot regiments was there any real discipline. Officers were abused or ignored, supplies looted, equipment neglected. Only in the workers' detachments were officers relatively sure of obedience. New conscripts were often sent to the front line without proper training, sometimes without uniforms or even weapons. Supply shortages meant that the individual soldier had often to live on what he could steal. Clothing stocks hardly existed and soldiers were sometimes obliged to fight and march barefoot. Thus the phenomenally high desertion rate is not surprising. One figure is eloquent: in 1919 in the Petrograd Military District no less than 119,000 deserters were apprehended, while the total strength of the District was only 150,000. It was circumstances such as this which prompted Trotsky to sanction the death penalty for desertion, or even for malingering.

With all its weaknesses and internal conflicts, it is creditable that the Red Army held together at all. There was conflict at the top (Trotsky versus Voroshilov, for example), among the officers (old specialists against promoted NCOs and the new officer-graduates unsympathetic to both), between the commissars and the commanders, between the peasant and proletarian soldiers (with the Red sailors holding both in equal contempt); and, in addition to all this, a chaotic supply situation.

The White Army, which was numerically inferior to the Red, was better supplied and disposed of more military talent and experience. In fact it had a surplus of leaders since it was recruited so much from the tsarist officers. Some of these consented to serve as ordinary soldiers, but many sought or invented safe staff positions in the rear, while others devoted much of their energy to intrigue. For its rank and file the White Army depended very much on the Cossacks, who fought well when they believed the Bolsheviks were threatening their privileges, or when loot was in prospect, but were otherwise unreliable, frequently refusing to fight. When the Whites resorted to conscription their recruits were no more enthusiastic than the Red conscripts. Even the ex-officers tended to melt away, claiming, quite logically, that since they had joined voluntarily they were free to quit voluntarily.

Until Wrangel took over the remnants of the White Army, its officers set an example of drunkenness, looting and violence which their soldiers willingly followed. Outrageous treatment of the local population, the outspoken intention to restore the landlords, and the greater social cleavage between the Whites and the peasantry made the latter finally prefer the Reds.

The battles of the Civil War were not especially bloody. It was after the battle that most of the savagery and killing took place. Prisoners who were willing to change sides were often spared. (Many soldiers, and whole units, did change sides, sometimes more than once. The Reds often employed non-Russian troops, Latvians and Mongolians, when they feared fraternisation between the armies.) Captured Bolsheviks and White officers were shot almost as a matter of course. Looting was quite normal, although the Red soldiers behaved better in occupied territory than did the Whites. Mutilation of prisoners as part of the execution process was not uncommon. Many of the Red soldiers, nominally fighting for an atheist cause, were deeply if malignantly religious, and would force local priests at bayonet point to give their comrades a Christian burial.

Independent or semi-independent peasant armies came into being, hostile to the Whites and usually suspicious of the Reds. The exploits of Chapaev, an enthusiastic Red, and his peasant army are still honoured in the Soviet Union—although if Chapaev had survived the Civil War his independent nature would probably have led to his downfall, as with other peasant leaders. The so-called Greens caused both the Reds and the Whites much trouble. These were bands of deserters, terrorists, idealists and others who could support neither the Reds nor the Whites and were the enemies of both, roaming the countryside and fighting all and sundry. Makhno's peasant army was in a similar position. It was well-led and won many victories over the Reds, Whites and Central Powers. Makhno was an anarchist and his troops carried the black flags of the anarchist movement. They were supported by much of the peasantry but were eventually driven into Rumania by overwhelming Red forces.

Both the Reds and the Whites employed cavalry on a large scale, usually Cossacks. The armoured train was also an important weapon of war, especially as the campaigns tended to be fought along the railway routes. All the armies made extensive use of captured equipment; in fact most of the Red Army's ammunition came from captured White supplies. A few aeroplanes were used by both sides, and the Whites used some tanks supplied by the Allies.

The Course of the Civil War

In the winter following the Revolution former tsarist generals made their way south towards the territory of the Don Cossacks, whose traditional spirit of independence had resisted Bolshevik agitation. In January 1918 a Don Republic was declared, but when the Germans moved into the Ukraine the Cossacks began to favour the Bolsheviks for patriotic reasons. The White Army was thus reduced to the 5,000–6,000 ex-officers who had trekked south to join the resistance. Komilov was initially leader of this volunteer army but was killed in action, being replaced by Denikin.

By the spring of 1918 the Cossacks and the Volunteer Army were again co-operating, though not always amicably. In May Novocherkassk and Rostov were captured, with some help from German and Austrian troops. Having mastered the Don and Kuban regions the White Army pushed eastwards with the aim of crossing the Volga and linking up with anti-Bolshevik forces between that river and the Urals. In the summer of 1918 Tsaritsyn was besieged and, more important, the Tsaritsyn–Moscow railway cut.

Tsaritsyn was vital to the Reds, because through it passed grain from the south bound for the Bolshevik-held cities of the centre. It was therefore decided to hold this city at all costs, and Stalin was sent there with the task of safeguarding the flow of grain. Also at Tsaritsyn were Voroshilov, Ordzhonikidze and Budyenny, who were later to be counted among Stalin's closest associates. Voroshilov, the son of a railwayman and a former Party secretary, was now in command of the 10th Red Army. Ordzhonikidze, the political commissar of the same army, was a Caucasian who, like Voroshilov, had previously worked with Stalin. Budyenny, an ex-cavalry sergeant in the Tsar's Cossacks, had cut a heroic figure as commander of a Red cavalry division. These four, and the efforts of their forces, saved the city, restored rail communications with Moscow, and blocked the Whites' eastward progress. Subsequently Stalin was given almost the entire credit for this success, and in 1925 Tsaritsyn was re-named Stalingrad.

Meanwhile a second threat to the Bolsheviks had appeared in Siberia. During the First World War, thousands of Czech soldiers who formed an unwilling part of the Austro-Hungarian army allowed themselves to fall into Russian hands, and these formed the nucleus of a Czech legion which was organised to fight on the Allied side. In early 1918 this legion (of about 40,000 men) was stationed in Russia and was the most effective and best organised fighting force in the country. The Soviet government agreed to allow these troops to transfer to the Allies' Western Front, via the Trans-Siberian Railway and Vladivostok. However, while the Czechs were proceeding along the railway Trotsky ordered local Bolshevik authorities to disarm them. The attempt failed and the Czechs turned against the Soviet government, routing Bolshevik power in the cities and areas through which the railway passed.

The Czech revolt provided an opportunity for anti-Bolshevik groups to organise themselves. In the summer of 1918 a government was formed at Samara, mainly from Social Revolutionary members of the ill-fated Constituent Assembly. This government raised an army and captured Kazan. Farther east, another anti-Bolshevik government was formed at Omsk, with the highly respected Admiral Kolchak as its figurehead. Although Allied recognition of this government was obtained only on condition that it promised free elections and no restoration of class privileges, it became more and more dominated by reactionary and chauvinistic groups. The Social Revolutionary Samara government eventually disintegrated after military defeats by the Reds and intrigues and repression at the hands of the Kolchak government.

In the late summer of 1918 the successful defence of Tsaritsyn, a recovery by the Red Army in the east with the recapture of Kazan, and the defeat of the Left Social Revolutionaries' revolt gave the Bolsheviks a breathing space. At the beginning of 1919 the Soviet government no longer faced the possibility of war with Germany, which was defeated and apparently on the brink of a Communist revolution. On the other hand, White armies with western material support were threatening from three directions. In the east Kolchak's Omsk government ruled from Lake Baikal almost to the Volga (the fact that White territory was larger than that of the Bolsheviks was one reason why the Allies were reluctant to recognise the latter as the real government of Russia). Behind Kolchak in eastern Siberia the terrorist Semeonov maintained a savage regime with Japanese support. Kolchak's supply line, the railway from Vladivostok, was operated largely by Americans and defended by troops of various countries. In the south of Russia, Denikin's White Army was preparing another offensive and in the Ukraine a joint Franco-Ukrainian Nationalist offensive was planned. In the north-west General Yudenich, with British naval support (more apparent than real), was preparing to advance on Petrograd from his stronghold in the Baltic provinces.

Kolchak began his attack with over 100,000 men in March, expecting his offensive to coincide with the Franco-Ukrainian advance in the south. But it was at this point that the Allies decided to withdraw their forces. French withdrawal from Odessa and Sevastopol opened the way to Soviet occupation of the southern Ukraine and the declaration of a Ukrainian Soviet Republic. Thus the Reds were able to send more forces to meet Kolchak than the latter had expected. Nevertheless the White Army captured Perm and Ufa and approached Kazan. Meanwhile Denikin won victory after victory, capturing much of the Ukraine in the west as well as Tsaritsyn in the east, then advancing to capture Orel in October. Peasant revolts in Red territory and the Politburo's initial refusal to approve Trotsky's countermeasures made Denikin's task easier; at the height of his success he was only 200 miles from Moscow.

As for Yudenich, he began his drive on Petrograd in October, confidently expecting support from the British fleet. However, the Royal Navy withdrew without firing a shot, and internal dissension or sheer incompetence resulted in failure to fulfil the order to cut the Moscow–Petrograd railway. The Red defenders of Petrograd fought courageously and Yudenich's army was forced back to Estonia where, the following year, it was demobilised.

Meanwhile, Kolchak directed most of his forces towards the north-west so that they might link with hitherto inactive White troops around Archangel. However, this move exposed the centre of his front in the Samara region to strong Red attacks under Frunze and Kuibyshev. Also, the increasingly reactionary policies of Kolchak's Omsk government led to revolts and partisan activity in the rear. These revolts were fostered by the Social Revolutionaries, who were more anti-White than anti-Red. Kolchak's Czech allies became more and more unco-operative, and soon the White Army was making a miserable winter retreat back towards the east. By the time this retreat reached Irkutsk Kolchak was of no further use to the Allies, and the French handed him over to his enemies for execution. Soviet power reached Lake Baikal but it was not until 1922, after the withdrawal of the Japanese, that the Russian Far East came under Bolshevik control.

The Red counter-move against Denikin's advance in the south was delayed because Stalin and others were opposed to Trotsky's plan. But Lenin eventually backed the latter, and a drive on Orel with a cavalry sweep through Denikin's rear started a White retreat which ended in the Crimea, in March 1920. At this point Denikin resigned in favour of Wrangel. The latter had much greater political and practical awareness than previous White leaders. He reorganised his troops, introduced stricter discipline, and at last caused the Whites to adopt an agricultural law which would satisfy the peasants' demand for land. But all this was too late. Britain refused further support and after a brief offensive Wrangel's army was pressed back. In November 1920 Red troops broke into the Crimea and the Whites carried out a successful evacuation, over 100,000 soldiers and civilians being shipped to Constantinople, whence they swelled the pockets of Russian refugees which had appeared in various cities of Europe and America.

This was the end of the Civil War. But meanwhile the Red Army had been engaged against Poland. The Poles were not satisfied with their new eastern frontier, the Curzon Line, which had been fixed by the Allies. They took advantage of the Reds' other preoccupations to advance into territory which was not Polish but had once been part of the Polish Empire. General Pilsudski captured Kiev in May 1920, but a wave of genuine patriotism (or traditional anti-Polish feeling) led to spirited Russian resistance. Many former opponents as well as tsarist officers, including the famous · General Brusillov, chose to throw in their lot with the Bolsheviks at this time. The tide turned and the Poles were thrown back. But instead of halting on the Curzon Line Lenin (against Trotsky's advice) decided to capture Warsaw, envisaging the establishment of a Polish Soviet government. The Russian advance in turn ignited Polish patriotism (or traditional anti-Russian feeling), while the French sent General Weygand as military adviser to Pilsudski. Tukhachevsky's Red Army was defeated on the Vistula, largely because Budyenny, Egorov and Stalin decided not to support him. The Reds were driven back in disorder as far as Minsk, an armistice was declared, and in 1921 a treaty allocated to Poland much Byelorussian and Ukrainian territory east of the Curzon Line. This area was not recovered until Russia's attack on Poland in 1939.

Daily Life During the Civil War

Living conditions in Moscow and Petrograd were not quite so extreme as in some provincial cities, but the essential feature of the time was common to all parts: a feeling of living on an active volcano. All the old laws of society, accepted modes of behaviour, measures of respect and value, had been destroyed or distorted or reversed. Poverty became an advantage, riches a dangerous handicap, careful upbringing a liability. Dishonesty was one key to survival, illiteracy no bar to power, violence nine-tenths of the law. And yet while everyone felt rootless, conscious of living on very thin ice, to many the Revolution had brought immediate benefit, or better prospects. In the villages and in the army children of illiterate but now land-owning peasants were being taught to read and write; in the factories workers who had been at the mercy of their employers felt that they were beginning to have some control over their own lives; and the power of moneylenders, priests, officers and old-style policemen had been replaced by the power of the soviets, which, however savage and obtuse they sometimes might be, at least were trying to repair the neglect of centuries and make Russia fit to live in.

But, despite the frequent speeches of Bolshevik agitators in public places, in the factories and in the army, the main interest of the ordinary Russian was not so much politics as survival. Death was advancing on three fronts against the individual: deprivation, execution and conscription. Deprivation took two main forms: deprivation of nourishment, and of warmth. In general, the territory held by the Reds was a net consumer of foodstuffs; normally the cities of the centre drew their grain from the south, which was now largely outside

Bolshevik control. Bread-rationing was in force but was discriminatory; the ration was a privilege, not a citizen's inalienable right, and workers and soldiers had extra shares. After labour conscription had been introduced any person of working age unable to produce a 'worker's book' (which indicated place of work) could not officially obtain food, fuel, clothing or lodging (and would probably be arrested anyway). The ration varied from place to place and from time to time, according to the particular supply situation. Moreover, it was sometimes quite unavailable, or, even worse, available at one store but not at the next; as each person was allocated to a particular store this kind of situation was explosive.

Even at the best of times the food legally available was insufficient, and recourse was had to extra-legal and unofficial channels of supply. The Black Market flourished, and since the official sources of supply were so chaotic the government allowed this kind of speculation to exist. (Shops and stores had been taken over by the co-operatives, which more and more acquired the bureaucratic characteristics of the government departments.) However, the life of stall-holders was not a secure one; from time to time the Cheka would make raids, arresting some of the sellers and buyers. Sometimes the Cheka could be bribed with gifts of food and materials, but sometimes it could not, and the arrestees swelled the prison population. Occasionally food speculators were shot.

The biggest of the Black Markets was the Sukharevka in Moscow. Here the former propertied classes traded the remains of their possessions for scarce foodstuffs. In time these supplies of fine china, furniture, jewellery, clocks, pianos, ball dresses, silver and paintings were exhausted, and their owners denuded. But new sellers appeared with new commodities: tools, equipment and materials purloined from government factories and army depots by workers and soldiers. Some private barter was quite legitimate. Since workers were paid largely in kind there was nothing wrong, say, in a non-smoker selling his tobacco allocation on the Sukharevka. Again, peasants could come into the town markets with dairy products, honey and any other products not subject to compulsory government purchase, and make a fortune of paper money. Apart from open Black Markets there were semi-secret establishments performing the same kind of economic function. Illegal restaurants, for example, were usually inside private houses and clients came only by personal recommendation. These offered at astronomical prices meals which were relatively nourishing.

There were those, too, who did well out of newly-acquired power.

Bribery and corruption, so typical of tsarist Russia, flourished. Any official with any power at all was able to supplement his rations from bribes. The most unscrupulous, or the highest-placed (and this included occasional Party members), could make private fortunes by misappropriating supplies entrusted to them. Although conventional prostitution had been brought to a forcible end in 1917 there developed a new class, popularly known as 'Soviet maidens'. Typically, these worked in government offices and gave themselves to their superiors in exchange for food or clothing. One of Trotsky's friends is reliably reported to have boasted that she was the only one of his mistresses who had never demanded food from him.

For those who chose, or were obliged, to rely on official supply sources life was simply a succession of queues as the bureaucrats took over and multiplied. An American journalist has described how she bought a saucepan in 1920 Moscow. First she went to a trade office for a buying permit. This had to be signed by three officials in the food administration, whose signatures took a whole day to obtain. The following day the permit was exchanged for an inspection order, which allowed a visit to a store where various types of saucepans were on display. When she had chosen the saucepan type, the inspection order was exchanged for a purchase coupon valid at a particular co-operative store. After ascertaining which day this store would be selling saucepans the purchaser rose early and queued until opening time. When the saucepan was finally acquired it proved to be of good quality and cost three roubles. A similar saucepan on the Black Market would not have taken several days to obtain, but would have cost more than 2,000 roubles.

Undernourishment sometimes led directly to death, but more often weakened resistance to fatal epidemics, whose spread had been facilitated by lack of soap and hot water. Cholera, influenza and typhoid took their toll, but typhus was the most deadly. Spread by the movements of lousy troops and refugees, it claimed more than two million deaths in 1919–22. Lack of medical supplies and of proper care made matters worse. Patients in hospitals sometimes froze to death. The few passenger trains still running had a box-car attached, reserved for travellers succumbing en route.

The activities of the Cheka have already been described. But their physical was perhaps less than their psychological effect. Apart from genuine plotters and speculators their victims included the entirely innocent. A denunciation of one citizen by another, even though voiced to satisfy personal rancour rather than from genuine belief, was often sufficient to condemn a man to imprisonment or worse. The Cheka itself not only sought to uncover plots, it sometimes constructed its own to trap the incautious, or even invented conspiracies. The saying 'Every Russian has been, is, or will be in prison' was heard more and more. However, while there was no guarantee of freedom from arrest, order was kept in the towns. One could safely walk the streets at night in Soviet cities and the same could not be said of towns held by the Whites.

People tended to become inconsiderate, even cruel, in their relations with each other. On crowded trains carrying hungry people out of the towns in search of food passengers would fight for a foothold at each station, the weak or the undernourished being thrown off and left behind. One class of people which endured extra suffering was the Jews. Although many Communists, including Trotsky and Zinoviev, were Jewish (in origin if not in sentiment), the Revolution did not benefit the Jews as much as they had hoped. The nationalisation of trade caused severe unemployment among them, and anti-semitism did not die out under the soviets. Although the Bolshevik leaders repeatedly stressed that rich Jews were enemies and ordinary Jews were friends, Red soldiers organised their own pogroms against all classes of Jew. In White territory the situation was worse; to tsarist anti-semitism was added a belief among the unperceptive that Jewry and Bolshevism were synonomous.

Moscow and the other Bolshevik cities at this time were more drab than usual. Shops were closed, the streetcars rare or non-existent, a few automobiles carried important functionaries, public buildings were unheated and poorly illuminated, people died in offices and on the streets, Red revolutionary posters were everywhere. Surprisingly, in Moscow and Petrograd the theatre was flourishing, even if the audiences were obliged to huddle in their overcoats. Poetry-reading became popular; in fact because of the paper shortage poetry was the only feasible form of literature. It was at this time that revolutionary poets like Blok and Mayakovsky attracted mass audiences.

Allowing for loss of territory, the estimated number of deaths attributable to the First World War and Civil War is no less than 16 million, of which only two million were soldiers' deaths in action in the First World War. About two million refugees emigrated. So about one Russian in every ten disappeared during those seven years.

The Economy

In Lenin's view the October Revolution had achieved a transfer of effective power from the bourgeoisie to the representatives of the workers and peasants, and there could be a gradual transition from the capitalist to the socialist economic system. Emphasis was on gradualness; there was no intention of immediately nationalising or confiscating industry. But some government control over firms was required, and this control was to be exercised both from above and from below, by the government and by the workers of each enterprise.

In mid-November the Decree on Workers' Control formalised the participation of workers' representatives in the running of enterprises: they had the right to supervise the management, to approve production targets and inspect documents, but they were forbidden to interfere with the management's executive decisions, or to take possession of the enterprise. Up to the summer of 1918 only a few enterprises were nationalised by the government: the banks were the first (because they were financing a strike by employees of the State Bank), then certain categories of trade (the grain trade had in fact already been nationalised by the Provisional Government), and individual enterprises (like Wagon-Lits) because their managements departed, or closed down, or otherwise refused or were unable to co-operate. Finally, a few key companies (such as the Putilov armaments works) were taken over. Nationalisation was without compensation for the original owners.

But for every one factory officially nationalised, four were taken over by local soviets against the wishes of the central government. Workers often expelled the managements and began to run their factory for their own benefit. This syndicalism was more harmful than, and as self-interested as, capitalist ownership: a factory expropriated by its own workers would not co-operate either with the government or with connected enterprises. It would sell its products where it could get the highest price, not where they were most needed, and moreover the new worker-managements lacked the skill and the experience to organise production efficiently. Meanwhile the government tried to maintain its concept of State capitalism, organising central boards for given industries on which the trade unions, the proprietors and the government were all represented, and which had wide powers over the industries they controlled. For the most basic industries, such as coal, the boards had the additional task of preparing for, or consolidating, nationalisation. Against much opposition, the subordination of the workers' committees to the official trade union organisations was achieved and responsible one-man management was imposed, at least in theory. But piece rates could only be introduced gradually, so great was the resistance of the workers. At the same time the arbitrary 'taxation' of the bourgeoisie by local soviets (often achieved by arresting individuals, then confiscating their property) was condemned.

The assistance of foreign capitalists was also canvassed, but the situation changed too rapidly for this to bear fruit. The relatively moderate approach to industry, with its purpose of pacifying bourgeois managers and specialists whose skills could not be replaced, did not last long. Both the Left Social Revolutionaries and the Left Communists deplored such moderation. Moreover, the intensifying Civil War meant that there could be no toleration of munition and supply difficulties caused by reluctant proprietors or self-interested workers' committees. Hence the pace of nationalisation quickened and in June 1918 the Decree of General Nationalisation was passed, clearing the way for the nationalisation of all enterprises. This decree was hurried through because it was believed that many Russian firms had been surreptitiously acquired by German citizens (by constraint in German-occupied areas, or by share dealings), and that the newly-appointed German ambassador was about to present a list of these German-owned firms, demanding for them immunity from nationalisation.

By 1920 industry employed only about half the number of workers it had used before the war, and the output per worker had fallen by two-thirds. Thus all manufactured products were scarce, and many non-existent. During the Civil War the Donetz Basin and the Urals, which together with Poland had accounted for almost all the Russian iron output, were not available to the Bolsheviks. Cotton from Central Asia was cut off, and so were imports (which often put factories out of action for lack of spare parts). Coal and oil were at times unobtainable and the railways had to use wood for their locomotives. Shortage of metal, among other difficulties, led to transport chaos because engines and track could not be renewed; by 1920 two-thirds of the locomotives were out of service. Transport difficulties aggravated the food situation and famine appeared in the cities. Workers deserted their jobs to look for food in the countryside, uncounted infants, invalids and old people died from starvation and cold. At one point even workers, who were specially favoured, were issued only one ounce of bread each day—a starvation ration which could be supplemented only by the Black Market, theft or migration to the home village. The government resorted to inflation in order to obtain its needs, but this was a self-accelerating and self-defeating process, for as the quantity of money in circulation increased so did the new banknote issue needed to achieve a given end. Inflation proceeded rapidly and came to a head in 1922. For example, in May 1922 railway fares were one million times the 1917 rates. They were doubled in June, and again in the autumn. Apart from wiping out any savings still in the possession of the former richer classes, inflation also hurt the peasantry, for the latter sold their crop in the autumn and saved the receipts for expenditure during the following year.

Because money lost its value so quickly, barter arrangements multiplied. Deals were arranged between factories and local authorities in the countryside, whereby output would be exchanged for grain. In time these exchanges were arranged on a broader basis, perhaps with the participation of an entire industry. Wages began to be paid increasingly in kind, which simultaneously ensured that labour would not starve and gave managements a weapon against recalcitrant workers. There were those among the left wing of the Party who regarded rampant inflation as an essential part of the Revolution: one enthusiast described the note-printing press as 'a machine-gun attacking the bourgeois regime ,in its rear, that is, through its monetary system'. Others envisaged the complete abolition of money and in fact transactions were carried out more and more by book entries without any financial exchange. However, after War Communism came to an end a more or less stable currency was re-established, in 1923.

During this period nationalisation proceeded until by 1920 even firms employing a single worker belonged to the state. The free market, whose law of supply and demand hitherto had roughly ensured that the goods produced were in fact the goods required, was replaced by a system of priorities, allocations, and targets set by government organisations. A given enterprise no longer produced what it thought it could sell, itself arranging to purchase the required materials from other firms. Its production was now fixed for it, government departments ensured its supplies by instructing other firms to supply it with what was needed. Each enterprise was either subordinated to a central board (if it was large-scale, or its output was of national importance) or to a provincial economic soviet (if small-scale and of purely local significance). The central board for each industry, and the economic soviet of each province, took their instructions from the Supreme Economic Soviet, which was intended to be a central body making general plans for the entire economy.

In practice the orders from the Supreme Economic Soviet frequently took little account of local conditions, and this council became so overloaded with minor questions that it was unable to function in its co-ordinating role. Similarly the central boards and the provincial economic soviets often had little knowledge of the enterprises under their jurisdiction. So there was a downpour from the top of orders, instructions and recommendations having little relation to practical possibilities, and in each enterprise there was conflict, or at least confusion, between the new organisers—politically reliable, sometimes imaginative, but inexperienced—and the old specialists, who had experience but lacked enthusiasm. The new central and local organisations which were supposed to plan economic life provided a haven for unenterprising bureaucrats of the old school, who multiplied as the economy became more and more divorced from the old market relationships. It is said that by the end of this period no less than one Petrograd adult in four was an office worker. In these circumstances enterprises could only survive by going through the motions of obeying instructions while actually following their own advice. When it became obvious that industry was being suffocated by paper, the 'shock' technique was introduced. This entailed giving high priority to a vital industry or firm, by-passing the usual paper-logged channels, and giving favourable treatment in the allocation of materials and organisers. This method worked at first, but like inflation soon lost its efficacy: more and more enterprises were declared 'shock', so that enterprises which were not so favoured were forced out of production and could only be revived by receiving equal treatment. Soon almost every firm was a 'shock' firm and the priority lost its meaning.

The essence of War Communism was the replacement of the free market by controlled production and distribution, backed by armed force. It was in food supply that the system was most crucial and most harmful. As the value of money declined peasants, instead of immediately selling their crop, preferred to store it (in such conditions of scarcity this was described as hoarding or speculation). Compulsory requisitioning of stored grain was the answer to this, with armed detachments from the towns being sent to uncover and take away whatever was found, leaving the peasant only with his seed corn and his own food requirement. To help in this the poor peasants were enlisted to spy out the stocks of their better-off neighbours, and to force them to deliver it 'voluntarily'. But while many of the richer peasants fully deserved the description *kulak* ('fist'), ruthlessly forcing poor peasants by virtue of unpaid debts to work on their land, the majority of peasants were of the so-called 'middle' type, men who by hard work just managed to exist and produce a small surplus of foodstuffs for the town market. Thus the fanning of the class war in the villages, with the government's weight on the side of the unproductive poor peasant, did not improve the production of grain. Either the peasants with a surplus managed to hide it from their village enemies and from the requisitioning detachments, or they reduced their sowings in the following season. This antagonising of the most productive peasants, together with the damage done by the First World War and the Civil War, meant that Russian grain production in 1920 was only half that of pre-war years.

Peasant risings and the not infrequent murder of requisitioning detachments caused a slight relaxation in policy towards the peasants, but the much advertised and always exaggerated revolutionary solidarity of the town proletariat with the peasantry was clearly broken. At the same time discontent grew in the towns: semi-starvation, the subordination of the trade unions to central policy, the appearance of careerist Party officials leading lives of luxury and misapplied power, all combined to create a spirit of rebellion.

When the Civil War was over, the pressure of popular dissatisfaction could be contained no longer. In March 1921 the Kronstadt sailors revolted. These Red sailors, the heroes of the Revolution, were recruited largely from the peasantry and reflected the peasantry's discontent. They made no secret of whom they were fighting against: 'Soviets without Communists' was their most frequent slogan. Although the revolt was suppressed after two weeks of bitter fighting and its leaders executed, the revolt was a damaging psychological blow to the Bolsheviks. It was clear that War Communism could not be continued.

III

Moderation and Restoration

The New Economic Policy

THE DEMANDS of the Kronstadt rebels—soviets without Communists, free and secret elections, freedom of the press and of assembly, nondiscriminatory rationing, the ousting of Party functionaries from government posts, freedom for small-scale industry, concessions to peasants—were echoed in part by a number of peasant revolts which occurred at the same time. Although Tukhachevsky's troops put a bloody end to the Kronstadt rising, and the peasant revolts were similarly crushed, the crisis did at least make the Bolsheviks more receptive to a radical change of policy.

There was no question of reducing the role of the Party, but Lenin felt that if the economic situation could be remedied then a better-fed population would forget its hostility towards the Bolsheviks. By 1921 the peasants had been driven by violence and armed requisitioning into a state of mind where they planted only enough grain to feed themselves. Hunger in the towns had been one of several reasons why Russian industry had been producing only about 15 per cent of its pre-war output. Private trading was prohibited from 1920, so that even the goods which were produced were unevenly distributed.

The basic economic problem was the relationship between the town and the country, that is, between the worker and the peasant. The towns were not producing enough goods to send to the villages in exchange for food. Hence the forced requisitioning of food. Requisitioning, by alienating the peasants, reduced food supplies still further, which in turn meant that the town workers produced even less. Also important was the fact that the workers and the soldiers still had their roots in the peasantry; many were former peasants and most had family ties in the villages. The conciliation of the peasantry seemed therefore the obvious first step, and the main proposal of

Lenin's 'New Economic Policy' (NEP), presented to a Party Congress in March 1921, was the abolition of requisitioning.

At this Congress Lenin admitted that War Communism had not been a success, that socialisation must proceed more slowly (as in fact he had intended before the unrestrained confiscation and national-isation of 1918). A tax in kind, fixed in advance, was to replace grain requisitioning. Hence the peasant would know that whatever he produced in excess of the tax could be sold for his own benefit. From this concession other changes, politically more important, followed. The acceptance of peasants producing a marketable surplus implied an acceptance of the market, hence trade and money had to be revived. In turn the previous system of supplying food and agri-cultural raw materials by allocation to various industrial enterprises was replaced by a decentralised system whereby individual enter-prises made their own arrangements for obtaining their materials and selling their production.

Thus the revival of private enterprise was seen primarily in trade. Retail trade became the province of the private dealer, and so did much of wholesale trade. The 'Nepmen' played an important part both in channelling food and industrial goods to the consumer, and in helping industry to find markets and materials. Some Nepmen enriched themselves ostentatiously and led a riotous existence for a few happy years. Others were simply peasants who happened to own a horse and cart and could thus act as middlemen between their neighbours and the nearest town.

Private enterprise also returned to industry. In December 1921 all enterprises with less than 20 workers were restored to their former owners (if these could still be found) or to new ones (often local co-operative groups formed for the purpose). Large enterprises remained in state ownership, as did all the vital industries and services (what Lenin termed the 'commanding heights'—heavy industry, foreign trade, railways, banks). But administration of state-owned enterprises was decentralised. The old system of central boards was largely abolished, individual enterprises became indepen-dent and usually united with similar or complementary enterprises to form trusts chartered by the state. Each enterprise had a manager, appointed by the trust, who had more-or-less complete authority inside the factory.

Co-operative trading was also revived, and in 1923 a new currency issue marked the end of inflation and the restoration of money as the prime unit of exchange. The practice of paying wages in the form of food or clothing died out. The State Bank was empowered to make loans in aid of industry and trade.

It was a year or two before the NEP could show results. Its first year was marked by the 1921–22 famine, during which about five million people died of starvation. The famine was not entirely a surprise, nor did the Party at first show much anxiety; in the previous hungry periods discriminatory rationing had usually ensured that the workers and Party members would survive while 'class enemies' might not. But this famine passed all expectations: workers and peasants began to die. A special Famine Aid Committee was established, including in its membership bourgeois representatives, and in August 1921 the writer Maxim Gorki made an international appeal, which resulted in Herbert Hoover's relief organisation, and Fridtjof Nansen's appeal. The Quakers and Russian immigrants in the USA also made important contributions. Three-quarters of a million tons of American food and medicines (of which five-sixths were supplied free) helped to reduce the casualties, but relief work was sometimes hampered by the activities of the GPU. Bourgeois members of the Famine Aid Committee were arrested, and the Russian employees of the Hoover mission were likewise subject to Party or GPU bullying.

Industry was slow to recover. Railway transport was always chaotic and several times on the point of complete breakdown, partly because of, and partly causing, the internal fuel shortage. Giving the railways priority in coal supplies meant that many factories ceased production. At first the shortfall of farm products meant that the villages were not able to buy all the output of the towns, so there was an apparent paradox of industry limiting its production at a time when its products were badly needed. Then when the 1923 harvest was gathered the town–country terms of trade were reversed, and the peasants grumbled that they could not obtain enough manufactured goods. Probably in 1923 the unpopularity of the government was as great as it had been two years earlier; the workers were still underpaid, underfed and unproductive, while the peasants had never forgotten their treatment during War Communism and were incensed by antireligious activity, particularly the desecration of churches and confiscation of valuables. In both town and country there was a feeling that every Communist was a little tsar.

But in time the position improved. Industry in general reached its pre-war level in 1926 or 1927. Harvests were better. There were some imports; more than 1,000 new engines from Sweden and Germany helped to restore the railways, and the fuel crisis was overcome. The population felt more prosperous. But as things got better the concessions to private enterprise became fewer. Lenin had always said that NEP was a partial, and in particular a temporary, restoration of capitalism. His successors, perhaps feeling that if the trend towards capitalism was not reversed it would become irreversible, began to put pressure on the Nepmen. State trusts formed their own syndicates for procurement and distribution. Goods produced by private enterprise faced higher railway tariffs. But the moderates inside the Politburo still held that the key to economic progress lay in appealing to the peasantry's self-interest. Bukharin even proposed to the peasants the slogan 'Enrich yourselves!'. He later had cause to regret this suggestion, but at the time it was in accord with the idea that if only the peasants could be induced to produce for the market more grain (which could be exported, or used to feed a greater number of industrial workers), then the USSR's economic problems would be half-solved.

Some, however, felt that the dividing up in 1917 of the large estates (which had previously been the source of Russia's marketable grain) could only be undone by merging the individual peasants' holdings into large farms, which would be worked collectively, and would be large enough to use modern equipment. At the same time large-scale farming would need fewer peasants for greater output, and this would provide a source of labour for operating new industry. This concept, and the feeling that capital for industrialisation could be amassed by taking the peasants' food output and giving little in exchange for it, was the economic basis for farm collectivisation—although it is a moot point whether collectivisation was genuinely taken seriously before the crises of 1928 and 1929 drove the Party to drastic action.

The Formation of the USSR

The Bolsheviks had always proclaimed the right of nations which had formed part of the old Russian Empire to either secede from, or federate with, Russia. It was expected, however, that even the nations which seceded would sooner or later enjoy proletarian governments which would wish to associate with the Moscow government. The former Duchy of Finland was the first to break formally with Moscow, and in January 1918 the Soviet government recognised its independence. Local Bolsheviks then engineered a revolt but in the consequent civil war the Finnish anti-Red forces under General Mannerheim, with German assistance, crushed the rebellion and established an independent government in May 1918.

Difficulties in the Ukraine caused the Russian Bolsheviks to modify their acceptance of the right of secession. (Stalin, then Commissar of Nationalities, changed the formulation of this from 'the right of non-Russian peoples' to the 'right of the non-Russian working class' to secede.) What happened in the Ukraine was that a national government was formed, independent of Moscow. A local Bolshevik revolt only forced the nationalists to seek help from the Germans. Thus the Russian Bolsheviks were presented with a hostile, 'bourgeois', state right on their border and this danger was not finally removed until the end of the Civil War. Byelorussia (White Russia), even closer to Moscow, also declared its independence, but was not recognised by Germany. Also in 1918, the Baltic nations (Latvia, Estonia, Lithuania) and the three main Transcaucasian colonies (Georgia, Armenia and Azerbaijan) declared their independence.

In these circumstances Moscow made efforts to bring the new states back into the fold. In 1919 Communists in Byelorussia gained power and reunited that nation with Russia, and in the same year a Ukrainian Soviet Republic was formed (but it was not until the end of the Polish war that this could be considered as secure). The defeat of the Red Army by Poland in 1920 ensured that the three Baltic states remained independent, and enabled Finland successfully to claim from Russia the White Sea port of Petsamo.

In the Transcaucasus British troops were present until 1920, having replaced Turkish forces after the Armistice. After the departure of the British a Bolshevik revolt was arranged in Baku, the capital of Azerbaijan, and a Soviet Republic proclaimed. At the end of 1920 Russian and Turkish troops occupied Armenia and agreed to split this nation between the two countries. Georgia, however, was recognised as independent in May 1920 by the Moscow government. It had a moderately efficient non-Bolshevik socialist government, dominated by the Mensheviks, and the new nation enjoyed a certain respectability in the West. Ramsay MacDonald was one of several socialist leaders who visited Georgia at this time. But the existence of an elected Menshevik government so close to Bolshevik territory could not be tolerated, and Stalin contrived an invasion in 1921. Tiflis fell after a few days, the non-Bolshevik parties were suppressed, and a Soviet Republic of Georgia was proclaimed.

The various new Soviet republics tended to be more and more organised from Moscow, by Stalin's Commissariat of Nationalities.

As their interests became more obviously subordinated to those of Russia, their local Communists became disenchanted. In Georgia the local Party's Central Committee voiced its discontent openly, but was suppressed by Stalin and his fellow-Georgian Ordzhonikdze. After this, apart from an unsuccessful revolt in Georgia in 1924, there was little open opposition to the new (1924) Constitution, which formalised the subordination of the Soviet republics to Moscow.

According to the 1924 Constitution the government structure was headed by the All-Union (i.e. federal) Congress of Soviets, which had its executive the Central Executive Committee, which in turn had its small Presidium where the real decisions were made. On the lower levels there were local, district, provincial and republic soviets. All adults except 'non-citizens' had a vote, but it was confined to the elections of their own local soviet. In turn the members of the local soviet would elect from among themselves members to the next highest soviet, and so on. Thus the members of the higher and influential bodies were passed through the filter of several elections and this, combined with the influence permeating from Moscow, ensured that only approved people would be elected. (Influence over local elections to government and Party offices was exerted by sending a Party member from a higher body to 'suggest' which of the aspirants should be nominated as candidate. This advice was usually followed, but until the thirties local bodies sometimes succeeded in ignoring the recommendations.) Each of the Soviet republics had its own soviet, and this was allowed to administer certain activities (such as local trade) with only general supervision from Moscow. This division of responsibility satisfied neither the local Communists demanding more autonomy, nor those Russian Communists who demanded greater centralisation. But it was backed by Lenin and Stalin and was adopted. Earlier, it had been decided to call the new federation the Union of Soviet Socialist Republics. Its first President (technically the President of the Central Executive Committee) was Kalinin, an old revolutionary of peasant origin. His was never a decisive role, but he played a great part in mollifying the peasantry.

The governmental structure and the Party structure were apparently separate, but in reality the acts of government bodies accorded with Party policy. This was because at every level of government there was a parallel Party organisation, and the higher the body the more closely were the two sides intertwined. While in the formal sense meetings, say, of the government's Presidium were quite separate from the gatherings of the Party's Politburo, the same persons belonged to each. However, this did not always prevent differences between those whose prime loyalty was to the Party and those who acted in the name of the government. Often there was a conflict between ideology and expediency (as for example, in a later period, over the question of the role of the profit motive in the Soviet economy). Before Stalin became in effect both Party and government such conflicts could be resolved by discussion; during his ascendancy they were naturally muted, but after his death much of the manœuvring which appeared to be between personalities was in fact a reflection of differences between Party and government.

The Party

In 1922 the last effective remnants of the Menshevik and Social Revolutionary parties were eliminated by the GPU, and show trials were held in which 14 Social Revolutionary leaders were condemned to death (although execution was delayed for two years). Henceforth, although there remained inside the bureaucracy and taking part in policy discussions former members and sympathisers of the non-Bolshevik parties, the struggle between different policies and philosophies increasingly took place within the Party, rather than between the Party and its opponents. This threatened Party unity and in 1921 (after a dispute over the role of trade unions had split the Bolsheviks) there had been a formal prohibition of dissident groups inside the Party. But this prohibition did not prevent the emergence of opposing factions and personalities.

The Party itself was changing in character. The old revolutionary and idealistic members were being joined by newer adherents, many of whom were careerists and most of whom were administrators rather than critics. Organisation, obedience and pleasing the right people became more important than courage and thinking. At the same time those persons, Party and non-Party, who had enjoyed the violence of War Communism, distrusted the moderation of the NEP, and hankered for the good old days, were able to some extent to satisfy their nostalgia by participating in the GPU, which was virtually the Cheka under another name. Greater economic freedom under the NEP tended (in theory at least) to strengthen those classes most likely to subvert the regime. Hence greater economic freedom had to be matched by restrictions on political freedom, and the GPU was an essential weapon in this.

This situation provided an opportunity for an ambitious personality to climb towards the top, the qualities required being absolute ruthlessness, patience and calculation, and a realisation that the methods used by Lenin to bring his minority Bolshevik Party to power might also be used to bring to power a minority within the Party. Stalin had these qualities, and in addition he benefited from two pieces of good fortune: his colleagues chose him for seemingly innocuous posts which in fact enabled him to use the only two forces which would really count, violence and the Party members' votes; and Lenin died just as he was on the point of acting against him.

Stalin was the son of a shoemaker in Georgia, a land where men were quick on the draw, where blood feuds were taken seriously, and where men killed frequently. This background, and his education in a church school where he was trained for the priesthood, probably explains why Stalin developed into a nonconformist and confused teenager, was expelled from his school, and became a revolutionary. As a member of the Social Democratic Party (later to give birth to the Bolshevik Party) Stalin distinguished himself in banditry and conspiracy. He was involved in bloody bank robberies carried out to raise Party funds, and his taste for intrigue led him in his mid-twenties to contrive a split in the Baku Party. After the Revolution of March 1917 he returned to Petrograd from exile in Siberia and supervised the editing of the Party's newspaper *Pravda*.

Stalin had been a member of what was later to be called the Politburo from 1917, and from the start was entrusted with the unglamorous organisational tasks in the Party: selecting the right member for the right job, influencing Party elections, learning the strengths and weaknesses of individual members. At one period Stalin was the only person who was in both the Party's vital bureaux, the Politburo and the Orgburo. Moreover, when the Party Secretariat was established, Stalin's old crony Molotov soon became its *de facto* head. Meanwhile in 1919 the government office of Workers' and Peasants' Inspection was opened. This was intended to supervise and in fact to create a civil service. It was to eliminate the traditional bureaucratic evils of corruption and incompetence. It had the power, and the duty, of making a thorough investigation of any governmental department or office. Stalin became the head of this organisation. Subsequently, in 1921, a parallel Party organisation was formed (the Control Commission) with the same objects of weeding out careerism, misbehaviour and incompetence in the ranks of Party members. The periodic purges, when unsatisfactory members were expelled from the Party, were based on evidence supplied by the Control Commission. When in 1922 Stalin replaced Molotov as head of the Party Secretariat he was able to influence the work of the Control Commission. At the same time, his Party position and his direction of the Workers' and Peasants' Inspection meant that he had great influence in the GPU's policing activities; in fact after the death of Dzerzhinsky in 1926 Stalin had more weight in the GPU than Yagoda, Dzerzhinsky's successor as nominal head of the organisation.

Right from the start Stalin used his advantages to appoint his own supporters to key posts in the Party's bureaucracy or 'Apparat', as it began to be called. These supporters in turn would supervise the filling of vacancies in their own spheres of influence. Thus as time passed Stalin's strength in the Party increased and he could ensure a preponderance of his own supporters in elections to the more important policy-making bodies. Almost without exception Stalin's lieutenants were mediocrities in the intellectual and moral sense, just as he was. The dog-like Molotov, without a grain of originality or a spark of warmth, was not untypical. He bore the nickname 'Stone-bottom' because of his nature, and his apparently permanent posture as he sat behind his card index. But he was absolutely loyal to Stalin and would carry out the latter's instruction inflexibly.

Trotsky described Stalin as 'the Party's most eminent mediocrity', and probably regarded himself as the most eminent brain in the Party. He may have been right in both propositions, but what perhaps he did not realise was that Stalin's mediocrity was no bar to power. In the new Party what counted was the ability to find a majority of loyal, even if unthinking, votes. Trotsky relied on the old revolutionary weapons of fiery speeches and clever pamphlets, which in the new conditions had lost their effectiveness. Inflexible votes could crush incontrovertible arguments.

Lenin's health began to deteriorate in 1921 and from the beginning of 1922 until his death in January 1924 his participation in government and Party life was only sporadic. It was during these last two years that his distrust of Stalin's growing power intensified. The first big difference between Lenin and Stalin concerned the latter's overriding of the Georgian Communist Party in 1922, subordinating the Georgian Communists to Moscow and enforcing the resignation of the local Party control committee. In three notes on this question Lenin blamed himself for not intervening previously against the policies of Stalin and his assistant Ordzhonikidze. He also perceptively remarked that Stalin, being non-Russian, was a more blatant example of Russian chauvinism than the home-bred variety.

Stalin heard of Lenin's strictures and tried to see him, but Krupskaya (Lenin's wife) refused to admit him because Lenin was too ill to endure an argument. Stalin abused her, but without swaying her. Subsequently Lenin wrote to Stalin demanding an apology and more or less broke off relations with him. At the same time he instructed Trotsky to defend the interests of the Georgian nationalist Communists against Stalin's Apparat. A few days later another stroke finally removed Lenin from political activity.

Probably because he did not wish to break Party unity at a time when the Bolsheviks were desperately unpopular in the country, and because Stalin seemed indispensable, Trotsky did not reveal the contents of Lenin's notes on the Georgian question, and Stalin was able to ensure that they were not published. At the Party Congress in 1923, which was carefully packed with Stalin's protégés, Trotsky remained silent and the overthrow of the Georgian local Communists by the Apparat was approved. Thus Georgia lost any semblance of independence within the new USSR, and Trotsky lost the last chance to attack Stalin with the unquestioned authority of Lenin.

In retrospect, Lenin's death in 1924 was the most disastrous blow suffered by the Bolsheviks. If he had lived a few more active years the USSR might have escaped its subsequent misfortunes. Among the Bolshevik leaders he was the only one who combined the honesty to admit his mistakes, the courage to change course accordingly, and the authority to ensure full support for such changes. After his death Kamenev, Zinoviev and Stalin formed a collective leadership of the Party. On the government side Rykov was chosen as Prime Minister (i.e. Chairman of the Council of Ministers). Rykov was partly a figurehead—he was probably chosen because he was wholly Russian—and took his instructions from the Party. One of the Party's triumvirate, Kamenev, was Rykov's deputy, while Rykov himself was a member of the Party's seven-man Politburo.

Before he died Lenin had composed what was to be known as his 'testament', in which he evaluated his possible successors. Trotsky he characterised as brilliant but not entirely suitable as a leader and Bukharin was perhaps the most highly praised. Lenin did not in fact name, or even hint at, his successor, but he left no doubt that Stalin did not have his approval. He worried about Stalin's accumulation of power and doubted whether the power would be used with moderation. About the same time Lenin wrote two articles in the Party's newspaper *Pravda*, criticising Stalin's activities. Then he added a postscript to his testament, characterising Stalin as 'rude', and proposing that he be removed from his post as General Secretary of the Party. At the meeting of the Party's Central Committee after Lenin died, his testament was read, but at the instance of Zinoviev, supported by Kamenev, it was agreed that Lenin's fears about Stalin were, happily, groundless. The testament was suppressed and not published in the USSR until 1956, although the *New York Times* printed an accurate version of it as early as October 1926.

Those like Zinoviev, Kamenev, Bukharin and Rykov, who were neither Trotskyists nor Stalinists, were confronted with a choice of evils and their own freedom of action was limited by their refusal to create an open split in the Party at a time when it was unpopular. Trotsky, too, was reluctant to split the Party and this was one reason why he did not put all his energy into the internal Party struggle. He enjoyed in any case two great advantages: his popularity, based on his oratory and his real achievements in the Civil War, and his control of the Red Army. Stalin's position was not absolutely secure in the early twenties, and he was careful to display a certain obsequiousness and modesty in his dealings with the Party. Although he had lost his position as head of the Workers' and Peasants' Inspection when that body was merged with the Party's Central Control Commission, the new, even more powerful, combined organisation with its influence on the GPU was headed by his associate Kuibyshev. This enabled Stalin to interfere with policies approved by Rykov's government. For example, the GPU might arrest foreigners or others serving the government and although Stalin could never be shown to have initiated such moves only a humiliating approach to him by the government could effect a release, and this not always.

Trotsky made his first attack on the Kamenev-Zinoviev-Stalin triumvirate during Lenin's last illness, accusing the three of fostering the disappearance of democracy within the Party. This led to a castigation of Trotsky at a Party conference in early 1924, and the posting abroad of a number of his supporters. For example, Rakovsky, the prime minister of the Ukraine, was appointed ambassador to Britain, and after his departure Stalin's friend Kaganovich was sent to purge the Ukrainian Party organisation. Stalin also secured an increase of Party membership, ostensibly to strengthen the proletarian element, but in fact to improve his own position.

Trotsky was absent from Lenin's funeral (he later claimed that

Stalin had deceived him about the date) and, at this ceremony and the Party Congress which followed it, Stalin both established the sanctification of Lenin and played the role of first disciple. Some months later Trotsky published a pamphlet, *Lessons of October*, in which he again bewailed the disappearance of Party democracy, and scathingly attacked Kamenev and Zinoviev. The resulting controversy between Trotsky and this pair had the effect of damaging the public image of both sides, while Stalin remained aloof. By this attack Trotsky also damaged his position in the Politburo, and the latter removed him from his post as War Commissar, a demotion which he accepted meekly. This weakening of Trotsky enabled Stalin to pay less and less attention to his two co-leaders Zinoviev and Kamenev, and in 1925 he added three of his supporters (Kalinin, Molotov, Voroshilov) to the existing Politburo (Stalin, Trotsky, Bukharin, Kamenev, Rykov, Tomsky, Zinoviev).

By 1925 the Politburo was split between the Stalinists, the so-called leftists (Kamenev and Zinoviev) and the moderates (Rykov, Bukharin and Tomsky), with Trotsky maintaining his independence. The 'left' gave priority to ideology and to the spread of revolution abroad, in the meantime making a balanced investment in light and basic industry and in agriculture. The moderates gave priority to the solution of internal problems and regarded concessions to the peasantry and agricultural investment as the best economic policy. Stalin supported the moderates for tactical reasons, and in December 1925 a Party Congress condemned the left. Both sides claimed Lenin as their guide, but when Kamenev proposed a vote of no-confidence in Stalin the majority against him was overwhelming.

After the victory Stalin sent his supporter Kirov to Zinoviev's stronghold, Leningrad, where he undermined the latters' support in the local Party. Kamenev and Zinoviev were more or less forced into alliance with Trotsky, and in October 1926 at a meeting of the Central Committee Trotsky and Kamenev were expelled from the Politburo, and Zinoviev was replaced as head of the Communist International. But diplomatic reverses, particularly the massacre by Chiang Kai Shek of the Chinese Communists, encouraged the three dissentients to again attack the leadership (i.e. Stalin and the moderates). In 1927 Trotsky and Zinoviev were expelled from the Party, and at the Party Conference in December 1927 even the moderates were shouted down by cries of 'Long live Stalin!' when they asked that the leftists should be given a fair hearing. The Congress expelled about 75 major 'opportunists' from the Party. Zinoviev and Kamenev made public

68

recantations, and one night a squad of GPU men bundled Trotsky, still in his pyjamas, into a train to Alma Ata.

After a period of exile at Alma Ata, Trotsky was deported to Turkey, and then driven from country to country until he finally found haven in Mexico. Reprisals were taken against his family. He became the leader of an anti-Stalin émigré movement and was finally murdered in 1940. The Trotskyist parties which still existed, sometimes even flourished, outside the USSR, together with his often brilliant writings, were all that remained of him. Inside Russia, his writings were banned, and his existence hardly mentioned. He disappeared without a trace, except when some unfortunate was branded as a 'Trotskyite'.

After the elimination of the leftists, Stalin in 1928 proceeded to liquidate his former allies, the moderates.

Social Policy

Education of the workers and peasants had always been one of the Bolsheviks' first priorities. But even though teachers' salaries were exceedingly low, there were not enough resources to provide a good education for all. By 1928 almost every town child received an elementary education, but only about two-thirds of country children. The literacy campaigns had met with some success: by 1928 almost half of the Russian population was able to read and write, and this proportion was much higher among the younger people. The educational service provided for Red Army conscripts was the biggest single factor in overcoming illiteracy. In the schools new methods were introduced. The rigid divisions between different subjects were broken down, and there were some interesting discussions, and some action, directed towards bringing education and productive labour closer together. In some cases a factory would adopt a given school to give pupils practical experience at the workbench which they could relate to what they were learning at the school desk. An attempt to replace strict discipline with voluntary self-control by the students was not successful, and the frequent arrest or expulsion of teachers on political grounds was an additional hindrance. As in other fields, there was a great difference between theory and actuality, and between one place and another, but nevertheless Soviet educational innovations during the twenties deserved more attention than they in fact received in other countries. In the 1930s, when social initiative fell on stonier ground, there was a partial return to tradition: marks, grades, old-fashioned discipline, and even Latin were reintroduced in the high schools.

New universities were established, but later these and the older institutions suffered from political causes. The teaching staff of the universities could only be provided by using the old scholars and specialists, most of whom were hostile to the regime. Control over these teachers and occasional expulsions could only harm the teaching process. Moreover, the raw material entering the universities was inferior, for it was largely composed of children of manual workers and peasants. Children of the non-citizens* were usually excluded, but sometimes penetrated the class barrier by fraud. There was a blossoming of vocational and part-time education; the universities had their own workers' faculties ('Rabfaks'), and many factories organised their own schools or classes.

It was during the twenties that in reaction to the distorted family and moral life imposed by the old regime and its church an equally extreme but opposite concept appeared. At one time it almost seemed that the Bolsheviks were attempting to end the family as a social unit, but in fact only a handful inside the Party envisaged this. However, free love was accepted, and instant divorce and instant marriage were made easy. (Divorce was immediately granted at the request of one of the partners.) Easy divorce and the critical housing situation often resulted in ludicrous and tragic situations. Depending on which of the marriage partners was the legal tenant of the home, a husband or wife could without warning lose both spouse and house. A wife might learn of her divorce only when her husband brought his new wife home. Sometimes the legal tenant would allow the ex-wife or ex-husband to remain. Because in the towns the home consisted usually of a single room, there were cases when a husband and wife slept in the same room with two or three of their previous partners. At the same time there was a good deal of orgy-going, especially among the newly rich Nepmen and government and Party functionaries. Scandals occasionally came to a head and local Party organisations would be purged, the enquiries often revealing fresh scandals. In general, the free love experiment, pursued with typically Russian over-enthusiasm, was a failure and became a danger to the state. One reason for its failure was that it was neither free nor love: with influential men obtaining unwilling women by threat or bribe, it seemed that not

---

* The Soviet term for these people was 'the deprived ones'. They were priests, former merchants, etc. who did not enjoy the rights of citizenship (including the right of higher education for their children).

only was food distributed unfairly, but also women. In later years divorce was made a more serious process, although it remained easier than in most countries. In time, too, most Party members were persuaded that, being an élite, they should set a high moral standard.

After 1922 life for the ordinary Russian was plainly getting better, and those who had survived were adequately fed in the ensuing years. But the Civil War had left hordes of orphans and homeless children (estimated at more than two million in 1920) and these banded together and roamed the countryside as bandits, presenting a serious danger in some localities. There was a genuine intention to capture and re-educate these children, but many were already too dehumanised, and were killed by the Cheka.

The Cheka itself at one time seemed likely to disappear. At the time NEP was introduced many prisoners were released and the Cheka (or GPU as it became) was ordered to pursue a more moderate policy. However, as NEP progressed, and as the Stalinists gained Party office throughout the country, arrests of 'hostile elements' (especially of the bourgeois experts on whom the government relied to rehabilitate industry) became more frequent. Justice leaned towards class principles; convicted workers and peasants received lighter sentences than those of more suspect social origins. Occasionally the GPU men themselves were arrested for the misuse of their powers, but they too were usually treated lightly. In one locality some railway workers were shot for stealing sugar, while almost at the same time Cheka men convicted of stealing meat received one year's imprisonment. In general, the GPU had plenty of work; apart from investigating crime and counter-revolution its operatives reported the mood of the people, kept individuals under quiet observation, and ran the censorship. There was a peculiar and often disturbed relationship with the Party. The GPU was responsible for checking the loyalty of Party members, while the latter were often members of the GPU. When the local Party organisations were being purged of Trotskyites, and at other times, there was much tension between the two bodies, resulting from the arrest of Party members by the GPU.

As always in Russia, there was a clear distinction between what was intended to be done, what was done, and what was said to be done. It was in the towns that reality corresponded most closely with the Party's conception. In the countryside the Party and government had less impact than they imagined. Party members in the villages did not last long, soon abandoning their membership. Local Party officials were arbitrary in their actions, incompetent in their decisions, and

frequently drunk. Both in town and country restriction of news produced an information vacuum filled by tenacious and fantastic
rumours. A Japanese invasion, the murder of Trotsky, a certain
famine, the flight of the Bolsheviks, were all announced by these
rumours, among many others. Probably the majority of peasants had
little idea who the Bolsheviks were, and what they were trying to do.
Most, at least in the villages of Western Russia and the Ukraine, still
thought the Bolsheviks were Jews.

World Revolution

Marx had emphasised that a new socialist society could only be built
in conditions of prosperity, and the doctrine of 'permanent revolution', associated with Trotsky, was a development of this theme.
In theory, the Russian Revolution had been premature, for it should
have followed—not preceded—revolutions in more advanced
countries which had long since entered the capitalist phase. For the
prosperity which was a prerequisite of socialist society Russia needed
large-scale production and capital equipment. 'Permanent revolution'
implied the engineering (or at least the inevitability) of socialist
revolutions in the more advanced countries of Western Europe, which
would then consolidate the Russian Revolution by giving economic
help to the Soviet Union. Eventually, socialism would spread everywhere, to achieve the 'world revolution'.

After 1917 the Bolshevik leaders expected an almost immediate
series of revolutions in Central and Western Europe, and did what
they could to trigger them. They had strong hopes that a mere
declaration, like that on peace which urged the soldiers of the
western powers to stop fighting for the capitalists, would spread
revolution. When it appeared that more concrete stimulation was
required, money and trained agitators were made available. But in
defeated and impoverished Germany, which seemed most ripe for a
Bolshevik takeover, the 1919 Revolution was defeated and the
Bavarian Soviet Republic lasted only a couple of months. The
Hungarian Revolution likewise failed to survive.

To organise revolutionary activity outside Russia the Communist
International (Comintern) was used. This was quite separate from
the Commissariat of Foreign Affairs and it happened sometimes that
the latter would busily cultivate friendly relations with a foreign
government which the Comintern was simultaneously working to

overthrow. At times it seemed that the Soviet government was genuinely surprised that foreigners refused to believe its claim that Comintern activities were quite independent.

The Comintern had been founded in 1919, to provide a Bolshevik alternative to the old Socialist Second International which hitherto had co-ordinated the activities of the socialist parties of the various countries. The Communist International—or Third International— held its first Congress at Moscow in March 1919, but was attended by no outstanding foreign delegates. Its second Congress was more impressive, with delegations from nearly 40 countries. Zinoviev became the head of the Comintern, and its policy, which earlier had consisted of generalities about agitation in armies and in trade unions and about the need to crush moderate socialists, became more and more concerned with an obedient and disciplined execution of directives from Moscow. These directives tended in later years to give priority to the Soviet Union rather than the various national Communist parties.

At times Zinoviev and the Comintern officials seemed to live in a fantastic world of their own. In 1923 another rising was engineered in Germany and in its course the Comintern telegraphed directives which had little relationship with the actual situation. Because military advisers had been sent from Moscow, it was imagined that thousands of armed proletarians were on the march, whereas in fact the German Communists not only disposed of negligible armed strength but even proved unable to initiate a general strike. This failure not only made ordinary Germans more receptive to Nazi propaganda about the Bolshevik menace; it discredited the German Communist Party, the Comintern and Zinoviev. The prestige of the latter was similarly shaken by a futile attempt to infiltrate Red Army men into Estonia and start a revolution there.

In the twenties, as the prospect of world revolution receded, the concept of 'socialism in one country' appeared. This was favoured by the moderate Bolshevik leaders, and was adopted by Stalin as a useful weapon against the 'permanent revolution' theories of Zinoviev and Trotsky. Socialism in one country implied the strengthening of the USSR in order to withstand the expected capitalist attacks, without the support of revolutions in the West. After a decade of waiting in vain for world revolution, the new doctrine had overwhelming attractions and was certainly more practical than the 'permanent revolution' theory. It was the manner in which the USSR was to be strengthened that became the contentious issue between the moderates and the Stalinists. When the latter gained power, socialism in one country took the form of massive industrialisation with the aim of providing the USSR with the defensive and economic power already possessed by the capitalist countries.

Diplomatic Recognition

By the end of the Civil War few of the Bolshevik leaders still expected an immediate world revolution, but they continued to believe that the capitalist powers would sooner or later attack Russia to put an end to the threat of international Communism. The Allied intervention during the Civil War had strengthened this belief. The second great danger was the probability of a final economic collapse; the abandonment of War Communism coincided with an unusually bad famine, industrial production was only a fraction of the pre-war level. Trade with the West seemed to offer the best chance of countering both these threats: Leninist doctrine suggested that if western businessmen found trade with Russia profitable they would encourage their governments to seek better relations rather than war. At the same time trade might be accompanied by investment, with western capital and experts helping to reconstruct Russian industry.

In fact, although Russia had some raw materials to export, any worthwhile trade would have needed credit. To obtain credit, not to speak of capital investment, was not easy after the Soviet government's renunciation of foreign debts and nationalisation of foreign investment. These disclaimed obligations were so large that Russia would have been unable to pay, even if the government had wanted to. However the Soviet government was willing to pay extra interest on new credit received, as a gesture towards meeting western claims. But this in itself was not enough; few capitalists would invest in the Soviet Union so long as that country's existence was not recognised by the West. Hence the quest for diplomatic recognition could not be separated from the search for international credit.

Russia's first success was achieved just as the Civil War was ending. In May 1920 Krassin led a trade delegation to London and, in spite of right-wing hostility and British feelings about the Russo-Polish war, an agreement was signed ten months later. This agreement implied *de facto* recognition of the Communist government. The next move was to cultivate relations with Germany.

At this time Germany and Russia seemed natural allies, for both were the black sheep of the international community, and the Franco-British policy of squeezing immoderate reparations payments from Germany drove that country more and more towards an eastern alliance. The *rapprochement* between the two countries began in late 1920, and was peculiar in that it took place on two levels. Taking advantage of the demilitarisation forced on Germany by the Allies, Russia offered the German military authorities a clandestine arrangement whereby, in return for tank and aircrew training facilities and the manufacture in Soviet factories of aircraft and weapons, the German army would give the Red Army technical assistance and training, and reconstruct the Soviet weapons industry. These arrangements (of which for some time the German government had no knowledge) proved useful to the armed forces of both countries.

Meanwhile the British government had arranged the Genoa Conference for April 1922, and one of its results was expected to be an agreed and co-ordinated policy for the economic reconstruction of Russia. The Soviet government did not relish a joint approach to its problems, feeling that economic agreements with the West were best made with individual countries so that one could be played against the other. Germany was still theoretically liable to pay war reparations to Russia, and although the Soviet government did not seriously intend to press for these, the mere possibility provided a bargaining counter for obtaining concessions from the German government. En route to the Genoa Conference Chicherin and his Soviet delegation had talks in Berlin, but were unable to persuade the Germans to sign any agreement. However, confronted at Genoa by French venom and British superciliousness, and fearing an Anglo-Franco-Russian agreement behind its back, the German delegation felt compelled to sign with the Russian delegation the Treaty of Rapallo.

This agreement, signed during the course of the Genoa Conference, shook London and Paris and elated Moscow. The Soviet government had at last achieved *de jure* recognition by a European power. Economic agreements followed the exchange of ambassadors, each country waived financial claims against the other, and for a time relations were very friendly. But Chicherin's pro-German policy did not enjoy unanimous support among his colleagues. On the one hand, the Trotskyites and others who hankered after world revolution continued to prod the German Communists towards an uprising and in 1923 succeeded in provoking disturbances (these were suppressed and damaged still further the reputation and prospects of the German Communists). On the other hand, Stalin, with his habitual suspicion of any action taken without his participation, used his influence in the GPU to create 'incidents', like the framing and show trials of Germans working in Russia. Incidents like these, together with a softening of Allied policy culminating in the Locarno agreement (1925) by which Germany was admitted to the League of Nations, led to growing estrangement between Germany and Russia, but no real crisis developed between them until the thirties.

Meanwhile a Labour government in Britain had in 1924 granted *de jure* recognition to the Soviet government, and this example was followed by several other countries (including France, but the USA withheld recognition until 1933, although this did not prevent private commercial agreements with the USSR). A general settlement between Britain and the Soviet Union, including compensation for British property nationalised after the Revolution, proved impossible. But agreement on most issues, while postponing a decision on the matter of compensation, was incorporated in a draft treaty. The ratification of this treaty, however, was prevented by a British general election.

Some mystery still attaches to this election of October 1924. It was called after the Labour government had been defeated on a resolution accusing it of lenience towards an insignificant Communist weekly paper, which had appealed to British soldiers to disobey orders. Five days before polling, Conservative newspapers published a letter from Zinoviev to the British Communist Party in which, among other things, revolutionary activity in Ireland and in the British army was recommended. Since the Conservative campaign had been based on Labour's softness towards Communism, this letter made effective electoral ammunition and helped to defeat Labour in the election. One of the first acts of the new Conservative government was to refuse ratification of the Anglo-Russian treaty negotiated by its predecessor.

The 'Zinoviev Letter' was almost certainly a forgery and was entirely successful; it ended what was to be the last attempt to reach an all-embracing Anglo-Russian accommodation. Moscow's support for British workers in the 1926 General Strike, and Communist activity in China, encouraged the newly elected Conservative government to pursue an anti-Russian policy and in May 1927 the British police raided the Soviet Trade Delegation. This raid, which was an infringement of diplomatic privilege, produced little which could be called incriminating, but nevertheless two weeks later Britain broke off diplomatic relations with Russia. This, apart from gratifying Conservative supporters, helped Stalin in his campaign against the moderate Bolsheviks, whose policies depended on good relations with the West. The restoration of relations in 1929, after a new Labour government had been returned to office, did not repair the damage.

Asian Policy

With the exception of Japan, the countries of Asia were undeveloped and lacking an industrial proletariat capable of creating a revolution. They were, however, very much under the influence of the West and any move they might make to free themselves from foreign dominance was considered useful by the Soviet government. The latter believed that while any new regimes in these countries would be 'nationalist-bourgeois' (like the Russian Provisional Government of 1917) they would still weaken and divert the West, and would eventually be replaced by truly proletarian governments.

Soviet policy towards China was based on these considerations. China at this time was split between the old Pekin government and the revolutionary Kuomintang regime in the south. The latter was regarded as potentially the most effective anti-imperialist force in the east, and to develop the military side of the movement some Chinese officers were trained in Moscow. One of these Russian-trained officers was Chiang Kai Shek, who on his return established a military school where more officers were trained on the Soviet pattern.

The Kuomintang was a nationalist movement and the extent to which it should have Russian support was one of the issues separating Trotsky from Stalin. The former, still believing in World Revolution, wished to build up the Chinese Communist Party, which was gaining strength at the time. Stalin, apart from his antipathy towards any Trotsky-inspired advice, felt that a Kuomintang victory would be one way of confounding the British, whom he suspected were planning war against the USSR. Stalin's policy was put into effect, and the Chinese Communists were instructed to identify themselves with the Kuomintang, working with the latter and refraining from any action or propaganda which would alarm it. In 1926, under the leadership of Chiang Kai Shek, the Kuomintang began a year's successful offensive against the Pekin government, and extended its territory up to the Yangtze. The Kuomintang then turned against its Communist allies. Many were murdered and the survivors forced into hiding. Eventually Mao Tse-tung and others rebuilt a small Party nucleus and led it to safety into Western China, but until the forties the Chinese Communist Party was incapable of effective action on a national scale. The disastrous consequence of following Soviet advice was never forgotten by the Chinese Communists.

Although in 1920 Russia made an unsuccessful attempt to annex Northern Persia, by 1921 it was possible to sign a treaty giving Russia control of Caspian Sea fishing rights, and permitting Russian occupation of Persia should any other country threaten the USSR from Persian territory. A treaty with Afghanistan was also signed in 1921. Relations with Turkey were friendly. In 1921 Kars and its surroundings was returned to the Turks, who immediately began to massacre its Armenian population. Some Soviet aid was given in the campaign against the Greeks; Kemal's Turkey seemed an obvious example of new nationalistic forces attacking the old imperialism, and it was this feeling which ensured that Russo-Turkish relations remained good until 1939. During the thirties Russia gave Turkey some economic and technical aid.

Religion under the Bolsheviks

The established Church of tsarist Russia, the Russian Orthodox, was an institution more tenacious than tsarism itself. Russia was predominantly a country of peasants, and the latter had a deep, if crude, belief in God. Yet the Church as an organisation was probably held in less respect than it believed. It was in any case split by a distinct class division: the 'black' priests (so called because of their dress) led a monastic life, were the traditional guardians of what religious learning there was, and supplied from their ranks the higher dignitaries of the Church. The 'white' clergy consisted mainly of the local priests. Their promotion was restricted, they were allowed to marry (but not with completely free choice), were usually semi-educated, and were responsible for the spiritual needs of their parish. The Church took full advantage of the ignorance of its adherents, village priests leaned towards the witchcraft aspects of their profession and were neither able nor willing to raise the cultural level of their flock. Moreover, as the Bolsheviks liked to point out, the priesthood did nothing to relieve the traditional repression of the common people, in fact it encouraged it by teaching that the humble suffered by God's will, and that suffering was good for the soul. The Church's moral bankruptcy was largely a product of its vested interest in the established order, however bad. Tolstoy, whom many regard as the greatest Russian Christian, was excommunicated by the Orthodox Church. Rasputin, the self-styled Man of God whose moral degeneracy was obvious, was not.

Communism was an atheistic movement, but atheism was not its main concern, and Lenin tolerated church-going Party members. Soviet religious policy was influenced by the knowledge that the Party was (and outside the towns still is) an atheistic minority surrounded by a numerically overwhelming Christian majority. While continuing to regard religion as the people's opium the Soviet authorities rarely prevented believers attending Orthodox worship. They did, however, make great efforts to kill religious belief by propaganda, and at certain periods persecuted the clergy. But, ignoring the occasional excesses, and respecting the atheistic beliefs of the Communists, Soviet religious policy was not unreasonable; the individual might still enjoy the comforts of his religion, but the Church's social impact (or, in some opinions, social harm) was restricted.

While the Bolsheviks were reaching for power in 1917 another revolution was taking place in the Orthodox Church. Taking advantage of the general confusion, a Church council elected a Patriarch. The office of Patriarch had been abolished by Peter the Great and the revival was intended to strengthen the Church by providing a leader around whom all might rally. The person 'elected' (he did not receive the most votes: the election was to some extent fixed) was Tikhon, who late in 1917 had to face damaging anti-Church legislation. When private property in real estate was abolished, the Church lost much of its wealth. This blow was followed by the confiscation of the Church's schools and seminaries, which were transferred to the Ministry of Education. Then a decree established the civil wedding as the only valid form of marriage ceremony, and in early 1918 the Church was finally separated from the state, denied the right to own any property, and the teaching of religion in schools was forbidden.

Patriarch Tikhon's reaction to the Bolsheviks was unambiguous: 'Come to your senses, ye madmen, and cease your bloody doings . . .' However, the new laws were enforced even though blood was sometimes shed. Churches became the property of the believers who worshipped in them, while the monasteries were taken over by the state. This latter led to the discovery that many of the sacred relics of the Church were fakes: the 'miraculously preserved' remains of one saint were found to be of wax, the 'bones' of another were of cast iron. These revelations prompted a complete investigation and to their joy the authorities discovered that all kinds of rubbish had been presented for the reverence of the ignorant faithful. The publicising of these frauds was probably the most successful atheistic propaganda ever used by the Communists.

During the period of War Communism hundreds of priests were killed, but this provoked little active discontent among the religious masses; the peasantry apparently loved its God more than it loved its clergy. By 1920 the monasteries and convents had been converted to hospitals, schools, sanatoria, prisons, and barracks. The Orthodox Church was threatened also by the development of sects. In the disturbed conditions and with the troubles of the traditional Church, old sects attracted new members and new sects were established. Even more damaging were the splits in the Church itself. The most significant splinter group was the so-called 'Renovationist' Church, which split from the Orthodox ostensibly because the latter in 1922 resisted the handing over of church valuables to be sold for famine relief, as ordered by the government. The Renovationists were against the privileges of the black clergy (which is why they gained so much white clergy support), replaced Church Slavonic by Russian in their services, and were openly, and not without servility, pro-Soviet. There were also the Regenerators, somewhat similar but even more progressive, whose leader described the Orthodox and the Renovationists respectively as black crabs and red crabs: their colour was different but neither could crawl forwards. The government in the early twenties tended to regard the Renovationists as the lesser of several religious evils, and made some efforts to widen the split. At one time it seemed that the Renovationists would rout the Orthodox, but when government encouragement of the splinter groups ended in the late twenties most of their supporters returned to the old Church as eagerly as they had earlier abandoned it.

In 1922 Tikhon was at last arrested for his hostility, and preparations were made for a show trial on the usual charge of counter-revolutionary activity. But before this could take place the Patriarch made a complete recantation, regretting his previous anti-Soviet actions, repudiating tsarism, and pledging his support for the government. After this he was released, the more savage pressures were removed from the Orthodox Church, and when Tikhon died in 1925 he was allowed a prestigious and public funeral ceremony. Tikhon's successor was Sergius, whose first two years of office were spent largely in prison. He was finally released from gaol in 1927, after he and his colleagues signed a declaration which identified the Orthodox Church with the Soviet Union, so that any action against the government was to be regarded as ungodly. This declaration was not accepted by all priests. Those Church leaders already interned in a White Sea island concentration camp disowned it, and so did many high priests still at large. The Church in Leningrad was the most significant opposition, but preaching by Sergius's supporters, backed by violence from the GPU, soon silenced the dissidents.

Higher ecclesiastical politics was only one field of anti-religious activity. More important in the long term were efforts at the local level designed to disillusion believers. At first local action was crude, consisting typically of desecrations and violence by Young Communists. This strengthened rather than weakened the faith, so more emphasis began to be placed on persuasion and propaganda. The newspaper *The Godless* was published and in 1925 its supporters founded the Godless League, which was to co-ordinate anti-religious propaganda. The League supplied atheistic literature, lecturers and banners. Its speciality was exposing biblical teaching to scientific facts. But government support of the League was lukewarm because there was a reluctance to antagonise further the peasantry. Moreover, the 'godless cells' which had been hastily set up all over the countryside were frequently lacking in enthusiasm; in fact among the local leaders of the League were many churchgoers who had joined because they were afraid to refuse. Above all, the League's activities were attended by atheists while the believers mostly stayed at home; the godless were always preaching to the converted.

In minor ways, too, attempts were made to weaken the hold of Christian tradition on social life: the official celebration of New Year's Day rather than Christmas, of May Day rather than Easter, and the efforts—partly successful—to give civic weddings some of the atmosphere of the church ceremonial. Quite unsuccessful in the long run was the abolition of Sunday: from 1929 to 1940 there were (officially) six days in the week, on each of which one-sixth of the workers were enjoying their day of rest. This made Sunday church impractical, at least in the towns, but was universally unpopular: husband and wife rarely had the same free day and the concept of the six-day week was passively resisted by most people (like the stall-holder who wrote the notice 'No fish until next former Sunday').

Thus in the first decade of Soviet power, although the Orthodox Church had been broken and discredited as a social organisation the strength of religious belief had not diminished. It may even have been strengthened by the attacks made on it. But it had other storms to weather, notably the attacks on country priests during the collectivisation drive, and the purges of the mid-thirties.

During this period Moslems were treated relatively leniently. This was partly because to the Communists Islam was an unknown quantity. Its status as a hostile element was not disputed, but its place in Marxist social analysis was not clear and nor was the ideologically correct method of opposing it. Moslem Bolsheviks were not numerous, and most of them combined their Communism with traditional religious beliefs, seeing nothing incongruous in adjourning Party meetings when it was time for prayer.

Gradually the attitude of wait-and-see was replaced by encroachments on Moslem privileges. In the twenties the religious endowments were confiscated (there were mainly in the form of land, the income from which maintained schools and mosques). Then the Moslem schools were abolished, and also the Moslem courts of law. In the Caucasus and Central Asia wars and revolts occurred: the Reds did not subdue Moslem resistance in Bokhara until 1922, and it was only in the early thirties that the last armed opposition was wiped out. At the same time, just as the Orthodox Church had split into conservative and progressive factions, the 'New Mosque' movement broke with the traditional Moslem elders and took a pro-Soviet line. The progressive wing of the Ismailites even claimed that the Aga Khan was Lenin's father.

But like Christianity, the Moslem faith remained strong. In 1929, a Communist ex-Moslem school-teacher and leader of the Central Asian anti-religious movement was torn to pieces after he had erected a statue of Lenin in one of the holiest of Moslem shrines. The de-veiling of women campaign led to bloodshed, as incensed husbands or traditionalists murdered those progressive or pressurised Moslem women who had discarded their veils. Moreover, many local Communists failed to support the militant atheists. In the mid-thirties these moderate Communists, together with many Moslem priests (and also a few over-zealous atheist militants), were imprisoned or executed.

IV

The Five Year Plans

1928

ALTHOUGH MOST RUSSIANS probably did not realise it at the time, 1928 was a turning point in the history of the USSR, for it marked the beginning of forced industrialisation and forced collectivisation, which were to transform, for better or for worse, the life of every inhabitant.

The situation after 1925 was this: the fast rate of economic improvement of the preceding years was in danger of petering out, for it had been obtained by the relatively easy restoration of pre-war productive assets, and future increments could be gained only by investing in completely new plant; there was a large pool of unemployed labour; agricultural production had increased but this had meant the emergence of a class of successful peasant farmers—and all Bolsheviks, even of the Bukharin type, remembered the pre-1914 years when the government had tried with some success to foster a class of prosperous peasants which would support the tsarist regime; the prospect of revolution in other countries, whose industry might have helped the USSR, had receded still further; and most Bolsheviks believed that sooner or later the capitalist powers would attack Russia. Fascism had already appeared in Italy.

Economic stagnation was not to the taste of a Party which regarded itself as a dynamic vanguard. But within the Party there were disagreements about what the next move should be. All were agreed that further industrialisation was necessary; but how, and how fast, was unresolved. The moderates felt that industry should be geared to the peasantry, supplying its wants and prospering as the peasants prospered, and that the political danger of the emergence of prosperous peasants—land-owning, labour-employing and anti-socialist—could be contained by taxation and legislation. Those, like Bukharin and

Rykov, who held these views, pointed out that the mildly socialist agricultural co-operative movement was already embraced by one-third of the peasants. They also advocated better relations with the West so as to obtain capital and experience, and to counter fascism. They were confident that a steady economic improvement would lead to greater popularity for the Party.

Others, notably the leftists led by Zinoviev and Kamenev, gave equal priority in investment to heavy industry, light industry and agriculture, so as to achieve a balanced expansion of production which would keep Russia on the move until world revolution came to her aid. But there were also some leftist theorists who advocated a very fast rate of industrialisation, to be financed mainly by paying low prices to the peasants for agricultural products, which would then be exported, or sold in the towns at higher prices (which would, however, still be moderate prices, so that low wages could be paid to the workers, thus reducing manufacturing costs). Collectivisation of agriculture to facilitate farm mechanisation, to release labour for the towns, and to make easier the unpopular grain collection, was a prerequisite of this policy. Collectivisation also appealed to many Party members because it would break the power of the richer peasants, of whom the Bolsheviks seemed to have an exaggerated fear. (This fear was the reason for the unmentioned inconsistency between the Party's acceptance of bourgeois specialists in industry and its hostility towards rich peasants, who in essence were bourgeois agricultural specialists capable of doing for agricultural production what the industrial specialists were doing for industrial production.)

Stalin may have adopted the policy of rapid industrialisation as early as 1926, but he did not reveal his defection from the moderates' view until after Zinoviev and Kamenev had been defeated. Apart from the economic arguments for a great leap forward, it gave him a tactical weapon inside the Party, a policy with which to oppose the economic views of his Party rivals. But at the time he probably did not foresee another great advantage: that the revolution in the economy would be accompanied by a revolution in society, with the stirring-up of all possible social and political differences into violent conflict. (This process, a partial return to the heady atmosphere of War Communism, Stalin termed the 'intensification of the class struggle'.) In this period of continual crisis and induced conflict the Party was more ready to accept a strong leader such as him.

In October 1927 the Party Congress voted for the formulation of a five-year plan based on a rapid industrialisation, as advocated by Stalin.

The different opinions in economic policy had not only been debated inside the Party, but were also the subject of the various economic plans worked out by the State Planning Commission (Gosplan). This, since 1926, had been tentatively formulating five-year plans of economic development, and produced several variants, based on different rates of growth and different proportions of heavy (basic) and light (consumer) industry. The First Five Year Plan, which was unanimously accepted by a Party conference in spring 1929, stipulated a very fast growth-rate and an enormous preponderance of heavy industry. The proposed speed of development far exceeded what even the most optimistic of left-wingers had envisaged, because they had not regarded as practical the social upheaval which such an extreme programme would involve. But the agricultural crisis of 1928 which had led to collectivisation (itself an extreme measure) was probably among the factors persuading non-Stalinist delegates to vote for the Plan. And given the need to industrialise, the desire to maintain the Bolsheviks in power, and the belief in an inevitable and imminent capitalist attack, it was an arguable alternative to the more moderate proposals. It was a policy of extremes, but because of this perhaps had a better chance of quickly attaining enough momentum to get off the ground. On the other hand, the excess of extremism with which it was carried out was at best harmful and at worst a crime against humanity. Forced economic development naturally required coercion, and hence increased police power and the repression of opposition, but under Stalin these unpleasant but necessary by-products seemed to become ends in themselves. Nowhere was this more evident than in the collectivisation campaign.

Collectivisation

At the end of 1927 rumours spread of an impending famine, though in fact the harvest had been good. Stalin blamed hoarding and specula-tion by the so-called 'kulaks' for this artificial crisis, and there began harassment and persecution of the more prosperous peasants. Then, in 1929, Stalin announce his intention 'to liquidate the kulaks as a class'.

These kulaks were not the kulaks who had been liquidated in the Civil War period. They were the peasants who had become more prosperous than their fellows by dint of hard work and good manage-ment, obeying government exhortations to produce more food. Forced collectivisation involved the incitement against the richer farmers of the unsuccessful poor peasants, and as many of the average peasants as possible. Sometimes this was easy, sometimes not, but when the poorer peasants did not manifest the prescribed measure of class enmity, there was always the OGPU,* and in some cases the army, to support the 'dekulakisation' squads. The division of peasants into kulaks, middle and poor was an abstraction rather than a reality. Many kulaks were respected by their poorer neighbours, who were often of the same family, and it could happen that kulaks were prominent members of village soviets. Thus it is not surprising that when kulaks were attacked they were often defended by the poor and middle peasants.

Nevertheless the kulaks were duly expropriated and killed or deported to work camps of doubtful survivability. With them went a proportion of middle and poor peasants who had resisted collectivisation and thereupon had been labelled also as kulaks. For the majority of poor peasants collectivisation was not unattractive, for they themselves had little to contribute to the new amalgamation of holdings which constituted the collective farm ('kolkhoz'); most of the land, animals and implements for the kolkhoz came from the richer peasants. Moreover, remuneration of the new collective farmers was to be on a basis of man-hours worked and to have no relation to the value of the property handed over by each peasant on joining the kolkhoz.

1929 and 1930 were the years of the collectivisation drive. The richer peasants, who saw they had nothing to gain and then discovered they had nothing to lose either, expressed their despair by burning their crops, killing their cattle and destroying their machinery. In places there was armed resistance and in March 1930 Stalin (perhaps affected by his second wife's suicide) realised that he had gone too far too fast. Accusing officials of being 'dizzy with success', he implied that collectivisation had been rushed against his wishes. Many farms were de-collectivised but nevertheless by the end of 1934 87 per cent of farmland was collective, and 99 per cent by 1937. The slowing down

* As the organ of state security repeatedly changed its name and status, the following account may be useful: in 1922 the separate (i.e. republican) GPU organs were amalgamated with the central OGPU (Unified State Political Board) which in 1931 became the UGB of the Peoples' Commissariat for Internal Affairs (NKVD). The latter, apart from this security board, also had sections dealing with such matters as crime, fire brigades, frontier troops, highways and police. In early 1941 the UGB became a separate ministry (NKGB) and Beria co-ordinated the activities of the NKGB and NKVD. After people's commissariats were retitled ministries these two became the MGB and MVD respectively. In 1953 the MGB was reincorporated in the MVD but in 1954 its functions were transferred to a state committee, the KGB (Commission for State Security).

of collectivisation, however, came too late to avoid famine. The chaos of collectivisation—peasant resistance, lack of machinery, no clear concept of how the new farms were to be organised—led naturally to poor harvests. Nevertheless, all grain in the growing areas was collected by actual or implicit force and taken to the towns or exported. The peasants then began to die of starvation. About 10 to 15 million people died in the 1932–34 famine and its attendant epidemics. The government made every effort to conceal the famine from the outside world and this meant there could be no appeal for international aid. The USSR continued to export grain in exchange for industrial plant. It has been alleged, probably with some truth, that the famine was not unwelcome to Stalin; it was an effective way to break peasant resistance.

Although even Khrushchev after 1956 never acknowledged it, the manner and form of collectivisation was probably the most disastrous act of Stalin: for it sooner or later alienated the peasants, liquidated the most energetic, halved the number of cattle, horses and pigs, and replaced small but highly productive holdings by larger but less productive collective lands. Lenin's first priority—amicable co-operation between worker and peasant—had thus been rendered impossible for at least a generation. Even when town workers were in their turn impoverished, the peasantry remained as an underprivileged class, depressed, deprived and resentful.

The collective farms formed in this manner were ideologically quite acceptable but nevertheless regarded as a second-best form of social organisation. They were not 'state property', the land being granted to the collective peasants in perpetuity. There was also a State Farm concept (Sovkhoz) in which ownership was vested in the state and whose peasants received a wage like factory workers. But the Sovkhoz farms were relatively few and tended to specialise in work such as cattle breeding or fish farming.

Typically a kolkhoz consisted of 50–100 families, who divided their time between the collective land and the small private plots which each household was allowed to keep. They were organised into labour brigades and paid according to the work-days they registered on the collective land. The wages were paid from the farm's income; if, as often happened, the farm made a loss, there were no wages. Each kolkhoz was managed by a chairman and his assistants. These were appointed from above (that is, by the local Party organisation) and frequently had no knowledge of agriculture. Most of the farm's produce (from the collective and, later, from the private holdings) was taken at rock-bottom prices by the state; this was the compulsory delivery, the size of which was fixed in advance by the government through the Ministry of Agriculture and was often more than the farm could grow. Any surplus left after the compulsory delivery had been made could be sold at higher prices. At kolkhoz markets in the towns surplus produce, usually in the form of dairy products, eggs, vegetables and fruit, was sold to the urban population at prices which reflected true market value (and were therefore higher than prices in the state shops, which obtained their supplies from the compulsory deliveries, but which were often empty). This system meant that bread and some of the basic foods were cheap, while the citizen could often obtain more varied supplies by paying high prices in the kolkhoz market. On the other hand the inevitable tendency was for peasants to neglect the collective fields (mainly devoted to grain) and to work hard and intelligently on their private smallholdings, on which they could produce milk, poultry, eggs, honey, vegetables and fruit, fetching high prices in the market. The low yield of the collective lands was depressed even further by a deluge of impracticable instructions from the local Party organisations, each fearful of the consequences if the farms under its jurisdiction failed to fulfil the production plan.

The achievement of collectivisation before the production of tractors and farm machinery was organised, and the slaughter of horses by resentful peasants, was a problem which could be solved only in the long term. To make the best use of machinery, Machine and Tractor Stations (MTS) were organised to maintain and allocate the new implements. One MTS served several farms and rent for the use of its machines took the form of additional deliveries of produce. The MTS also disposed of most of the scarce specialists and rural Party members, who were thus well-placed to exercise surveillance over the neighbouring farms.

Agricultural collectivisation was expected to stimulate peasants to seek work in the towns, and there was in fact a large-scale migration of young farmers to the somewhat better-paid work offered by new industry. (This had started in the NEP and was already causing a town housing crisis. The departure of the younger and more energetic peasants was to be one more factor contributing to agricultural stagnation.) At the same time impoverishment of the peasantry meant that few resources were needed to supply the country population (that is, the majority of Soviet citizens) and what was thus saved could be devoted to the development of heavy industry.

The Five Year Plans

Collectivisation was one half of Stalin's economic policy for 'socialism in one country'. The other half was rapid industrialisation. This did not signify simply an increase of production, but rather the equipment of the USSR with the means of production; the manufacture of goods required by the population was regarded as a very secondary necessity.

The First Five Year Plan was worked out to cover the years 1928–32, and its main emphasis was on the production of energy and of construction material: coal, oil, electricity, steel and other metals, timber and cement. Tractors also had high priority. By 1930 the pace was being forced and the slogan in most use was 'The Five Year Plan in four years!'. In these years, while the Donetz Basin remained the mainstay of coal production, there were massive mining developments east of the Urals. A new iron and steel industry—the Urals-Kuzbass Combine—was established on the basis of the rich and easily mined ores of Magnitogorsk in the Urals and the good coking coal of the Kuznetsk Basin. (Smelting was done at both ends of the combine: trains carried Urals ore to the Kuzbass and returned with Kuzbass coal. Artificially low railway tariffs concealed the wastefulness of this scheme, which did, however, boost Soviet iron and steel output.) Other big projects of the First Plan included the Stalingrad Tractor Plant and the completion of the Dneproges hydro-electric station, which at 650,000 kwt was the biggest in Europe. These projects were often poorly planned and wastefully executed—in terms of human life as well as of resources. On the other hand, they did constitute a great leap forward in the transformation of Russia from an agricultural to an industrial nation, and they did at times inspire a real patriotic fervour in those who carried them out.

The First Five Year Plan in a few of the sectors regarded as important was in fact overfulfilled, but was underfulfilled in steel and electricity. The meagre provisions for consumer goods like food and clothing, as well as housing, were not achieved. The Second Plan (1932–37) was on the same principles but paid more attention to productivity and the quality of output. (The latter had been, and continued to be, bad, for in the anxiety to meet high targets inferior products were accepted.) Consumer goods production was again minimised, heavy industry was fostered especially in the Urals, and some reluctant measures were taken to improve the railways whose

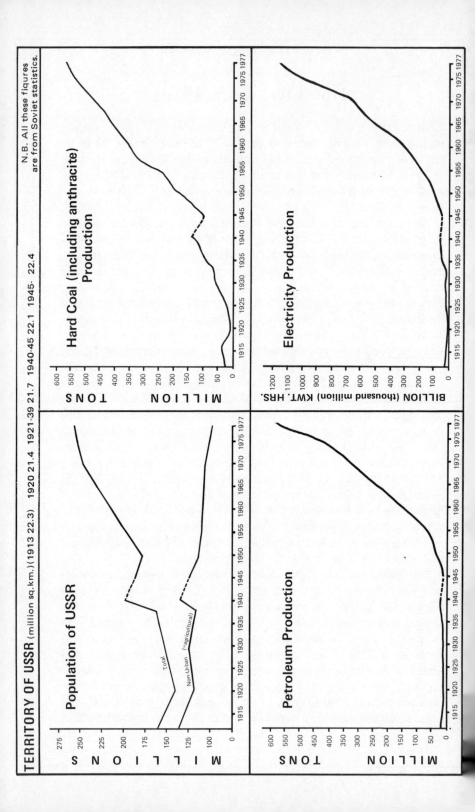

TERRITORY OF USSR (million sq.km.)(1913 22.3) 1920 21.4 1921-39 21.7 1940-45 22.1 1945- 22.4

N.B. All these figures are from Soviet statistics.

Population of USSR

Total

Non-Urban (=agricultural)

Hard Coal (including anthracite) Production

Petroleum Production

Electricity Production

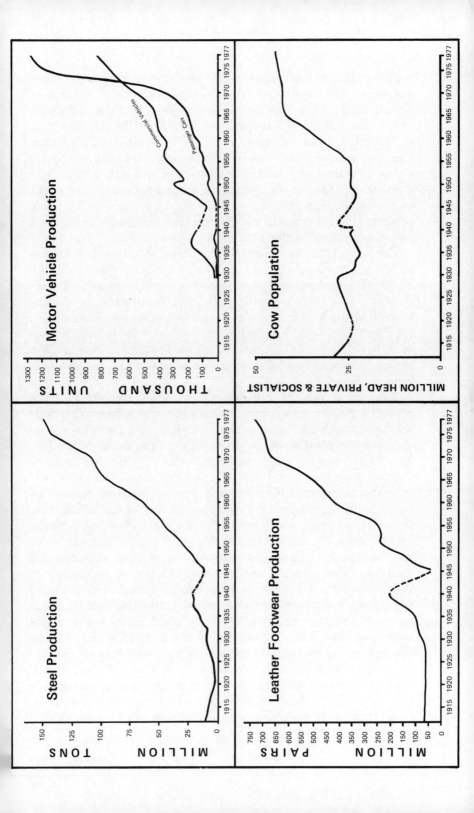

deliberate neglect had cost the nation dear in successive winter transport crises. The standard of living fell in reality, but rose officially—a phenomenon which contributed a new riddle to Russian folklore: 'Why were Adam and Eve like Soviet citizens?' 'Because they lived in Paradise and had nothing to wear.' As in the NEP and First Plan, much technical assistance was obtained from abroad, either by buying a few examples of western products and redesigning them for domestic production, or by hiring foreign specialists, especially engineers. Foreign exchange was obtained by exports of primary products, including grain, but the economic depression in the west meant that prices for these were low.

The Second Plan was underfulfilled in most of its sectors, but nonetheless registered a great increase of heavy industrial production. But quality of output was still poor, there was much waste, and although the USSR was becoming stronger industrially the standard of living was still falling. Workers were driven like slaves and only just managed to subsist. The Third Five Year Plan (1937–41) tried to remedy some of these defects, and there were for a time hopes of a better life, but the imminence of war led to a revision of targets and an increase of arms production.

Although it was the Five Year Plans which received the most publicity, they were only one part of the planning process. They were interlocked with long-term perspective plans, and shorter (i.e. one-year) current plans which might modify the provisions of the Five Year Plan. The economic justification for the fully planned economy was that at this time the USSR was striving to make full use of very scarce resources, and only a central body with an all-embracing view could decide and impose the most fruitful way of employing those resources. Planning was entrusted to the State Planning Commission (Gosplan), which was answerable to the government and which was assisted by planning departments in each of the industrial ministries. Full planning involved the collection of statistics from which forecasts were made, deciding what targets should be set and co-ordinating the targets of each industry, and checking the fulfilment of these targets. It was the Party which finally approved the targets and the Party in addition to the ministries and Gosplan checked the fulfilment. Enforcement was simplified because the Five Year Plan was a law, and its infringement therefore a criminal offence. However, the ease with which managers and administrators could be imprisoned for non-fulfilment of plan did not in itself ensure the achievement of impossible targets, and encouraged book-cooking.

The federal ministries in charge of each industry, having received the approved plan for their sector, would break it down into the targets for the individual republics, the corresponding ministries in which would thereupon break down their figures into the targets for each individual enterprise in their jurisdiction. Thus the director of an enterprise would be told the quantity and categories of his production, and its cost in terms of money and resources. The supply of materials was the concern of his ministry, which would negotiate with other ministries and with the Ministry of Transport. Theoretically, although the plans were imposed from above, they incorporated the suggestions of the individual enterprises which in the preparatory stage had the opportunity of discussing the proposals. But in fact this was largely meaningless. Factory meetings were dominated by Party and Komsomol agitators and it was hazardous for individuals to propose a reduction of the targets. Thus factory meetings to discuss the plan would usually result in resolutions to increase the target, resolutions which would be dutifully accepted unanimously by a raised-hand vote.

The difficulty with the planning system was that it involved the transfer of decision-making from the people on the spot to people sitting in offices. Although the latter had a broader view, they were usually ignorant of local circumstances. Also, the pressure to over-fulfil ever-higher targets led to confusion when one branch of an industry merely fulfilled the plan while dependent branches over-fulfilled. This kind of situation was very common: in one year the railways received a surplus of fishplates to join the rails, but not enough rails; factories would cease production because one raw material was lacking; finished products would pile up awaiting the arrival of one component. There grew up a shady profession of middlemen, whom factory managers would reward highly for obtaining materials and components through a network of illegal channels. Much falsification was perpetrated, sometimes with the acquiescence of local Party officials (whose own prospects depended on how well targets were fulfilled). Statistics were sometimes fraudulent, and more often simply distorted or misleading. One common tactic, encouraged by the practice of measuring output by weight, was to make articles more heavy, that is, to use more materials than were necessary. Another, more fundamental, drawback was that planning mistakes became big mistakes because it was perilous for a perceptive individual to suggest that any feature of the plan (which in effect was the Party line) was misguided. Only when the result of a mistake became glaring did the Party itself (on the national scale,

Stalin and his associates) make corrections. The show trial of a scape-goat 'wrecker' or 'saboteur' or 'enemy of the people' was the usual accompaniment to the official acknowledgement of error. Some of the bigger mistakes of this period were the retardation of oil production in favour of coal, investment in canals rather than in the more-needed railways and highways, the building for the Moscow Metro of underground palaces masquerading as stations at a time of cruel housing shortage, and the undertaking of gigantic industrial projects when a larger number of smaller projects would have been more economic.

Thus total planning, while it certainly made possible the rapid development of a few key industries, was cumbersome and inflexible. By denying the citizen significant influence in decision-making it not only deprived him of satisfaction of his personal wants (which may have been desirable in the circumstances) but it also failed to make the best use of its resources. Moreover, total planning involved the planning of labour. By 1941 the situation of the Soviet worker resembled Marx's description of the nineteenth-century European proletariat.

The Trade Unions and the Workers

The role of organised labour in a proletarian state had been a thorny question ever since 1917. In 1920 Trotsky had attempted to sub-ordinate the trade unions absolutely to the state, but had been resisted. During the NEP period, however, the trade unions had gradually lost the confidence of the workers. There was a high proportion (almost one in ten) of Communists among trade unionists and in the higher union organs the Party was dominant. Thus the unionist Party members were in complete control; they fixed elections to union organs, and they could, and did, arrange the expulsion of hostile workers from the union, thus making them unemployable. Although the ordinary unionist Party member was inclined to put the workers before the Party, the threat of expulsion usually compelled him to comply with Party policy, which meant siding with the management (and with the government) in disputes. Production was all-important so, even though strikes were 'legal', strikers (and especially strike-leaders) received little protection from their unions. It was said that since government was a workers' government, strikes in socialist industry could only be regarded as anti-worker. Tomsky, until 1929 the trade-union leader and a member of the government, acquiesced in this, even though he felt genuine concern for the workers. Fortunately living standards were improving in the NEP period, and the resentment of the workers was accordingly mollified.

With the trade unions enforcing and interpreting government or Party policy to their workers there was no obstacle to complete subordination of the proletariat. In the First Five Year Plan the workers were relatively enthusiastic, but when they realised that the 'labour heroism' and hardships were not going to bring immediate rewards, and were to continue, they no longer responded so voluntarily to exhortation. Accordingly other incentives were used. Wage discrimination replaced the egalitarianism hitherto favoured: the difference between the highest-paid and the lowest-paid was far wider in the USSR than in any other industrial country. Piece-rates, once condemned as the capitalists' favourite method of exploitation, were reintroduced and applied in a way which no capitalist would have dared to use. The wage-rate for a unit of output was ostensibly fixed so that the normal wage would be received by an average worker, but the 'average' worker chosen by the Soviet norm-fixers was invariably the most productive who could be found. This meant that all except the most skilled (or strongest, or best equipped) worker received a wage less than the 'norm'. A sophistication of this form of exploitation was the Stakhanov movement. Stakhanov was a miner who one day in 1935 was given the easiest seam, the best tools and the best assistants, and succeeded in his man-shift at the coal face in producing no less than 102 tons. His example was widely publicised and other industries and enterprises produced their own Stakhanovites. The Stakhanovite output tended to become the 'normal' output on which piece rates were based. So, while the Stakhanovites were fêted with red carpets, visits to the Kremlin, Party membership, seaside holidays, medals and cash prizes, the mass of their fellow-workers, unable to attain the new norms, sank even further into impoverishment. However, there was one genuinely good feature; the speed with which useful technical innovations were adopted so that a new method which increased output at one place would be introduced quickly all over the country, rather than become, as in the West, a closely guarded trade secret.

The pressure on the worker, no longer the élite of the Revolution in fact, though still enjoying that status in propaganda, increased especially after 1938. By 1941 there were compulsory internal passports and labour-books: each worker had a labour-book, in which were entered his changes of job—which in themselves were a misdemeanour—and any infringement of 'labour discipline' for which he had been convicted. Severe penalties, including wage cuts, imprisonment or labour camp, could be imposed for lateness or for slackness. Fourteen-year-olds were conscripted for training in trades suffering from a labour shortage—the celebrated narrow-gauge children's railways, built in parks, were used to train those teenagers conscripted for railway service. The standard of living of the average worker had fallen. His wages may have risen on paper, and he was eligible for a variety of bonuses and prizes for good work, but his food and clothes had been better in 1928. Despite this, he could each year be persuaded at mass meetings, with the usual vote by hand-raising, 'voluntarily' to give up a month's wages to subscribe to the State Loan.

For the most arduous and dangerous work the NKVD was the appropriate organisation. The NKVD was not only a conventional home affairs ministry with a swollen security service. It was also a major industrial ministry in its own right. How many millions of people worked in its labour camps is unknown (the peak may have been around ten million) but it was responsible for many large-scale works: the 970-mile Pechora Railway and its associated Arctic coal mines at Vorkuta, the White Sea Ship Canal and the Moscow–Volga Canal, the Kolyma gold mines, and many other railway, mining and timber projects in inhospitable regions. The death rate was very high, both from hunger and cold and from hazardous working conditions. Moreover, with their half-starved and apathetic work force the NKVD enterprises were remarkably inefficient.

The Great Purge

Having by the close of 1927 defeated and discredited the leftists— Trotsky, Zinoviev and Kamenev—Stalin turned against his allies the moderates—Bukharin, Rykov and Tomsky. In early 1928 this trio seemed well-placed: Rykov was premier (although with little real power), Bukharin was in charge of the Comintern, and Tomsky of the trade unions. But inside the Politburo Stalin could muster a majority of votes. Of the nine full members he could count on four supporters (Molotov, Kuibyshev, Rudzutak, Voroshilov) and one sympathiser (Kalinin), and of the candidate members Andreyev, Kaganovich, Kirov and Mikoyan could be relied on. With this backing Stalin felt able to weed out Bukharin's supporters from the more important Party and government posts.

Those who opposed rapid and involuntary collectivisation and the policy of forced industrialisation favoured the moderates, so, until Trotsky was safely exiled from the USSR in early 1929, Stalin contented himself with staging a show trial of 'saboteurs'—Russian bourgeois and German mining experts. At this trial an unscrupulous lawyer, Vyshinsky, succeeded, with bullying, deception and the aid of the OGPU, in obtaining verdicts of guilty, thus discrediting the moderates' conciliatory policy towards bourgeois and foreign experts.

In early 1929 Stalin began to accuse Bukharin openly of right-wing opposition. The latter, rather ineptly, tried to obtain the support of the disgraced Kamenev, whom he had earlier helped to defeat. About the same time Bukharin, Rykov and Tomsky opposed Stalin's policies inside the Party's Central Committee, were outvoted, resigned, and were accused of sabotage. In 1929–30 Bukharin was expelled from the Politburo and the chairmanship of the Comintern, Molotov replaced Rykov as Prime Minister, and Tomsky lost his control of the trade unions to Shvernik, a devoted Stalinist. After a massive campaign against the 'right opportunists' in the Press and among the Party the unfortunate trio recanted. They remained members of the Party Central Committee but were thoroughly discredited. There followed a purge of their supporters and another show trial of 'rightist saboteurs' in industry.

Party purges had been frequent in the past, aiming at the elimination of those who had joined to feather their own nests. The usual technique was to call in Party cards, reissuing them only when the lives and actions and social origins of their holders had been scrutinised. In the purge of 1929–30 members who lost their cards included, apart from the opportunists and drunkards, many who were suspected of favouring the moderates' agricultural and economic policy, or who had not participated in the collectivisation campaign with the required severity, or who as trade unionists had sought to defend the workers from the ever-growing pressure of the Party and state. Loss of Party membership often entailed loss of job and unemployability for the former member, and frequently also for his family and friends. Those expelled for ideological reasons faced the possibility of imprisonment or deportation, or both.

Stalin's treatment of the moderates, and his economic policies, were not displeasing to those who had formerly supported the leftists, and many of them, including Radek, after showing the expected contrition were re-admitted to the Party. On the other hand, a widespread feeling in the Party that it was high time for Stalin to be replaced was reflected in a number of small groups which actually discussed among themselves how this might be achieved. But with OGPU informers everywhere these groups were soon arrested. Stalin wished to put them on trial but was opposed by many of his colleagues who, though they had not disapproved of the use of terror tactics against non-Party enemies, could not accept its use against fellow-members. The use of the address 'Comrade' between Bolsheviks did mean something to these people. Of the nine members of the Politburo at this time probably only two (Molotov and Kaganovich) were unquestioning supporters of Stalin on this issue. The others (Kirov, Kossyor, Kuibyshev, Ordzhonikidze and Rudzutak) are believed to have opposed violence against Party members. But by placing devoted and tight-lipped supporters in key positions in the Party apparatus, the OGPU, and the judiciary, Stalin was often able to circumvent the resistance of his colleagues. His protégé Yezhov conducted a Party purge in 1933. Poskrebyshev was put in charge of Stalin's private, shady, but powerful secretariat. The untalented and unscrupulous Vyshinsky climbed higher and higher in the judiciary.

But by 1934 it was evident that Stalin, with his policy of excesses, was still not in absolute command. At the Party Congress of that year Bukharin and other self-confessed one-time oppositionists were allowed to speak. Policy had been somewhat moderated; the OGPU was taken over by the NKVD, some show trials of specialists were halted, bread rationing was abolished, the Second Five Year Plan had been slightly scaled down, and peasants were allowed to produce more from their private plots. Significant also was the fact that Kirov, the head of the Leningrad Party organisation, received as much applause at the Congress as Stalin. In view of the Stalin cult, with its public praise and worship of the Party Secretary from Georgia, this open and genuine popularity of the handsome Russian from Leningrad could only mean that many regarded him as a fit replacement for Stalin.

Kirov's popularity, and his resistance to the use of terror against Party members, proved fatal. On the first of December he was assassinated, almost certainly with Stalin's connivance, and the key witness was killed in a staged car accident before he could be interrogated. The murder was blamed on leftists, and provided an excuse for the mass terror after which Stalin hankered. For a time non-Communists were the victims, many of whom were executed accused of 'preparing terrorist acts', a charge which by decree was denied a proper investigation in court. Kamenev and Zinoviev were also tried and imprisoned for 'opposition', but were not yet directly accused of Kirov's murder. The imprisonment of these two was Stalin's first major step against the Party, but he was not yet strong enough to make a massive assault on those whom he suspected of opposing him. However, it is possible that he arranged the death of Kuibyshev and of the popular writer Gorky, both of whom are believed to have remonstrated with him. In 1935 he also strengthened his position by appointing his devoted supporters Zhdanov and Khrushchev to head respectively the Leningrad and Moscow Party organisations, and to carry out purges therein. Yezhov, assisted by another Stalinist, Malenkov, became head of the Party Control Commission, which was a useful starting point for a new purge. The Komsomol leadership was reorganised. Vyshinsky became Chief Procurator.

In mid-1936 local Party organisations received a secret letter entitled *On the Subject of the Terrorist Activity of the Trotskyite-Zinovievite Counter-revolutionary Bloc*. This demanded vigilance against hidden foes and was dutifully followed throughout the country by denunciations of enemies, their expulsion from the Party, and arrest. A month later Kamenev and Zinoviev, with other former leftists, were accused of planning political murders, including that of Kirov. Both confessed and were shot. Their confessions implicated many others of Stalin's real and imagined opponents, including Rykov, Bukharin and Tomsky. Vyshinsky promised at the trial that these three would be 'investigated', and various workers' and peasants' organisations passed well-publicised resolutions demanding their execution.

However, Stalin was thwarted in this matter. After a year's investigation it was announced in September 1936 that Rykov and Bukharin had been cleared (Tomsky had in the meantime committed suicide). Stalin's response was the liquidation of the Deputy Minister of Justice and the replacement of Yagoda, in charge of internal security, by Yezhov. Yagoda apparently had resisted measures against Party members; he did not survive long after his demotion, which was followed by the removal of his assistants in the NKVD.

All this cleared the way for a second show trial of various Party members in January 1937. Radek was among the victims, who were accused of conspiring with Trotsky to betray the USSR to Japan and Germany. Radek made an artistic confession implicating, again, Bukharin and Rykov, and also the Red Army's Commander-in-Chief

Tukhachevsky. Vyshinsky, the chief prosecutor, ended his savage and humiliating peroration with the words 'I demand the shooting of all these mad dogs'. Most of the defendants were duly shot but Radek's co-operation saved him from execution: he died later in a labour camp.

Bukharin, who since his recantation had become editor of *Izvestia* and was also the main author of what was later to be known as the Stalin Constitution, was arrested as a result of his incrimination by the victims of this trial. With other moderates, including Rykov, Yagoda, Krestinsky and 17 other prominent Bolsheviks, Bukharin was put on trial in 1938 after a year's investigation. At this 'Trial of the Rightist-Trotskyist Bloc' the victims were accused of conspiring with the British and German secret services since the twenties and planning to restore capitalism in Russia. Bukharin was additionally charged with having conspired to murder Lenin and Stalin. Yagoda was alleged to have poisoned Kuibyshev and Gorky. The trial went smoothly, with the defendants duly confessing and incriminating others, except that Krestinsky revoked his confession in court—upon which Vyshinsky promptly adjourned the sitting. Krestinsky was returned to the NKVD investigators to refresh his memory, and in court next day revoked his revocation. With the exception of the minor defendants, all were shot.

Meanwhile the Red Army was undergoing the same treatment as the Party. Its commander was Tukhachevsky, a genuine Civil War hero who had recently introduced useful reforms and was widely popular both inside and outside the army. Apart from this dangerous popularity, he was no doubt disliked by the Civil War's pseudo-heroic trio—Stalin, Voroshilov and Budyenny. To this was added the fact that the Red Army was the only organised force in the USSR not securely under the detailed control of Stalin's protégés. Tukhachevsky was arrested in May 1937 and almost all the top army leadership followed—about two-thirds of all officers of the rank of colonel or higher, including 13 of the 15 generals. With the help of incriminatory evidence which the German Gestapo had been only too glad to supply, Tukhachevsky and other high officers were accused at a secret military court (presided over by Voroshilov) of spying for Germany and Japan. They were convicted and shot in June 1937.

Outside the USSR there were many besides stalwart Communists who claimed that the public trials were fair and the accusations properly proven. Allegations that confessions were faked or obtained by torture or threats were dismissed as the fictions of unscrupulous anti-Communists. The readiness with which most defendants made their confessions was probably the main reason for this delusion. However, post-Stalin revelations, including the memoirs of victims, confirm that mental and physical torture was indeed the main weapon of the interrogators. Defendants might be interrogated for days, even weeks, without a break by relays of inquisitors, would be confronted with implicating confessions of other victims, would have their bones broken, were promised release or mild sentences if they co-operated in concocting confessions which would involve the next wave of intended victims, were threatened with measures against their families if they refused, were persuaded that the Party needed their sacrifice, were assailed by a feeling of aloneness evoked by their deliberate isolation.

In addition to the public trials, literally millions of citizens were arrested and sentenced quietly. Even prominent Bolsheviks were sometimes spared the indignity of a show trial, perhaps because they refused to confess, or because a quick execution was desired. Among others who met their end at this time were Ordzhonikidze, whose reported 'heart attack' was in fact suicide induced by Stalin and Beria; Yenukidze, who like Ordzhonikidze was a former Georgian comrade of Stalin and Beria; and Rudzutak and Kossyor. Of the Party Central Committee's 139 members elected in 1934, more than 90 were arrested and punished, mainly by shooting. Of the 1,966 delegates to the 17th Party Congress, 1,108 were subsequently arrested. The arrest of one person was generally followed by the arrest of his associates, friends and family, so that the purge was an ever-accelerating process which if unchecked would sooner or later have dragged every citizen into the hands of the NKVD. In the first wave of victims were those who had sympathised with Trotsky or Bukharin, surviving ex-Mensheviks and ex-Social Revolutionaries, people who had been abroad (even on official missions like the Spanish Civil War), foreign Communists (Bela Kun, the exiled Hungarian Communist revolutionary, many German Communists, and almost the entire leadership of the exiled Polish Communist Party were killed at this time), Kirov's old friends in Leningrad, and members known to have opposed the purge or collectivisation. Soon ordinary non-political citizens were involved. The labour camps grew and multiplied. It could happen that a labour camp inmate might meet a fellow prisoner who a few weeks before had been his accuser, interrogator or torturer. Many citizens, to save themselves or to pay off old scores or to exercise their talent for denunciation, indulged in accusations of others. However wild the denunciation, there was little hope of victims escaping. Some of the atmosphere of this period is revealed in the NKVD documents and reports captured by the Germans in 1941: the peasant women discovered to have a portrait of Trotsky among her ikons and accordingly denounced as subversive and corrupt; officials who years previously had argued against the Stalinist line; people in authority who had written favourable testimonials for persons later accused of Trotskyism; and individuals who did not join in the chorus of accusation and denunciation at Party and other meetings held to 'unmask the Trotskyite-Zinovievite counter-revolutionaries' (meetings which ended with incantations like '. . . under the wise leadership of Comrade Stalin and the banner of the Party we shall rout out the counter-revolutionary sediment and lead the toiling masses to a better (etc.) life. Long live Comrade Stalin!').

But by 1938 it was evident that the purge was seriously weakening, even destroying, the USSR. In the Red Army inexperienced junior officers had been promoted to high ranks to fill the gaps, and industry was threatened by the deportation of technicians and specialists to labour camps. Among the free population the fear of the NKVD's knock on the door in the night led to nervous breakdowns and suicides. Apathy and fear was the ruling mood. So in 1938 began a purge of the purgers. Stalin's fellow-Georgian, Beria, who had gained favour by writing a history of the Revolution in Georgia which portrayed Stalin as the main hero, succeeded Yezhov as head of the NKVD security service. Yezhov and other NKVD officials were executed and it was implied that the excesses of the purge had been their doing, and against Stalin's wishes. Some arrestees were released, but by 1941 the labour camps still held millions of prisoners; those who had died or been released had been replaced by new victims.

The Stalin Constitution

After the Five Year Plans, Soviet propaganda's favourite subject was the 1936 Constitution. It bore much the outward form of the US constitution, but in fact most of its provisions were either meaningless or misleading. After Stalin died it was condemned, but the commission appointed in 1962 to devise a new constitution had produced no results when Khrushchev retired.

The 1936 Constitution proclaimed the USSR to be a federation of Soviet republics (in 1936 these were the Russian, Ukrainian, Byelorussian, Georgian, Armenian, Azerbaijan, Kazahk, Kirgiz, Uzbek,

Turkmen and Tadzhik union republics. Later these were joined by the Latvian, Lithuanian, Estonian, Moldavian and, from 1940 to 1956, the Karelo-Finnish union republics). The Federal (i.e. Union) government in Moscow had complete jurisdiction, through All-Union ministries, of fields such as defence and foreign affairs. Other matters, like particular industries, were administered by union-republic ministries (the federal ministries acted through parallel ministries in each republic); and some affairs, like basic education, were the sole concern of the individual republics. In reality, because of the primacy of the Party, the central control over the republics' budgets, and the fact that Union laws overrode conflicting republic laws, the separate republics neither demanded nor enjoyed real independence. Nor did the so-called autonomous republics, set up to accommodate certain nationalities which did not warrant full union-republic status. However, the formal existence of these divisions, and the encouragement of national cultures (which could be 'national in form' even though 'socialist in content') no doubt pleased their inhabitants, and the use of local languages in the various administrative and judicial organs was to their advantage. The Constitution acknowledged the right of any union-republic to secede from the USSR (but in 1951 Party leaders in Georgia were purged for allegedly planning secession).

The Supreme Soviet of the USSR was given the exclusive right to make laws (but in fact the most common forms of rule-making were not laws but edicts, decrees and instructions, which were not issued by the Supreme Soviet but by other bodies such as individual ministries). The Supreme Soviet, like the US Congress, had two houses. The Soviet of the Union had one member elected by each electoral district of 300,000 people, while the Soviet of Nationalities consisted of 25 members from each union republic, 11 from each autonomous republic, five from each autonomous region, and one from each national area.

The Supreme Soviet of the USSR was to meet twice yearly. In practice each session was for a few days only. This meant that members (who were henceforth selected so that about one-quarter were non-Party members) could continue their regular employment and thus remain truly representative, not a class apart. The main function of the sessions was not legislative but had the aim of associating the electorate, through its representatives, with the machinery of government and to give it a sense of participation. The member of the Supreme Soviet had the role not so much of expressing his constituents' views to the centre, but carrying back the centre's views to his constituents.

Before 1936 only the soviets in the villages and towns were directly elected, but the new constitution provided for direct elections to all soviets, including the Supreme Soviet. Elections were not contested, but there was some competition at the candidate-selection stage. The local Party had a dominating influence in this, but because the aim of elections was to demonstrate the support of the masses by achieving a vote as close to 100 per cent of the electorate as possible (that is, to achieve a full turnout and a minimum of spoiled ballots), the candidate selected tended to be popular as well as ideologically sound. Elections were to be held every four years. Eighteen was the minimum voting age (raised to 23 in 1945). The 1936 Constitution was notable in that it restored voting rights to clergymen, former tsarist officers and other suspect categories. On the other hand, there was a growing number of persons deprived of the right to vote by the courts (and priests, among others, still did not have the 'right to work').

The Supreme Soviet elected from its members smaller bodies to carry out the day-to-day work of government: the Presidium (the chairman of which was the equivalent of President in the European sense) and the Council of Peoples' Commissars (Council of Ministers). The chairman of the latter was in fact, but not in name, the Prime Minister. The organisation of government in the union republics and autonomous republics were similar, but their supreme soviets were unicameral. Lesser administrative units (territories, regions, areas, towns, districts, villages) had their own local soviets.

The new constitution had a long section detailing the rights of citizens and it was this which propagandists inside and outside the USSR used to demonstrate the progressiveness and democracy of the Soviet state. However, these rights were meaningless. Some, such as '. . . no person may be arrested except by decision of a court or procurator' were simply ignored. Others, like the article '. . . placing at the disposal of the workers and their organisations printing presses and stocks of paper . . .' were full of loopholes in definition and in any case could never be enforced in the courts. Moreover, since these guarantees took the form of stating what the citizen *could* do, and not what he *could not* do, it could always be claimed that any action not specifically allowed in the constitution was illegal.

The Party, the real ruling power of the USSR, was hardly mentioned in the Constitution.

The Party

There were no changes in the Party necessitated by the 1936 Constitution. As before, the dual membership of those members who combined the functions of Party official with a corresponding office in the government structure guaranteed that government policy would conform to the Party line. With some variations, each level of government organisation was paralleled by a Party organisation and members of the latter would also be members of the former.

The supreme Party body was theoretically the Party Congress, which according to the Party *Rules* was to meet every three years but which in fact did not. The Party's Central Committee, elected by the Party Congress, was a small and at first powerful body intended to carry out day-to-day work between the sessions of the Congress. As the years passed this Committee grew but became less influential, the Party Presidium (an even smaller body formed from the leading members of the Central Committee) gradually encroaching on its functions. All the most important ministers in the government were also members or candidate members of the Party Presidium. Other ministers, together with the first secretaries of republican and regional Party organisations and the chairmen (prime ministers) of republic councils of ministers were among the members of the Central Committee. The Politburo of the Central Committee remained a very small group of top leaders. In Stalin's time the Politburo was often bypassed; Stalin entrusted his wishes to personally selected committees of the Presidium.

In the republics and lower government units there was a similar structure, with the members of local government bodies being also members of corresponding Party organisations. Below the republics came, in descending order, the Party organisations of territories, regions, and districts or towns. It was the last group which administered the primary organs (the 'cells') which were formed of three or more members at their place of work. There was a three-tier structure in each organisation: a conference which like the congresses of the federal or republican organisations met rarely, a smaller committee elected from the conference for day-to-day work, and a bureau of a few members of that committee, where the decisions were really made. Members of a conference were elected by and from the next lower Party organisation. For example, a district Party organisation would be composed of representatives from the cells and would itself elect one or more members to the regional organisation. Party organisations were not financed by the local governments but from the centre, which was in keeping with their function of supervising local affairs according to the policies of the central Party organisation. Each Party organisation had its own secretary, and it was the secretaries (or the First and Second Secretaries in large organisations) who were most important and influential both in the local Party and in local life.

From the age of 9 years an individual could belong to the Pioneers, a kind of Soviet wolfcub-and-brownie movement. A youth league with greater political content was the Komsomol, which could be joined at the age of 15. Since the more senior members of this were in their late 20s, and its leaders were Party members, it was a useful auxiliary to the Party in various campaigns, demonstrations and emergency measures. Komsomol volunteers were often drafted, or volunteered, for harvesting, or for construction programmes. The Komsomol, whose admission requirements were much less stringent than those of the Party, had a high membership turnover, only the most enthusiastic remaining members right up to the upper age limit. On the other hand most young people, at least in the towns, were members at some time. There were great social and professional advantages in belonging to the Komsomol: a sense of participation in Soviet development, a little inside political knowledge, better prospects of promotion, tickets to holiday camps, and so on. In the thirties membership of the Komsomol was around nine million.

The Komsomol was one route to Party membership. The Party was considered to be an élite, and admission requirements were usually strict. Those who had attained membership were expected to lead an exemplary personal and professional life. Membership fluctuated as purges alternated with recruiting drives. In 1933 there were between three and four million members, but by 1938 less than two million.

The ordinary member, though carefully selected, had little in-influence inside the Party, but considerable influence outside it. As one of 'the vanguard of the working class' he functioned as a leader among his non-Party fellow-workers. He might associate with other members in the same job to form a Party group—a sort of internal pressure group; he was expected to set an example, to be ready for special tasks which might be arduous, time-consuming and involve change of residence; to explain and popularise he needed a grasp, though not a detailed knowledge, of Party ideology.

The earliest age for admission as a candidate member was 18 and after serving a probationary period the candidate could be recommended for full membership. An increasing number of members joined the Party because membership oiled the wheels of promotion. This was not necessarily harmful, for the capable and ambitious were particularly useful in the Party. This trend, and the purges, meant that in the thirties the preponderance of manual workers began to be replaced by a preponderance of the so-called intelligentsia—office workers, factory managers, administrators, the young Soviet-trained specialists and officers.

The backbone of the Party, and in fact the Soviet Union's nearest equivalent of a ruling class, were the paid full-time officials—the Party Apparat—who numbered around one in 12 of the total membership. By successful fulfilment of Party policy in his area of responsibility a Party secretary might progress upwards until he became First Secretary of a higher body. Then, with the patronage of the right people, he might reach the very top. But, if his patron fell, so might he. Along with other present or future first secretaries, chairmen, editors and army commissars he might attend a Party school and have access to training and facts denied the ordinary member.

Functions of the Party officials included checking of membership, inspection and supervision of any activity—especially economic and governmental activity—in the locality, selection (or at least approval) of persons to fill vacancies in important positions (chairmen of farms, factory managers, government officials), organisation of propaganda work among the masses (for which the local Party had an 'Agitation and Propaganda Section') and, above all, ensuring that the current Party policies and directives were applied in the locality. The power of the Party official was unquestioned in his own area, even though he could easily be broken by a superior Party organisation (and in fact was: the Great Purge found its victims especially among Party officials).

While in theory the lower Party organisations through their representatives in the higher organisations moulded Party policy, in reality during the thirties they had negligible influence. Their task was simply to carry out the instructions of the highest Party organ which in practice though never in theory was Iosif Stalin and his personal secretariat.

Intellectual Life

The 1930s, while witnessing the relative subjection of the workers and peasants, saw also the elevation of the intelligentsia. In other words the post-1917 table of ranks was reversed. This was reflected in the growing proportion of white-collar workers and administrators in the Party. A new intelligentsia was being born: young technicians and specialists trained to replace the old so-called bourgeois specialists, who now began to disappear through retirement or purging. The 1936 Constitution restored some of the rights of the 'deprived' classes, and the children of bourgeois parents, apart from securing the privilege of voting and serving in the Red Army, found it possible to go to university. In 1932 the requirement that two-thirds of university students should be of working class origin was dropped and academic standards promptly rose as the children of functionaries and administrators began to grow to half the total intake. In 1940, just when labour conscription was introduced for children not proceeding to further education, free tuition in universities was abolished, making it even more difficult for children of workers and peasants to gain a higher education. The brainworkers, who in 1940 totalled about ten million, were firmly established as a definite and privileged class. In the post-Stalin years, despite some corrective educational reforms, most privileges, like the shorter period of military conscription for graduates, remained intact.

In the arts, the ascendancy of Stalin was accompanied by repression. In the twenties artists and writers had many genuine achievements and innovations to their credit, but the early thirties brought the imposition of the doctrine of Socialist Realism as the only possible basis of creative work. At various times Socialist Realism involved a multitude of restrictive concepts. In effect it meant that all artistic work should serve and further the Party line. Thus the hero in fiction was not necessarily to be lifelike; rather was he to be portrayed as the ideal Soviet man whom the Party was creating. Typically an upright and handsome young man, educated in Soviet schools, whose father was a lumberjack and mother a tram-driver (or vice-versa), who never wore a tie in his life, who was or would become a Party member, outproduced his fellows, overcame enemies of the people and saboteurs, loved Stalin and the Party, and never asked the wrong questions. Thus began a dreary succession of literary heroes like the champion tractor driver, or the grower of extra-large turnips with his hand on the spade and his eyes on the milkmaid (but never vice-versa) or the producer of double-norm and extra-quality ball-bearings who falls for a progressive bus conductress or revolutionary chambermaid. The Union of Writers was established as a means of control: membership was a precondition for publication, and nonconformists could be excluded. This situation, while discouraging the more gifted writers, some of whom like Babel and Pilnyak died in captivity, was ideal for the untalented, and in these years many hitherto unsuccessful writers reached the heights of apparent success. Small wonder that at this time there was an immense demand for the nineteenth-century classics, which in fact continued to be printed—and in larger editions than the new novels.

History was continually rewritten to fit the current Party line, and the old versions disappeared from bookstores and libraries. This cycle of gurgitation, expurgation and regurgitation continued in the post-Stalin years (to 'correct the distortions of the past'). Hence the new saying, 'Who can tell what is going to happen yesterday?'

The press was even more tightly controlled and even less informative. *Pravda* remained the Party newspaper, through which the ordinary member could be acquainted with the Party line on current problems. Apart from a small section on the back page it contained little news. In fact, like other papers, it tended to cancel publication when there were really big events, for, despite the ideological competence of its editor, there were occasions when news could only be released after consultation with the Party leadership. *Izvestia* was the government newspaper, read by administrators, while *Trud* was the central trade-union paper. Apart from these three there were numerous others for different places and professions but all were basically the same, carrying little news but much exhortation, propaganda and comment.

As living conditions deteriorated and the population grew more apathetic, as the Axis danger became more threatening, appeals began to be made to Russian patriotism as well as to socialist principles. Heroes of the past like Peter the Great and Kutuzov came back into favour. The Orthodox Church, which had been savagely persecuted, especially during collectivisation and in 1937, was tolerated after 1938. There was more and more emphasis on the new Soviet technological achievements: new canals, factories and the Moscow Metro; skyscrapers, aviation and arctic exploration; while at the same time, so that unfavourable comparisons could not be drawn, information about other countries became more meagre and distorted.

Foreign Policy in the Thirties

Like almost everybody else, the Bolsheviks misinterpreted Hitler. To the Russian Communists, National Socialism was a step towards Communism; Hitler's revolution was to them the nationalist-bourgeois revolution which in their scheme of things would be the predecessor of the final Communist revolution. So, while Hitler was reaching for power, the German Communist Party (which had recovered from the failures of the early twenties and was able to collect several million votes in the 1932 elections) spent its energies at Moscow's behest not in opposing Hitler, but in struggling against the non-Communist left, against the Social Democrats. At times the Communists and the Nazis seemed almost to be allies as both attacked the common socialist enemy. If, instead of attacking the socialists, the Communists had formed a common front with them against Hitler, the latter's grasp for power could have been blocked. The Russian mistake was soon realised, and in 1934 to forestall a similar disaster in France the Comintern sanctioned a Popular Front, whereby the French Communist Party joined with other socialist and liberal parties to prevent the emergence of a fascist regime in Paris.

Despite Hitler's liquidation of the German Communists, for some months after the Nazis' assumption of power Stalin continued to show friendship towards Germany, although in May 1933 he cancelled the long-standing clandestine military co-operation between the USSR and Germany. However, the Nazi leadership openly discussed Germany's future expansion in the East (the Ukraine in particular was to become a Germany colony) and the growth of the German army hinted that this was no idle dream. When, in January 1934, Germany and Poland signed a non-aggression pact, Stalin realised that this implied an eventual 'frontier adjustment' at the expense of Russia.

With the Nazi menace becoming daily more apparent the USSR began to cultivate relations with France and Britain. The Soviet foreign minister, Litvinov, had some success in this policy of 'collective security' between 1934 and 1937. The USSR entered the League of Nations in 1934 with French support, and there was a tripartite pact signed in 1935 by which the USSR was pledged to assist Czechoslovakia if the latter was attacked, provided France did likewise.

But these agreements with the West soon lost their glamour when it became apparent that neither Britain nor France had the will to risk open conflict with Germany. This became evident in March 1936, when Germany reoccupied the Rhineland without provoking any military resistance by the West. There was the Abyssinian crisis, and in mid-1936 the Spanish Civil War again showed that the League of Nations was as ineffective as its leading members, France and Britain.

Franco's fascist-style insurgents had substantial support from Mussolini's Italy, and in September 1936 the Soviet government decided to intervene on the side of the legal, Republican, government. The events in Spain were a great embarrassment to Stalin. A fascist victory might drive the French government into a closer alliance with the USSR, but it might also encourage a fascist coup to overthrow that government. On the other hand, a victory of the Communist-inclined Republicans might well drive France into an anti-Communist alliance with Hitler. Another factor was the Soviet Union's desired image as leader of the socialist world; failure to support the left in Spain would tarnish the image.

Soviet support was accordingly accompanied by advice to the Spanish left not to pursue too radical a policy, to respect private property and foreign investment. By the end of 1936 hundreds of Soviet advisers, together with war equipment and munitions, had arrived in Spain. Also a miniature export version of the NKVD's sercurity service. Soon Moscow had control of one of the most important fronts, and of the Republican air force. Soviet military enclaves, not open to Spanish enquiries, were established.

Russian intervention prompted German and Italian assistance to Franco on an even larger scale. Stalin realised that Russia alone was unable to match the fascists, and that neither France nor Britain would help. Henceforth, an eventual fascist victory was accepted, but it was to be delayed as long as possible, for until the Spanish war was settled Hitler was unlikely to attack the East. Meanwhile, Stalinism, with its customary accompaniment of purges, secret police activity, and assassinations, was rampant in the Republican territory. Stalin feared, among other things, that the efforts made in Spain by non-Communist socialists, or by Trotskyite-inclined Communists, would detract from his own image. So, apart from the already established Soviet controllers of the Republican secret police, assassins were despatched from Russia with the aim of removing ideological enemies, real or imaginary, also fighting for the Republicans. Eventually these high-handed manœuvres became obvious to all and in the final reckoning damaged the USSR's prestige more than did the fact of Franco's victory.

Failure of the West and of the League of Nations to act against the fascists, together with the foundation in 1936 of the Berlin-Rome Axis, and the obviously hostile Anti-Comintern Pact (between Japan and Germany) the same year, meant that the USSR might simultaneously be faced with its two worst nightmares: war against

Germany, with Britain and France neutral, and a war on two fronts against Germany and Japan. Relations with Japan had always been uneasy, and in the later thirties there were frequent incidents on the Manchurian border. In 1938 and 1939 the Japanese made strong probing attacks and although these were beaten off by the Red Army it was doubtful whether an all-out attack could be defeated.

The German occupation of the Rhineland meant that all the remaining overt territorial demands of Hitler lay towards the east. The annexation of Austria in 1938 seemed to show that further aggression in central and Eastern Europe could be expected. Unable to find reliable allies in the West, the USSR began to seek a reconciliation with Germany. Nevertheless, when in the autumn of 1938 Hitler lay claim to the German-speaking part of Czechoslovakia, the USSR took the initiative in offering to support the latter. However Britain and France again refused to risk an armed conflict, and the Russian offer was not taken up (partly because the West had little confidence in the Red Army, partly because of the fear of extending Bolshevik influence in Central Europe, partly because many Conservatives were not averse to German expansion in the east, but mainly for reasons of self-preservation). The refusal of France to act relieved the USSR of its own obligation to Czechoslovakia according to the tripartite agreement of 1935, and the Munich Conference allowed Hitler to take what he wanted. The entry of German troops into Czechoslovakia was accompanied by the Polish occupation of part of northern Czechoslovakia. When in 1939 Germany occupied the remainder of Czechoslovakia the USSR contented itself with a quiet refusal to recognise the new German protectorate.

By the spring of 1939 Stalin still apparently preferred an alliance with the West, but no longer excluded a deal with Germany: his own Munich. At the same time the German-Polish alliance was breaking up, and in March the Polish government rejected Hitler's proposals for the return of Danzig to Germany. This refusal coincided with, but was not connected with, a British guarantee to help maintain Poland's frontiers if Germany should attack.

This British guarantee of Poland's frontiers did not, as Chamberlain's government hoped, deter Hitler's planned attack on Poland. Instead it caused Hitler to seek an alliance with the Soviet Union as a preliminary to attacking the Poles, expecting (understandably but wrongly) that Britain would abandon Poland to its fate if Germany had Russian support.

At the end of April Hitler denounced Poland in a foreign affairs speech, and omitted any hostile references to Russia. The hint was not lost on Stalin, for a week later the pro-western Litvinov was replaced as Minister of Foreign Affairs by no less a personage than Molotov. Gradually, with both sides playing 'hard to catch', and suspecting each other's motives, Russia and Germany came closer together, and in August Ribbentrop arrived in Moscow.

The visit of the German foreign minister meant that Stalin was at last compelled to make a definite choice between Germany and the West. There was already in Moscow a team from the British Foreign Office which, in the intervals between tea and tennis, had been negotiating for several weeks with French and Russian representatives on the subject of an effective political-military alliance.

The situation facing Stalin was an inevitable war in Eastern Europe triggered off by Hitler's seemingly imminent invasion of Poland. He had the choice of an alliance with Germany by which the Baltic States and eastern Poland might be annexed by the USSR while western Poland was occupied by Germany, or an alliance with France and Britain, which were less uncongenial to the Soviet Union, but appeared to be spineless and in any case lukewarm in their wish for a Russian alliance. Moreover, a western alliance was hampered by the refusal of the Polish government to permit the passage of Red troops over its territory and by the reluctance of Britain to acknowledge Russia's strategic need to acquire the Baltic States and part of Finland. In these circumstances, and given the current weakness of the Soviet defences, alliance with Hitler seemed to offer the best prospect of preserving the Soviet Union.

Ribbentrop's discussions with Stalin led to a ten-year Non-Aggression Pact with a secret section which divided Poland into German and Russian 'spheres of influence', and acknowledged Finland, Estonia and Latvia to be Russian spheres, while Lithuania was to be Germany's concern. Russia was to have a free hand in Bessarabia. The public announcement of the pact, on 23 August 1939, caused shock and dismay to the outside world (many Russians were also alarmed, as well as Communists abroad). The shock and dismay would have been even greater if the secret codicils had been revealed.

On 1 September German troops invaded Poland and after a short campaign routed the Polish army. England and France declared war two days after the frontier was crossed, but Russia, despite German invitations, did not send troops into eastern Poland until 17 September. There were two main reasons for this tardiness: not until 15 September was an agreement signed between the USSR and Japan, ending hostilities in the Far East, and secondly Stalin had nothing to lose and everything to gain by delaying his advance until the Polish army had been broken by the Wehrmacht.

Ribbentrop revisited Moscow in September to revise and renew the Soviet-German accord and it was decided that Poland should cease to exist. The resulting partition of Poland must have been personally gratifying to Stalin, for it regained the territory for whose loss he was partly responsible in 1920. On the 13 million inhabitants of the newly acquired territory, ten million Ukrainians and White Russians already belonged, ethnically, to the USSR. The remaining three million were Poles or Jews. Hitler also allowed the Soviet Union a free hand in Lithuania, which had previously been allocated to Germany. Germans living in the Baltic provinces who wished to move to Germany would be allowed to do so, while Ukrainians and White Russians living in German Poland were likewise permitted to resettle in the USSR. Important economic agreements between Russian and Germany were signed at the same time, by which the USSR was to supply raw materials and food in return for manufactured goods.

Stalin's first move against the Baltic states was to mass troops on their frontiers and then invite them to sign military and economic agreements with the USSR. By these, Soviet troops were allowed to establish bases, and the Baltic states supplied goods in overwhelmingly large quantities for ruinously low prices. In May 1940 anti-Soviet provocations were arranged or imagined in Lithuania, Estonia and Latvia and this provided an excuse to move in the Red Army, depose and deport the existing leaders, and with an accompaniment of planned spontaneous demonstrations to create Communist governments which unanimously voted for incorporation in the USSR as union republics. At the same time hundreds of thousands of inhabitants, suspected of being potentially or actively anti-Soviet, were deported to concentration camps.

Finland, which according to the Russo-German agreement was in the Soviet sphere of influence, had friendly relations not only with the West but with Germany too. However, Stalin considered that the Soviet alliance with Germany was sufficiently strong to stand the strain of a possible Russian conflict with Finland. In fact a conflict was at first thought unlikely, as Soviet demands were not entirely unreasonable. The essential fact was that the USSR's second city, Leningrad, was within shelling distance of Finnish territory. In any future conflict with Germany (which Stalin still expected to occur eventually) this might well prove to be the Achilles' heel of the Soviet defences. The nearby Soviet naval base of Kronstadt was similarly uncomfortably close to Finland.

In October 1939, as soon as the Baltic states had been satisfactorily dealt with, negotiations were started with Finland. Apart from rectifying the frontier so as to make Leningrad and Kronstadt less vulnerable, the USSR wished to build bases at the entrance to the Gulf of Finland, and near Petsamo on the Arctic Sea. In exchange the USSR offered an area in Karelia which although less valuable economically was double the size of the territory which Finland was asked to cede. Many Finns were inclined to accept these proposals, but the Soviet treatment of the Baltic States aroused resentment, and also a fear that Soviet bases in Finland would be stepping-stones for further pressure. Accordingly negotiations were broken off on 13 November and two weeks later the Red Army attacked, while Russian aircraft bombed Helsinki. A new government for Finland had already been assembled from Finnish Communists living in the USSR and this was kept in readiness.

But the Red Army was badly mauled by the small Finnish Army. In the Winter War of 1939–40 Russian losses were high and successes few. The USSR appeared to the outside world in the image of tsarist Russia, bullying and ineffective. But France and Britain were prevented from sending soldiers to Finland by the refusal of Norway and Sweden to risk their own involvement by allowing troops to pass through their territory. Thus the only positive result of international resentment was the expulsion of the USSR from the moribund League of Nations.

In the spring the USSR brought in overwhelming numbers of troops and the Finns were finally compelled to ask for negotiations. By the terms of the treaty Finland lost rather more territory than the USSR had originally demanded. The city of Vyborg was lost and the Russo-Finnish border was moved farther west where it had been uncomfortably close to the Murmansk Railway. Russia's acquisition subsequently became the Karelo-Finnish Union Republic of the USSR.

The end of the Finnish war and Hitler's preoccupation with the defeat of France provided an opportunity for further Soviet expansion. In June 1940 Moscow demanded from Rumania the return of Bessarabia, which had been part of tsarist Russia. And because Bessarabia had traditional and linguistic ties with Northern Bukovina, the latter was demanded too. The Rumanian government was unable to resist, and the two territories were occupied by the Red Army,

Bessarabia later becoming the Moldavian Union Republic of the USSR. Although Bessarabia had been included as a Russian sphere of influence in the Russo-German Non-aggression Pact, the timing of the Russian move and the addition of Northern Bukovina annoyed Hitler and was undoubtedly one of the factors leading to his decision to attack Russia sooner rather than later. The Russo-German alliance was further weakened in 1940 by conflicts of interest in the Balkans, especially in Bulgaria and Rumania. It was only after protests by Molotov that the USSR was allowed to participate in the German-organised Danube Conference.

The rapid collapse of France dismayed the Russian government although its feelings were well-disguised, the Soviet press maintaining its pro-German line. It began to seem that the war would strengthen, not weaken, the most stridently anti-Communist powers, Germany and Italy. Moreover, the several years' breathing space on which Stalin had counted to re-equip and re-officer his armed forces seemed to be expiring after a few months. The feeling that a victorious Germany might soon turn against the USSR, together with the already existing tension between the two countries over the Balkans, prompted Stalin to send Molotov for further talks in Berlin. These talks of November 1940 were also welcome to Hitler, who felt that, if the USSR could be induced to move against Britain in Persia and India, this would both assist the German Army and divert Russia's attention from German activity in the Balkans. However, the Molotov-Ribbentrop talks made little progress, as the Soviet Foreign Minister was much more concerned with German encroachments on Russia's claimed spheres of influence in Finland, Rumania and Bulgaria. After Molotov's return to Moscow a note was sent to Berlin accepting the German suggestion of Russia joining the Three Power Pact (between Germany, Italy and Japan) but only if the main Soviet needs were satisfied—a free hand in Eastern Turkey, Iraq, Northern Persia and Bulgaria, the right to build bases in the Dardanelles, and the withdrawal of German troops from Finland. Hitler never deigned to reply to these demands, and this convinced the Soviet government that he no longer desired friendly relations. Henceforth Stalin's policy was to postpone the final breach as long as possible. Meanwhile, in December of 1940, Hitler ordered the preparation of 'Operation Barbarossa'—the invasion of Russia—for May 1941.

The threat from Germany gave urgency to a re-establishment of friendly relations with Japan and in April 1941 the Japanese-Soviet Neutrality Pact was signed. The Pact tended to direct Japan's expected expansion towards the Pacific and this was desired both by Russia and Germany—although for different reasons. Stalin hoped to divert Japan from attacks on the Soviet Far East. Hitler hoped that Japanese attacks would weaken the British war effort in Europe, and he had no desire for his imminent invasion of Russia to serve as cover for Japanese inroads in Siberia.

As Stalin grew more anxious about Hitler's intentions, he made every effort to show the latter what a reliable and useful partner the Soviet Union could be. In the honeymoon period after the Non-Aggression Pact there had been, apart from economic co-operation, significant political and naval co-operation. As early as September 1939 Moscow and Berlin issued a joint statement accusing Britain and France of responsibility for the continuing war, and the various Communist parties, including those of France and Britain, were mobilised to organise public meetings and disseminate slogans against their allegedly war-mongering governments. Walter Ulbricht, a German Communist who had taken refuge in the USSR from the Nazis, called on German workers to support Hitler's policies. German aircraft dropped over France leaflets of a speech by Molotov. Meanwhile, until September 1940 the German navy had the use of a base at Murmansk (enabling among other things the German liner *Bremen* to escape the Royal Navy), and a German commerce raider passed between the North Sea and the Pacific with the help of Russian ice-breakers. In return the Russian navy received a new German cruiser and some technical help in modernising its ships. However, Hitler's suspicions prevented the hoped-for acquisition of U-boats and of valuable blue-prints.

It was in the economic field that Germany benefited most. From the USSR were shipped enormous quantities of oil, grain, cotton, ferrous and rare metals. Moreover, the USSR obtained for Germany supplies from the outside world, thus nullifying the Allied naval blockade; even British tin and rubber found its way to Germany via the Soviet Union. In exchange for these materials the USSR was to receive manufactures, but, while Soviet deliveries, despite shortages at home, were prompt, Germany was slow to keep its part of the bargain. As Stalin became more nervous he undertook to supply even greater quantities, and faster. Thus by the time the invasion began Germany had received much and given little.

V

The War

The Red Army

DURING THE THIRTIES a new conscription system had been introduced, and more funds invested in the armaments industry. So far as numbers of men and units of equipment are concerned, the Red Army was the world's strongest. When Hitler attacked in 1941 he used about 170 divisions against about 200 Red divisions, he committed about 3,200 tanks whereas the USSR possessed more than 20,000, and the German air force was similarly outnumbered. As the war progressed the disparity in numbers grew. Germany exhausted its resources while Stalin mobilised his immense reserves of manpower, new tank and aircraft production lines were started (an annual output of 30,000 armoured fighting vehicles was attained towards the end of the war), and guns were produced so rapidly that at times the Red Army was able to prepare its offensives with 300 pieces massed on each kilometre of front.

However, the Soviet advantage of numbers was accompanied by a pathetic qualitative inferiority, especially in organisation, tactics and leadership. The Russian infantryman was brave, enduring, obedient and patriotic: qualities which were exploited by inferior officers. Time and again massed waves of Russian foot soldiers were sent into battle against impregnable targets. Well-planned assaults were frowned on, especially if they needed time to prepare. Officers (of all ranks up to and including the Commander-in-Chief himself) at times seemed to know only one tactic: the massed attack. The fact that officers could be shot for failing to execute often impossible orders meant that, if an initial attack failed, it might be repeated again and again until all the troops and their commander had been killed. German accounts speak of vodka-primed Red infantrymen advancing shoulder to shoulder, shepherded on the flanks by their officers and commissars, cheering and shouting, being cut down by machine guns and immediately replaced by others.

There was a shortage of rifles, and the new models were defective. Soviet aircraft were inferior to German. Soviet tanks were numerous but obsolescent; their immense numbers had been attained by long production runs and the change-over to new models had only just started in 1941. The new designs, however, were exceptionally good. They had extra-powerful guns and thick armour. The T34 medium tank was probably the best tank to participate in the war. Although most of its best features had previously appeared in the West, the manner in which they were combined was superb. The KV heavy tanks also came as a surprise to the Germans. Both the T34 and KV were proof against the standard German anti-tank gun, and anti-aircraft guns had to be used against them. Their wide tracks made them more manœuvrable in snow and mud, while their engines, unlike the tank engines of other countries, were specially designed. Fortunately for the Germans, there were few T34 and KV tanks in 1941, and they were badly used. Using them individually to support infantry, rather than en masse like the Germans, made their destruction easy. The Soviet practice of shooting while the tank was in motion, rather than when stationary as favoured by other armies, was also mistaken. Later in the war the Stalin heavy tank appeared, and this was at least the equal of the newly introduced German heavy tanks. But the reluctance to risk tanks in battles against enemy tanks, and the conception of the tank purely as infantry support, died hard.

The Russians had always attached much importance to artillery and the Red Army had some notable gunnery specialists. But the artillery had perhaps suffered more than any other arm from the Red Army purge, for skilled gunner officers were hard to replace. At the lower levels also the technical skill demanded of artillerymen could not always be attained from recruits drawn from agricultural or non-skilled occupations. This is one reason why the Red Army specialised in the more simple kind of weapon, notably mortars, and was less competent in the use of indirect artillery fire in attack or retreat. Towards the end of the war the caterpillar-tracked, armoured, self-propelled gun was widely used, both as a tank destroyer and as offensive artillery. Another Soviet speciality was the 'Katyusha', a truck-mounted array of rocket projectors which could saturate a predetermined area with a pattern of high explosive missiles. When first tried at the front it caused panic in both the German and the Russian infantry. The latter, however, soon learned to appreciate it.

When the Red Army began its offensives it relied heavily on massive artillery preparation.

Remedial measures introduced in the Red Army in the early forties followed efforts to restore military pride and glamour which had already been begun in the thirties. Because of tsarist associations and the events of 1917, when a commissioned officer was a class enemy, certain ranks had been abolished in the Red Army and officers' distinctions removed. But in 1935 the rank of Marshal had been reintroduced, together with several other ranks. In 1940 saluting was reinstated, and in 1942 came the most symbolic change of all: the restoration of officers' epaulettes. New decorations for bravery were introduced, with traditional Russian rather than Soviet titles: the 'Hero of the Soviet Union' award was supplemented by the Kutuzov, Suvorov and Alexander Nevsky orders. Campaign medals were also widely distributed.

In 1941 the great defect of the chain of command was its inflexibility. To eliminate one cause of this in 1942 a new regulation stated that at battalion level and below orders could be given orally. (Hitherto officers refused to act unless their orders arrived in documentary form.) But the Soviet concept of initiative remained an obstacle to efficient leadership. On the higher levels a change in circumstances was not considered an excuse for modifying or failing to carry out orders, and offending officers were liable to court martial. In 1941 some generals and many other officers were summarily shot for failing to carry out impossible orders; others committed suicide. Absurd situations developed; on one occasion a Soviet army forming one arm of a pincer movement continued its planned manœuvre for three weeks after the other arm of the pincer had been routed.

The most important move to improve the work of the army officer was the final demotion of the political commissar. The commissar's essential role was to maintain Party control over the army, to watch and report what officers were doing. Hitherto the commissar was not subordinate to the commander of the unit to which he was attached, but to the commissar of the next highest military formation. Thus in each unit there were two centres of authority—the commander who bore operational responsibility and the commissar, who though theoretically confined to political duties, frequently interfered with the work of the commander. The danger of this situation had become evident in the Finnish war and in 1942 the political commissars were renamed 'Deputy commanders for Political Affairs'. That is, they were now subordinated to their commander. Their role as watchdog of the Party continued, as did their responsibility to organise the political indoctrination of their men, and to prod every soldier to maximum efficiency. German accounts describe them as varying in action from enthusiastic fighters, inspiring their men to acts of heroism, to cowards skulking behind the lines, spying on the men and making trouble for the commanders.

That the ordinary Russian soldier fought bravely (provided he was properly led) was not due entirely to natural courage. He really had no choice. Behind the Soviet lines lurked the special detachments of the NKVD called 'Smersh' ('Death to Spies') whose target was in fact not spies but Russian soldiers unwilling to 'die the death of a hero'. At times and in places there was one Smersh member to every nine soldiers, with the task of shooting any man who retreated. After the abandonment of Rostov in 1942 without the Red Army making what Stalin considered a heroic resistance, new instructions were issued reinforcing the existing measures against unauthorised retreats. Moreover, it was announced that any Red soldier allowing himself to be taken prisoner would be treated as a traitor and coward (signifying among other things that his family would also suffer). Also, the 'hate the Germans' propaganda which had begun in 1941 led the Russian soldier to expect no mercy from the Germans after being captured. (The Germans did treat their Red Army prisoners as if they were indeed the inferior racial types described in Nazi ideology. Many, perhaps as many as three million, died in captivity. Those that survived were treated as traitors when they returned to the USSR after the war.)

Another incentive to proper Soviet behaviour were the so-called penal battalions, to which were sent soldiers and demoted officers who had behaved badly, or had been denounced as suspect. These battalions were used for the most sacrificial tasks like frontal attacks against machine guns, or clearing minefields by marching through them. At the other end of the scale were the Guards divisions. The title of 'Guard' was granted to those divisions which had most distinguished themselves. They were an élite, received higher pay, were better equipped, and were not usually wasted in useless and badly planned operations.

As the war progressed, officers sacrificed their men more hesitantly. This was largely because the officers themselves were different. They were younger, better trained, and battle-hardened. In 1942 there had been a minor purge of the officers, starting at the top. This purge was on military rather than political principles. Voroshilov and Budyenny were among the first to be transferred to positions where they could do less harm. Both had little military talent and had owed their high position to Stalin's favour. Their departure coincided with more mobile Soviet strategy; no longer were withdrawals delayed until escape routes had been closed. At the lower levels, too, the pig-headed and mediocre officers were either killed in action, put into penal battalions, or transferred. Nevertheless, right up to the end of the war the Red Army casualties remained very high in relation to the work done. There are no reliable figures either for German or Russian losses in the Second World War, but a reasonable estimate would seem to be that on the Eastern Front the former lost less than 3,500,000 (killed or missing) against a Red Army loss of seven to ten million.

The behaviour of the Russian soldiers advancing into non-Soviet territory varied. In Yugoslavia the Red Army men were accused even by Yugoslav Communists of disrespect for the local women. In Poland soldiers relieved the local civilians of their watches. In Germany for a time behaviour was unrestrained. No female, however aged, was safe, and there was destruction for destruction's sake. Even factories which might have provided useful reparations were destroyed. The Red soldier had fought a long and bitter war, he had lost family and friends, he had witnessed German destruction in his own country and seen, or at least heard of, the extermination camps in Poland. He could hardly be expected to behave like a perfect gentleman.

1941

One advantage which Stalin enjoyed over Hitler was a superior intelligence service. The restrictions placed on Soviet citizens travelling abroad, and on foreigners entering the country, made difficult the establishment of contacts and the passing of information. Moreover, the Germans had been concentrating their spying activities in the West rather than in the East. These inadequacies meant that little concrete military information was available to the Germans. The USSR had more Soviet divisions than Hitler had expected, and the T34 and KV tanks were an unpleasant surprise when first encountered. On the other hand Germany was still relatively open and thus easily penetrated by Soviet spies, and there could often be found Germans in responsible positions whose disaffection with the Nazi regime, or whose communist leanings, made them willing informers. In 1941 a Soviet informer, Richard Sorge, worked in the German embassy at Tokyo, and another may have been quite close to the German High Command. These spies, and the British government, informed Stalin of the date of the German attack. Stalin, however, took no action.

As the danger grew Stalin appeared to become more and more convinced that, so long as the Soviet Union took care to placate Hitler, the attack would be postponed. This was not entirely illogical; or at least it was no more irrational than Hitler's decision to start 'Operation Barbarossa' at this stage of the war. To Stalin, who knew Russia was weak (but not so weak as Hitler imagined), a German attack on the USSR seemed to be a gamble so risky that not even Hitler would undertake it. So long as Hitler besieged Britain he could count on ever-increasing Soviet material support and, perhaps, an eventual Soviet military contribution. To attack Russia before Britain was defeated would mean a war on two fronts and a critical supply position.

Thus, as tension grew, Stalin ordered his frontier troops to take no action, even to refrain from manœuvres, which might provoke the Germans. Even when German reconnaissance violated the frontier no action was taken. The warnings from abroad were ignored. Churchill's messages may have been construed as provocations to split the Russo-German alliance; the warnings of Soviet spies may have been disregarded partly because their reliability was questioned after their forecast date for 'Operation Barbarossa' had passed uneventfully. (Hitler's unexpected need to quell Yugoslavia after its pro-German government had been overthrown by rebels, and temporary disagreement with Hungary, had in fact caused a postponement of the attack.)

Stalin seemed to have the pathetic belief that if he took a holiday the tension would relax. Evidently he thought that Hitler would attack him out of distrust and fear of a betrayal rather than for ideological, psychological and hair-brained strategic reasons. As Hitler's new deadline of 22 June approached, deserters from the Wehrmacht revealed to the Soviet frontier troops the precise hour and minute when the attack would begin. But Moscow still forbade any defensive measures: troop movements might be a provocation. Freight trains carrying Russian raw materials for the German war economy crossed the frontier right up to the last minute.

In the small hours of 22 June the invasion began, taking the Red Army leaders completely by surprise. Bridges over the frontier rivers were captured intact and most of the Red Air Force was destroyed on the ground. Later in the day Germany declared war. (Molotov's reported reply to the German ambassador was '. . . what have we done to deserve this?') Some hours later the Russian people were informed that they were at war. Stalin was still on holiday and Molotov was in charge. According to some accounts, during the first ten days of the invasion Stalin wavered between panic and depression and could not be persuaded to take decisive action. The only bright spot was the British promise of support. This was not only an encouragement but also a surprise, for it had been half-expected that Britain would stand aside or even join Hitler against the USSR. Britain's acquiescence in the occupation of Czechoslovakia had confirmed suspicions that many British leaders would like to see Hitler move east, and the fact that Britain and France finally declared war when Hitler moved against another country close to Russia had not changed this conviction. Then, Churchill was an uncompromising anti-Communist, and, swayed by their own propaganda, most Russians believed that the arrival of Rudolf Hess in Scotland had betokened Anglo-German conspiracies.

The German assault was three-pronged. The Northern Army Group was directed towards the Baltic States and Leningrad, the Central Army Group crossed the frontier at Brest and was to move against Moscow, while the Southern Army Group attacked the Ukraine. The invading armies included Italian, Rumanian and Hungarian troops. Finland contented itself with regaining territories lost in the 1939–40 war.

At the end of June, as the Germans advanced deep into Soviet territory, Stalin formed his State Defence Committee. This war cabinet had at first five members (Stalin, Molotov, Malenkov, Voroshilov and Beria) but Kaganovich, Mikoyan and Voznesensky were later added. Day-to-day control of the forces was in the hands of the 'Stavka' (Stalin and Molotov with the four soldiers Voroshilov, Budyenny, Shaposhnikov and Zhukov).

On 3 July, two weeks after the invasion, Stalin broadcast to the people, reminded them of the fate which had befallen Napoleon and the Kaiser, and called on them to wage total war on the invaders. For probably the first time the Soviet people, desperately needing leadership, genuinely began to look up to Stalin as a trusted, if feared, authority. In his turn Stalin treated the conflict not so much as a Soviet, but as a Russian war. Patriotism produced more fervour than ideology.

The German strategy was to thrust mechanised troops through the Soviet lines and then to unite the thrusts so as to prevent the retreat of the broken Red forces. Soviet military dogma and incompetent leadership made this strategy even more successful than had been hoped. The theory that a future war against the capitalists would take place on the capitalists' own territory had led to the doctrine of offensive war; the Red Army had been trained on the assumption that it would be an advancing, never a retreating, force. Thus it had little instruction in the technique of the fighting retreat, and its men and supplies were massed vulnerably on the frontier. Moreover, the High Command time after time refused to sanction retreats until it was too late. Its favourite exhortations of 'not a step back' or 'to the last man' usually did little to delay the German advance and only simplified the encirclement of the Red forces. The Soviet chain of command was faulty—officers were reluctant to act without the assent of their superiors, who in turn postponed their agreement until their own superiors had been consulted. Among other things, this enabled the Germans to capture intact so many vital bridges, even though most were protected by a Red officer with his finger poised over the demolition switch.

The German aim in the first stage of the war was to destroy the Red Army and to take up positions, well past Leningrad and Moscow, on a line drawn from Archangel to Astrakhan. This line would serve as the start line for a possible second stage, an advance towards the Urals. These were ambitious aims, especially as little real information was available about Soviet strength. Hitler's optimism seemed to be based on two questionable assumptions: that the Russian railways were as bad as they had been during the First World War, and that the Red Army was in fact as ineffective as it had appeared to be in the war against Finland. In the long run neither of these assumptions proved justified, and it was the Germans who were to suffer most from transport difficulties.

Nevertheless, despite the foolhardiness of the undertaking, it seemed at first that Hitler would once more be proved right. The Wehrmacht advanced so rapidly through the badly led and poorly equipped Red Army that at times the German troops entered towns whose population had no inkling of their proximity. Hundreds of thousands of bewildered Russian soldiers gave themselves up after being surrounded. In the Vyazma 'pocket' in the autumn about half-a-million prisoners were taken, at Kiev another half million. In October the Central Army Group after capturing Smolensk and Mozhaisk was within sight of Moscow. The Northern Army Group was besieging Leningrad, and in the south Odessa had been handed over to Rumania and much of the Crimea overrun.

Poised against Moscow, Guderian's armoured corps was held up for a few weeks while Hitler decided what to do next. It has since been claimed that this delay cost Germany the war, for it gave Stalin a breathing space in which to prepare the defence of Moscow. It may indeed have saved Moscow, although even this is not sure, for Guderian's tanks and men were worn out and depleted. But in any case the capture of Moscow would probably not have been decisive.

In Moscow, there was panic and disorder for a short time. The expected German capture of the city encouraged some of its anti-semites to make a premature emergence, and a few optimistic traitors prepared Swastika flags to welcome the invaders. Some Party members 'lost' their membership cards. The evacuation of the government departments stimulated much of the population to flock to the stations, bent on escaping while there was still time. There was some looting and rioting but order was soon restored, and the knowledge that Stalin was remaining in the Kremlin convinced both the faithful and the cynical that the authorities intended to defend the capital. The male population was organised into workers' detachments, to be thrown into battle after learning how to load, aim and fire a rifle, while the old and the adolescents and the women were sent to dig earthworks.

The first attempt to take Moscow began at the beginning of October, and after heavy fighting a few German troops penetrated as far as the suburbs, but no farther. After a second vain attempt, and the arrival almost simultaneously of bitterly cold weather and fresh Red forces from Siberia, the attack was called off. At the beginning of December Russian counter-offensives pushed back the German lines to beyond Mozhaisk. Here the Wehrmacht, ill-equipped for the cold, but still with high morale, endured the winter.

Farther north the siege of Leningrad had begun. Although there was an intermittent lifeline across Lake Ladoga the supply situation was desperate. Neither Budyenny, the romanticised cavalry hero of the Civil War who commanded the army group on this front, nor Zhdanov, Stalin's Party colleague who was responsible for Leningrad, proved equal to their responsibilities: the former failed to delay the German advance, the latter failed to evacuate the civilian population or to provide sufficient food stocks. For two years Leningrad was shelled by the Germans, who were plainly intent on starving it into submission. They succeeded with the starving—between half and one million died—but did not obtain the submission. Not for the first time in Russian history, sacrifice of the masses compensated for the failures of the leadership.

Thus the situation at the end of 1941 was that the Germans occupied the western part of European Russia—the territory which had contained two-thirds of Russia's heavy industry, four-fifths of its population and almost half the railway network. However, much of industry and the working population had been successfully evacuated to the Volga, Urals and Asian areas and was soon to be once more in production. Also on the bright side was the success, even if limited, of the Soviet counter-offensive, the beginnings of munition deliveries from the West (to facilitate these, Britain and the USSR had jointly occupied Persia), and Japan's attack on the USA which released Far Eastern and Siberian troops for service against the Germans.

1942

The winter of 1941–42 was grim for both sides—for the Russians, whose army had been decimated, and for the Germans, who had failed to reach the set objectives of the 1941 campaign: Moscow, Leningrad and the Caucasian oilfields were still in Soviet hands. Moreover, while the winter cold was unpleasant for the Russian soldier, for the German it was calamitous. Winter clothing arrived late and in inadequate quantity and at one stage the Wehrmacht was suffering a thousand serious and moderate cases of frostbite each day. The tight-fitting German army boots had no space for rag or newspaper insulation and their steel nails drained away the body warmth. (Russian soldiers wore boots a size too large, and without nails.) Not only this but tank and truck engines were put out of action, sometimes permanently by the low temperatures, and rifles and machine guns could no longer be relied on. The supply position was serious with long lines of communication, few good roads, shortages of railway rolling stock, and partisan attacks on road and rail convoys.

German casualties in the first 12 months of the Russian campaign had been heavy, about one-and-a-quarter million (compared to less than 160,000 on the Western Front in 1940) but Soviet casualties had been heavier: between four and five million. Whereas his generals, realising that the Russians were by no means finished, wished to draw back the army to shorter defensive lines, Hitler himself planned new offensives for the summer of 1942. The main aim was to be the oilfields of the Caucasus. As in 1941, Hitler considered Moscow to be only a secondary target; even the capture of Leningrad had greater priority.

In July von Manstein liquidated the bridgehead on the Kerch Peninsula which the Red Army had won in its 1941 counter-offensive, and after a heroic defence Sevastopol was taken. Thus the entire Crimea was conquered. A drive by the Wehrmacht towards Voronezh was delayed by Timoshenko's thrust on Kharkov (unsuccessful and costly, but winning a month's respite). Stiffening Soviet resistance around Voronezh caused Hitler to concentrate on Stalingrad, farther south. Meanwhile, Rostov had been captured and the German forces streamed into the Caucasus, capturing the Maikop oilfields, but failing to penetrate into the mountains barring the way to Baku and Batum. Hitler's insistence on dividing his attacking army into separate Caucasus and Stalingrad advances ensured that neither objective was secured.

Stalingrad, although an important transport centre and armaments producer, was absolutely vital neither to Stalin nor to Hitler, but both chose to treat it as such for largely symbolic reasons: it was, after all, 'Stalin's City'. An array of Soviet talent was concentrated there. Vassilevsky, who had just replaced a mediocre predecessor as Chief of the General Staff, was sent. So was General Zhukov, whose talented direction of the army had just earned his appointment as a deputy defence minister. On the political side, Malenkov represented Stalin, and there was also Khrushchev, the former Party leader of the Ukraine who had retreated with the Red Army from Kiev. The city garrison, which was not large, was commanded by General Chuikov.

Hitler, who did not know, or did not wish to know, that the Red Army still had considerable fresh reserves, envisaged a walkover both at Stalingrad and in the Caucasus. In fact some troops were sent from the south to assist in the assault on Leningrad, while vital mechanised troops were sent from the Eastern Front to France, to cope with a possible Allied landing. Even so, if instead of making a frontal assault on Stalingrad the Volga had been crossed and the city surrounded, the battle might have been won. But with Soviet resistance stiffer than expected, every ruined house and cellar being bitterly defended, the direct attack made ever slower progress. The Russian garrison received a trickle of fresh men and supplies from across the Volga while the main reserves were concentrated for an eventual counter-blow. From mid-September to mid-November, at the price of heavy casualties on both sides, the Germans reached the river at several points, but pockets of Soviet troops inside the city still continued to resist. German troops and supplies had to be diverted from the Caucasus front (thus crippling the German offensive there) and Paulus was appointed to command the 300,000-man army besieging the city. On 19 November began the Russian counter-attack.

For this counter-attack Zhukov disposed of the entire operational reserve, which had been assembled in the two months gained by the few but tough street fighters of Stalingrad. The Soviet forces were divided into three parts (under Rokossovsky, Yeremenko and Vatutin). Directing the first blows on the weakest sectors of Paulus's army—the Italians and Rumanians—the Red Army cut off the German rear. Hitler stubbornly refused to sanction a withdrawl, ordering Paulus to remain where he was until the spring (even though he had less than 50 tanks and two days' fuel left). A hastily organised relief army failed to break through, Goering was unable to keep his promise of an adequate supply airlift, and the German forces, demoralised by cold and hunger, were destroyed. Paulus was captured in Stalingrad on 2 February 1943 and the last German resistance ceased about the same time. Hitler had lost 300,000 men killed or captured and enormous amounts of equipment. It was not the first time the Wehrmacht had been defeated (its El Alamein defeat had occurred just as the battle for Stalingrad began), but it was certainly its most crushing and humiliating reversal. Although in the material sense Germany probably remained militarily superior to Russia, psychologically Stalingrad marked the turning point of the war. The Russians were now certain that they would win in the end.

1943

The Stalingrad defeat meant that strong Soviet forces threatened to cut off the German army in the Caucasus—and this was accordingly withdrawn. Good German generalship and Soviet failures permitted an orderly retreat. In the Ukraine the Germans were obliged to quit Kharkov. Meanwhile outside Leningrad a minor Russian victory obtained a precarious railway link with the city. In February, however, von Manstein out-manœuvred the Russians and recaptured Kharkov. After the spring floods a German counter-offensive near Kursk failed and was transformed into a retreat. The Red Army made a rapid advance and by the winter of 1943 had recaptured Smolensk, Kharkov, Kiev and Krivoi Rog. Apart from the Northern Army

Group which was still besieging Leningrad, the German army had been driven more than half-way back towards its 1941 start line.

Thus 1943 was the critical year of the war. Soviet victories alternated with reverses and the German army, while no longer victorious, was still a force to be reckoned with. If, instead of insisting on rigid defence lines and impossible offensives, Hitler had accepted a policy of elastic defence he might well have escaped the disasters of 1944 and 1945.

The Red Army Offensives

In early 1944 a series of small-scale offensives drove back the Germans from Leningrad, captured Krivoi Rog for the last time, brought the Red Army close to the Rumanian frontier, retook the Crimea and Odessa, and laid the foundations for the summer campaign of 1944.

By this time the earlier technical and supply deficiencies had been largely overcome. With its new Studebaker trucks the Red Army was just as mobile as the German, and could advance rapidly once a breakthrough occurred. Soviet strategy had likewise changed for the better; instead of concentrating all resources into a few elaborate large-scale, hoped-for master-strokes, a series of considerable but not exhaustive blows were struck all along the front, keeping the initiative, exploiting weak points, and disengaging when resistance became too strong. To meet these attacks the Germans were constantly shifting and dissipating their reserves and lost any chance of regaining the initiative. 1944 was propagandised as the 'Year of Ten Victories'. The first victory had been the relief of Leningrad, the second the drive towards Rumania, the third the recapture of the Crimea and Sevastopol, the fourth an offensive against the Finns in Karelia. None of these four, however, had significantly damaged the opposing forces. The fifth, sixth, and seventh blows thrust the Red Army to the Vistula in Poland, and inflicted heavy losses on the Germans. The eighth success brought the Red Army into the Baltic states, cutting off several German divisions in Courland, where they remained until the end of the war. The ninth blow took the Red Army to Yugoslavia and Hungary and the tenth was directed against Petsamo. These offensives, as usual, were accompanied by relatively heavy losses; the Red Army probably incurred three-quarters-of-a-million casualties during 1944. But Finland and Rumania withdrew from the war, Bulgaria (which had been at war against Britain but not against Russia) allied itself with the USSR, the pro-Soviet Poles were well established in the liberated part of Poland, while the surrender of Italy, with the opening of the Second Front in June 1944, meant that the Red Army was well placed for a final advance on to Berlin.

By the beginning of 1945 the Soviet Union had more than five million at the front in Europe, opposing less than two million Germans. The Red Army had more than 13,000 tanks, against the German eastern army's 3,000–4,000, and about seven times as many guns as the Germans. The Red Air Force, which in the 1945 offensive was under the direction of the armoured forces, also had numerical superiority.

The drive began in January, having been advanced by one week at the request of Churchill (who wished it to coincide with the Ardennes offensive). In the north, two army groups under Rokossovsky and Chernyakhovsky invaded East Prussia. In the centre, Zhukov drove from the Vistula directly towards Berlin, while farther south Koniev attacked Upper Silesia. Meanwhile, Malinovsky and Tolbukhin operated in the Balkans and after clearing Budapest in February liberated Austria and Slovakia.

The Oder was soon reached and large German forces in East Prussia were cut off. However, the advance was delayed for several weeks and the decisive drive on Berlin began only in April. On 2 May, after fighting desperate German resistance, the massed assaults of Red infantry succeeded in subduing the city and bringing the war in Europe to a close.

On the Home Front

Hitler had some hopes that his invasion would trigger off a revolt against Stalin, but in this he was disappointed. Russian anti-Stalinists lay low until they found themselves under German occupation; there was less outright opposition to Stalin than had been expected, and the NKVD had control of the situation. On the other hand, the Russians did not at first display much fighting spirit and this relative apathy was the target of successive propaganda drives. The first of these was the 'Hate the German' theme, to which many noted writers contributed. Aided by German behaviour, this campaign portrayed the invaders as savage barbarians, surrender to whom was unthinkable, who must be destroyed unmercifully. This propaganda was directed particularly at the Red Army soldier, who had shown an unheroic readiness to surrender in the first months of the war.

Right from his first wartime speech Stalin played down the ideological significance of the conflict. It was portrayed more and more as a struggle of the Russian people, helped by the other Soviet nationalities, to preserve their ancient civilisation against the Huns. Alexander Nevsky, who in the thirteenth century had defeated the Teutonic Knights, was among the stalwarts of Russian history whose exploits were recalled to the modern Russians. At the other end of the propaganda scale, slogans written on walls were generally of the 'Death to the German invader!' type, not of the 'Down with the German capitalists' genre.

Stalin's broadcast two weeks after the invasion with its emphasis on the patriotic nature of the war firmly established him as the only possible leader. Russians who had previously hated or resented or merely feared him were now prepared to follow his directives enthusiastically. In his broadcast Stalin denied that the earlier Non-Aggression Pact with Germany had been a mistake, for it had gained time and nobody could have foreseen that the Germans would be so cynical as to make a surprise and unprovoked invasion without first declaring war. The disorderly retreat was in this way ascribed to the lack of scruples shown by Hitler, not to Stalin's mistakes. Later in the war, and especially in 1942 after the fall of Rostov, there was a definite tendency to blame the Red Army for the defeats: there was in fact a press campaign alleging that the Red soldiers were not fighting bravely. Later still, after Stalingrad and the Soviet offensives, Stalin began to be portrayed as a military genius, and after the war Marshal Zhukov (whom the ordinary Russian regarded as the architect of the Red Army's victories) was soon removed from the limelight. Only after Stalin's death was the Stalinist myth destroyed; he was then alleged to have been responsible for the 1941 disasters, and for the bungling of several subsequent operations.

Rekindling of patriotic enthusiasm for Russia's glorious past, and for national traditions, as well as the prudent need to mollify a possible source of opposition, led Stalin to cultivate friendly relations between the government and the Russian Orthodox Church. In the occupied regions German promises to encourage religious observances had already led many priests to co-operate with the enemy, thus setting a dangerous example to their parishioners. Accordingly, anti-religious propaganda ceased, the newspaper *Godless* was suppressed, steps were taken to restore the most valued churches, a Synod was permitted, Patriarch Sergius was allocated a house consonant with his dignity—and after his death the new Patriarch Alexis was allowed an impressive inauguration. The Church was permitted to own property and to publish its monthly journal, and the government established a special department for Orthodox Church affairs (whose director was surreptitiously known as 'Peoples' Commissar for Opium'). In exchange for all this (which was partly responsible for a significant rise in church attendance) the Church gave wholehearted support to the war effort, preaching and praying on behalf of the Red Army, instructing its priests in occupied territory to refuse co-operation with the Germans, collecting money for munitions, and acknowledging Stalin as Russia's '. . . leader, chosen by God'. This concord between Church and Stalin persisted until the latter's death. The Church played a useful part in the post-war peace movement, and in gaining the sympathy of the religious in foreign countries. The Orthodox Church became almost an established church, and no doubt welcomed the NKVD's persecution of rival churches and sects.

Economic conditions were bad, but in general not so bad as during the Civil War. Except when cities were besieged, the food rationing system worked fairly well. Rationing was discriminatory, but the discrimination was applied not on a class basis but according to the individual's value in the war effort. Soldiers and workers were relatively well fed, but office employees, 'dependants' of soldiers or workers, and children had meagre rations. However, people did not starve to death, although malnutrition often led to fatal illnesses. In the cities a legal Black Market was established where shops sold semi-luxury food at inflated prices to those who could afford it. Urban transport was bad or non-existent.

In the main categories of basic industry, production was at about half or two-thirds the pre-war level—and was devoted entirely to the war effort. About half the labour force in the factories was female. Working conditions were bad and this, together with malnutrition, long hours, poor transport and housing, caused many a worker to die at his job. In all, probably about 15 million Russian civilians died unnatural deaths during the war.

Together with military casualties, the war therefore cost around 20 million lives—more than one in ten of the USSR's population. In the last years of the war it was evident that there would be a population crisis within a few years and measures were taken to increase the birthrate. Unmarried mothers were freed of financial responsibility for their off-spring (encouraging an increase of so-called illegitimate births which, with the war-induced shortage of marriageable men, was not unwelcome) and financial awards and medals (like the 'Mother-heroine' and 'Maternal Glory' awards) were introduced for prolific mothers. Divorce was made less easy, and abortion remained illegal, thus strengthening 1936 legislation which had reasserted the importance of the family as a social unit.

Throughout the war cultural life of a sort carried on. Soviet composers wrote new patriotic music, the ballet continued and there was a flood of poor-quality but morale-boosting novels, poems, plays and films. In some ways people liked the war atmosphere: after the nightmares of the thirties, it was agreeable to share a common purpose and a genuine comradeship with the Party and government. Many must have hoped that this new, real, partnership would continue after the war, replacing the repressions and coercions of the previous decade. However, towards the end of the war influential Party voices were heard demanding a return to so-called 'Leninist purity' and ideological 'vigilance'.

The Occupation

Policy in the occupied territory of the USSR was probably the most glaring example of Nazi ideology hampering the German war effort. A main tenet of this ideology was the proposition that the Slavic peoples were racially inferior, sub-human almost, and fit only to serve the Germans as quasi-slaves. Hitler's policy, following from this, was to regard occupied Russia as a colony, supplying Germany with food, materials and expendable labour.

Thus in 1941, when it became apparent that the German invasion had uncovered anti-Communist sentiment, as well as anti-Russian feelings in the non-Russian parts, the Germans were by their own pre-conceptions prevented from utilising this opposition. By the end of the war almost all the goodwill which some Soviet citizens felt for the German 'liberator' had been dissipated.

There was much resentment among the peasants against collectivisation, and if the Germans had decollectivised agriculture they could have established a strong class of peasant proprietors with a vested interest in the occupation. But the suggestions made by Germans on the spot for such a reorganisation were defeated within the Nazi bureaucracy by those who opposed it either for ideological reasons or because they believed (like Stalin) that the collectivised system would produce more grain. Only in Byelorussia were there taken a few hesitant decollectivising measures.

Exploitation of nationalist feelings might also have paid dividends, especially in the Ukraine where many still resented the subordination to Moscow. But the Ukrainian nationalists, although at first encouraged by the Germans, eventually decided that they had to kill both the German Nazis and the Russian Communists. This they did, and survived as guerrillas until at least 1947; among their victims was General Vatutin of the Red Army.

As the German armies advanced they attracted vast numbers of sympathisers, many of them prisoners or deserters from the Red Army. By the end of 1942 there were about a million of these serving the German Army in non-combatant occupations. There were also fighting units from the non-Russian nationalities, including an entire Cossack corps, commanded by a German. A new threat to the Bolshevik regime appeared in 1943 when General Vlasov, one of the most popular and successful Red Army generals until his capture, was encouraged to organise an anti-Stalin army from among the millions of Russians in German prison camps. A multitude of prisoners joined him, although most of them probably did so simply as a means of escape from the starvation regime of the prisoner-of-war camps.

Among Vlasov's supporters there was a former assistant editor of the newspaper *Izvestia*, and there were useful German advisers who visualised him leading his new Russian Liberation Army triumphantly into Moscow. However, this concept was distasteful to the Nazi Party: after the Master Race had failed to subdue Stalin it was hard to admit that a Russian army might succeed. So, although Russian units were formed and used as garrisons in Western Europe and elsewhere, they were never allowed to develop into a significant force. On the few occasions when they were used in small numbers on the Eastern Front they were very successful. When Hitler became desperate towards the end of the war, an attempt was made to breathe new life into the Russian Liberation Army, but it was too late. One Vlasov division joined the anti-German Czech rebels in 1945 and others were captured by the Americans. Vlasov soldiers of all ranks captured by the Western Allies were handed over to the USSR. Vlasov himself was publicly hanged in Red Square during 1946.

Extermination of the Jews was carried out by the German civilian authorities, often with the acquiescence and sometimes the assistance of the local population; the anti-semitism fostered by the tsars, in Poland, Ukraine and Byelorussia especially, was still strong. The most notorious massacre was at Babyi Yar, outside Kiev, where about 100,000 Jews were killed, and all over Russia similar slaughter took place. In the occupied zone were many camps for Red Army prisoners, where conditions were so bad that most died and cannibalism occasionally occurred. These were for the ordinary prisoners: army commissars and Jews were shot immediately after capture. If they did not admit they were in these categories there was usually somebody among their fellow-prisoners who would denounce them.

From the occupied territories about three million young civilians of both sexes were deported to work as slave labour in German industry. In general they were treated as badly as the prisoners-of-war and were driven and bullied until they dropped dead. (Nevertheless, those who survived were for about a decade after the war regarded in the USSR as highly suspect.) These deportations encouraged young people to flee from home to join the partisans.

As in other occupied countries, post-war accounts of partisan activity in the USSR tend to exaggerate their heroism and their significance and disguise the fact that their fellow-countrymen trying to lead a normal existence under occupation suffered from them just as did the Germans. Nevertheless, it can be said that the Soviet partisans were numerous and useful, and that among them were to be found many genuine heroes and martyrs. In 1941 at the time of the big retreat they did not play a great role, but as the war progressed their attacks on the German supply lines were a serious embarrassment to the invaders. The partisans consisted largely of men who had fled from the Germans to avoid deportation or worse, and soldiers who had been cut off during the retreat and retired into the woods. Organising these bands were a few Party or Komsomol members deliberately left behind at the time of evacuation, and specialists flown in from outside. As the supply position improved, Moscow arranged parachute drops and airlifts of weapons, munitions, radar equipment and medical supplies. Apart from their attacks on road and rail transport, the partisans were also a useful source of information for the Red Army's high command. The best partisan country was in the wooded terrain in White Russia and parts of the Ukraine, and there were large areas which were under partisan control day and night despite occasional German efforts to dislodge them. Often in the German-controlled areas the occupiers' authority existed only during daylight. In retribution for partisan attacks the Germans executed numerous hostages, and this was another incentive for populations to abandon their homes and live in the woods. Oradour-type destruction of entire villages with their populations were carried out by the Germans as reprisals. At the same time, inhabitants suspected of actively or passively collaborating with the Germans were murdered by the partisans.

When the Germans retreated they made every effort to destroy whatever might be useful to the Reds: houses and cattle as well as railways and bridges and factories. Nor were historic buildings or works of art spared.

There were some localities which because of peculiar circumstances suffered less than others. Near Orel there was an experimental administration run by anti-Bolshevik Russians. Odessa, which with its hinterland had become the 'Transdriestra' province of Rumania, was also lucky. Always rather cosmopolitan, the city was developed as a kind of Bucharest, with a gay and slightly decadent atmosphere. Many Odessans, perhaps a majority, enjoyed this transformation. Even the Jews had a chance of survival, for despite German pressure as few as possible were handed over by the Rumanians. In some of the national territories friendship of the inhabitants towards the German occupiers was exceptionally strong and the occupation regime was accordingly less rigorous. After the Germans had retreated some nationalities (notably the Volga Germans, the Crimean Tartars, and some Moslem peoples in the Caucasus) were deported *en masse* to less hospitable country east of the Urals, even though only a proportion of these people had actually collaborated with the invaders.

Russia's Relations with the Allies

Only a few weeks after the invasion, Roosevelt arranged for supplies, including military supplies, to be sent to Russia. Britain did likewise and was subsequently joined by Canada. It was the USA which sent most, and three of its exports were vital to the Soviet war effort: over 400,000 trucks, which proved far superior to the few Soviet-built vehicles available; army boots and Spam. Other Lend-Lease items included aviation fuel and various scarce materials, aircraft, warships, tanks, railway equipment, medical supplies and miles of gold braid for the new Red Army officer uniforms. The fighting equipment, though useful, was never as important as the non-combatant items. This was because it did not begin to arrive in quantity until the time of greatest need had passed, and by 1943 Soviet production of tanks and aircraft was overwhelmingly greater than the rate of import. The main factor determining the scale of Allied assistance was transport. The Arctic route to Murmansk and Archangel became more and more important, but being subject to attack from German bases in Norway entailed heavy losses. At one stage, and especially after the convoy PQ17 had been decimated, Churchill warned that the scale of assistance might need to be reduced. This provoked a bitter response from Stalin.

Soviet demand for the Second Front had its beginnings in 1941, became particularly strident during the critical year of 1942, and was maintained until the Normandy landing of 1944. When in September of 1941 Averell Harriman and Lord Beaverbrook visited Moscow to discuss Russia's material needs, Stalin indicated how useful a Second Front would be. Failing this he was willing to accept British and US forces on Soviet soil. (But owing mainly to transport difficulties this was never possible, although some British fighter squadrons were based near Murmansk, and for a short time towards the end of the war American bombers used Soviet air bases.) In 1942, when both Russia and the West feared that the other might make a separate peace with Germany, Molotov visited Washington and London, and the resultant 20-year Soviet-British treaty of friendship was felt to be a great success for the USSR. An ambiguous statement about a Second Front in Europe issued at this time led Stalin to believe that an Allied promise had been made, but Churchill visited Moscow in August 1942 to explain to Stalin why there could be no immediate Second Front in France, and that instead there would be an invasion in North Africa. As at this time the Red Army was hard-pressed, there was a strong feeling that the Allies were not pulling their weight and this feeling was expressed openly by Stalin and later in the Soviet press. In 1943 there was not only anti-British feeling, but also an anti-British campaign in the USSR, with newspapers publishing cartoons of cowardly and indolent British generals. The belief was that, while the USA was willing to open a Second Front in France, 'reactionary circles' in England were opposing it. This belief was strengthened by some inept remarks by Wendel Wilkie, Roosevelt's emissary in the USSR. It was also hinted that Rudolf Hess was not being tried as a war criminal in Britain because he was acting as Hitler's envoy and aiming at an anti-Soviet German-British accord. At the same time there was some anti-Americanism, especially after the US ambassador had complained that the scale of American material assistance was being concealed from the Russian people.

Towards the end of the war, especially after the opening of the Second Front and Churchill's second visit to Moscow in October 1944, relations between Britain and the USSR became warmer. But the Soviet Union still considered Britain a lukewarm ally; it never understood, or tried to understand, the efforts made by America and Britain in the Mediterranean and the Far East and at sea. Nor, apparently, did Stalin realise that neither the American nor British government could wage war like he did, selling lives cheaply.

Perhaps to placate the Allies, but also because it served no useful purpose, the Comintern was dissolved in 1943. Foreign Communist parties had already been instructed to support the Allies and this policy was maintained when occupied countries were liberated. In France and Italy in particular, this meant a sacrifice by the local parties, for both emerged from the occupation as the strongest political force, and both had acquired arms. However, in response to instructions from Moscow, they made no bid for power and supported the new provisional governments.

There were meetings between Stalin, Roosevelt and Churchill at Teheran in 1943 and Yalta in 1945. The first was devoted mainly to strategic questions, the latter to the problems of the post-war world. At both meetings the Russian negotiators maintained the initiative, largely because Stalin was unwilling to make real compromises and because he was able, to a limited extent, to play off the Americans against the British.

So far as Britain was concerned the earliest and most serious difference with the USSR concerned Poland. When Hitler invaded Russia there were several thousands of Poles in the USSR, who had been taken prisoner during the Red Army's advance against Poland in 1939. After 1941 many of these were organised into a Polish army under General Anders, being supplied with Russian equipment and being expected to fight on the Russian front against the Germans. However, these Polish forces showed no enthusiasm to fight alongside the Russians, and Churchill eventually persuaded Stalin to allow them to leave Russia and join with the Poles already fighting with the British forces. The British patronage of General Anders, who was known to dislike the Russians, was one of the factors preventing genuine friendship between Britain and the USSR.

Meanwhile about 8,000 Polish ex-officers held captive in the USSR had disappeared, and enquiries from the Polish government-in-exile and by Churchill only obtained evasive answers from the Kremlin. Then in 1943 German propaganda broadcasts alleged that near Smolensk, at Katyn, the Germans had discovered a mass grave containing these officers: it was claimed that they had been shot by the Russians in 1940. The Polish government-in-exile asked for a Red

Cross enquiry, and this refusal to accept the Soviet government's denial of complicity led to the breaking of diplomatic relations between the two governments. (After Smolensk was reoccupied by the Red Army a Russian investigating commission showed foreign correspondents evidence indicating that it was the Germans who had committed this atrocity. However, there was other evidence which tended to implicate the Russians rather than the Germans, and the role played in this investigatory commission by Vyshinsky—the impressario of the pre-war show trials—seemed almost a guarantee of duplicity. On the other hand, while Russians seemed to be the most likely perpetrators, this does not necessarily mean that Stalin ordered the killing, which may well have been a private NKVD affair. Certainly the NKVD would not have regretted the liquidation of these anti-Russian and anti-Communist officers.)

The departure of General Anders, and the break with the London Poles was followed by the establishment in the USSR of a rival Polish government-in-exile and rival Polish army. Henceforth British concern with Poland's affairs was to press the claims of the London Polish government, and to agree on Poland's post-war frontiers. While at first Britain intended that both the USSR's 1939 acquisition of eastern Poland and the absorbtion of the Baltic states would be reviewed after the war, as the war neared its close concessions forced by the USSR, together with the application of the Soviet policy for Poland regardless of western objections, meant that the Baltic states and eastern Poland remained in the USSR. Liberated Poland in compensation was allowed to occupy Upper Silesia and to move its western border as far as the rivers Oder and Neisse. The western governments stressed that this Oder-Neisse line was only a provisional demarcation, but the post-war deportation of its German inhabitants and the diplomatic situation meant that the whole area in fact became part of Poland.

When the Red Army entered Poland the Moscow Polish government-in-exile was installed. A premature rising organised by the Polish Resistance in Warsaw played into Stalin's hands. This Polish Resistance was orientated towards the London Poles and was anti-Russian. Realising the moral and tactical advantage of capturing Warsaw from the Germans before the Russians arrived, the leaders of the Resistance organised a revolt just as the Red Army reached the suburbs. But the Red Army did not proceed any farther into Warsaw and the Germans were able to concentrate their efforts on defeating the revolt. This they did, with many executions and the brick by brick destruction of much of the capital. It has usually been alleged that the Red Army halted its advance into Warsaw precisely because Stalin wanted the Polish Resistance to be destroyed by the Germans. This, however, is only partly true. The Red Army in fact encountered heavy resistance and operational problems just as it was poised to cross the Vistula into Warsaw proper: it could not have mounted an immediate attack without serious risks. On the other hand, Stalin's refusal to allow western planes to land on Soviet territory after dropping supplies to the Resistance shows that he did not regard the failure of the revolt as something to be avoided.

Although Soviet policy towards Poland from 1939 to 1945 is often quoted as an example of Stalinist bullying and duplicity, from the point of view of Russia's national interest it was not illogical. Stalin probably realised that the traditional enmity between Poles and Russians would need several generations to eliminate. In the meantime Russians would be safer if the affairs of Poland were in the hands of a pro-Russian government: before the war Poland had conspired with Hitler against the USSR, and had not hesitated to annex part of Czechoslovakia when that country was in difficulties with Germany. The parts of eastern Poland occupied by the USSR had ethnic ties with Byelorussia and the Ukraine, and the extension of western Poland at the expense of defeated Germany was good for Poland and an additional protection for Russia.

Elsewhere in Europe, the Soviet government was less inflexible. In a private agreement made during Eden's and Churchill's visit to Moscow in 1944 it was established that Rumania and Bulgaria would be Soviet spheres of influence but that the USSR would not interfere in Greece. This accord was honoured by both parties: the USSR did not help the Greek Communists in their 1944 rising. The USSR subsequently requested and received part of East Prussia, the Baltic city of Koenigsberg becoming Kaliningrad. Stalin's initial demand for a liquidation of the German officer class was not approved by his allies and he later contented himself with heavy reparations from defeated Germany.

Much of the Yalta Conference was devoted to the establishment of the United Nations, a project dear to Roosevelt and for Russia's co-operation in which he was prepared to make concessions in other matters. Stalin at first visualised the post-war world as the province of the Big Three, who would maintain peace and impose their own plans in the lesser countries. But when the Western Allies brought in France and China to make a Big Five, and when they proposed safeguards and rights for the smaller countries, Stalin lost some of his enthusiasm. He made sure that the veto power enjoyed by the USSR as one of the 'Big' countries would be a strong veto. He also proposed that all 16 of the USSR's constituent republics should have a UN seat and vote. (To give this some credibility, a constitutional change had been made in the USSR, allowing—in theory—union republics to maintain their own foreign services and armed forces.) In the end the USSR, alone among the other members, was allowed three seats— USSR, Ukraine and Byelorussia. Roosevelt refused Stalin's suggestion of three seats for the USA too.

Also at Yalta Stalin's promise to enter the war against Japan was renewed. In return for this, the USSR gained western acquiescence for Soviet influence in Outer Mongolia (subsequently the Mongolian Peoples' Republic), the repossession of the Chinese Eastern Railway, Soviet bases at Port Arthur, the acquisition of the Kuriles and South Sakhalin and (at least implicitly) Russian influence in Manchuria and Korea. The USSR was to enter the Pacific war not later than three months after the defeat of Germany. Between the German surrender on 2 May and the declaration of war against Japan the Potsdam Conference was held. Roosevelt was dead, genuinely regretted by all Russians, and replaced by the less friendly Truman. The Potsdam Conference was concerned mainly with putting previous understandings into effect and frontier changes (such as the Oder-Neisse line and the Russian acquisition in East Prussia) were accepted provisionally pending a final peace conference.

On 8 August 1945 the USSR declared war on Japan, a few days after the first atomic bomb had been exploded over Hiroshima and more or less simultaneously with the Nagasaki bomb. Japan was already willing to surrender. In the short campaign Soviet troops penetrated into Manchuria, reached Port Arthur and North Korea, invaded the Kuriles and South Sakhalin. On 2 September Japan surrendered. Thus the USSR's intervention had not been of great value, while the Soviet share of the fruits of victory was considerable. Roosevelt had enlisted Soviet support because at the time of the Yalta Conference it was thought that Japan's resistance would be long and costly. Nevertheless, Stalin's entry into the Pacific war when it was all but over was not (as is sometimes alleged) an act of cynicism, but the result of scrupulously honouring a promise. On the other hand, subsequent descriptions of the Pacific war describing how Russia defeated Japan singlehanded were, if not cynical, at least ludicrous.

VI

Stalin's Last Years

The Atomic Bomb

KAPITSA, who had worked at Cambridge under Rutherford, and Vernadsky, who had worked with Madame Curie, were among the pioneers of Soviet nuclear physics. From about 1930, encouraged by the grand old man of Russian science, Yoffe, and by the enthusiasm of Ordzhonikidze and Bukharin, the Soviet nuclear scientists went ahead. Special funds were allocated and by 1940 only American researchers were better equipped. The Russians had a cyclotron working from about 1937. Leningrad was the main research centre, both the Radium Institute and the Physical-Technical Institute being involved. The pre-war director of the latter's nuclear physics laboratory was Kurchatov, to whom was later credited the leading role in post-war nuclear developments. By the beginning of the war it was evident that Soviet scientists were well aware of both the military and economic potential of nuclear fission, and were on the brink of fundamental discoveries.

Nuclear research was slowed down in 1941, presumably because it was thought that no results would be obtained in time to help the war effort. Information about the US—British—Canadian successes was obtained through espionage, but was sometimes misinterpreted. American restrictions from 1943 on the sharing of certain secrets with British and Canadian scientists may have obstructed the flow of this information because Fuchs, apparently the main informer, was a member of the British team. From 1943, presumably encouraged by knowledge of progress at Chicago, the Soviet government sanctioned an accelerated nuclear research programme and even asked the USA to supply uranium. Even so, there seems little evidence that the Soviet government at that time realised the full significance of the western atomic programme, or that information about this

143

programme was a priority target for espionage. The Canadian Royal Commission on espionage in 1946, which was set in motion by the defection to the West of a key member (Gouzenko) of the Soviet Embassy in Ottawa, revealed the surprising depth and extent of Soviet espionage in North America during the war years, but also indicated that the search for atomic data was pursued neither urgently nor efficiently. When, later, Fuchs and Nunn May were tried, it again became evident that Soviet interest in western nuclear physics did not have great priority until after 1945.

American leaders and scientists almost up to the end of the war had doubts about the feasibility of the atomic bomb, hence the wish for Russian participation in the final campaigns against Japan. The successful test of the first weapon took place during the Potsdam Conference and President Truman, while informing Stalin of the new super-bomb, took care to conceal its atomic nature.

In the months before Hiroshima the 'peace' group in the Japanese government grew stronger, and there were attempts to use the USSR as an intermediary. However, the USSR had no desire for a Japanese surrender at this time, before Soviet forces had joined in and earned a title to the promised post-war territorial awards in the Far East. Japanese suggestions that the USSR convey peace feelers to the USA fell therefore on stony ground, while a direct proposal to the USA appears to have been misinterpreted. By this time the US government was regretting its earlier invitation of Soviet participation in the Pacific War, and the attack on Hiroshima may have been partly prompted by an unspoken wish to induce a surrender before the USSR declared war.

The Communist press in all countries at first approved the use of the atomic bomb, but the significance of this weapon was minimised in Soviet commentaries, presumably so as not to spoil the claim that the decisive factor ending the Pacific War was the Soviet intervention. Nonetheless, Soviet nuclear physicists received instructions for an intense programme to develop an atomic bomb, and Beria was entrusted with the supervision of this programme. Progress at first seemed slow and in 1947 several physicists, including Kapitsa, who were regarded as recalcitrant, were put under arrest (probably house arrest, so as not to interrupt their researches). The first Soviet reactor appears to have been working by the end of 1947, and bore a marked similarity to an earlier American design. In September 1949 the first Soviet atomic device was exploded. This was several years earlier than western scientists had expected; knowledge of what the latter had achieved probably enabled Soviet researches to be concentrated on projects known to be feasible. The acquisition of German scientists and experience in 1945 may also have helped. But the main contribution was undoubtedly by Soviet workers, who were much more competent than western experts sometimes alleged: three Russian nuclear physicists were among the recipients of post-war Nobel prizes.

In 1953 a thermonuclear (hydrogen) device was first tested. Although such a device had been exploded in the USA in 1952, so far as the hydrogen bomb is concerned (that is, a weapon which could be dropped from an aircraft) the USSR was first. The first Soviet H-bomb was exploded in 1955, the first American in 1956. Soviet testing was done in the Arctic and in Central Asia. The bombs produced relatively large quantities of radioactive fallout and at least once (in 1956) this failing necessitated special food precautions in China. On the other hand Soviet scientists had the credit of building the world's first civil nuclear ship (the icebreaker *Lenin*, completed in 1959).

Foreign Policy

The feeling of nuclear inferiority, and the realisation that the USA would not share its secrets, was one reason for the progressive deterioration of East-West relations in the last Stalinist years, with each side driven by the other to increasingly uncompromising positions. While from the very beginning Stalin believed that the West was working against him, it was not until about 1947 that the USA and Britain began to abandon their policy of firm patience and, concluding that the USSR was no misguided ally but a determined enemy, began to take counter-measures. These counter-measures (the Atlantic Pact, rearmament, establishment of the German Federal Republic, etc.) in turn seemed to the Soviet government a confirmation of its existing belief in western malevolence and inspired counter-counter-measures. And so on until Stalin died.

President Truman's ending of lend-lease to the USSR without warning as soon as Germany was defeated, and the growing improbability of American loans for post-war Soviet reconstruction seemed—and in fact were—unfriendly acts. Anti-Communist outbursts by well-known but largely powerless individuals in the USA and Britain were taken, incorrectly, to be expressions of official policy. The question of German reparations provided more food for Russia suspicions. As the war approached its end the USSR had, not without justification, advocated 20 billion dollars' worth of German reparations, to be taken over a given period from German production. The Soviet share of this was to be ten billion. The reparations were to be administered on an all-German basis, which among other things would have involved Russian participation in the Ruhr industrial area—which the Allies did not relish. The Allies had consistently opposed these Soviet demands for reparations. An impoverished Germany was not among their aims, for they realised that the crippling reparations enforced at the end of the First World War had been partly responsible for the emergence of Hitler.

The West would agree neither to the 20 billion dollars' reparations, nor to a four-power control of the Ruhr. The Soviet response to this was a refusal to participate in a German peace treaty, and a declaration that an Austrian peace treaty could only be discussed after a German treaty was signed. In its turn the West declared that the four-power division of Germany could not be continued indefinitely, as the consequent uncertainty and chaos prevented any German recovery. Accordingly at the end of 1946 the British and American occupation zones were amalgamated—a first step towards a separate West German Republic. In Russian-occupied Germany the Soviet position had already been strengthened by the incorporation of the German Socialist Party into the Communist Party, the new combination being called the Socialist Union Party (SED). Reparations demands were partly fulfilled by the removal to the USSR of factories and plant, sometimes with their skilled workers (as happened with the Zeiss optical works and other highly technical enterprises). This process had started as soon as the Red Army had broken into Germany. Later, the dismantling of German industry having proved wasteful, many remaining enterprises were taken into Soviet ownership and produced goods for the USSR.

Another source of tension in 1945 and 1946 was the Middle East. The Anglo-Russian occupation of Persia during the war had left the Soviet Union in control of northern Iran, and there was no sign of a Russian withdrawal by the previously-agreed date (March 1946). A pro-Soviet government had been installed and this, it was hinted, would become the nucleus of a new Kurdish state incorporating also the Kurdish parts of Iraq and Turkey. In addition, the USSR had been applying pressure on Turkey for a share in control over the Dardanelles and the return to the Soviet Union of Kars and other territories ceded after the Revolution. These demands, never satisfied, only drove Turkey towards alliance with the West.

Stalin's foreign policy, while opportunist, was also cautious, and firmness on the part of the USA and Britain, together with anti-Communist speeches by Churchill at Fulton and by Senator Vandenberg, persuaded him that the Persian issue was one which could not be forced. Accordingly the Red Army left Persia in May 1946 and the leaders of the pro-Soviet government took refuge in the USSR.

Churchill's speech at Fulton, Missouri, was a well-planned occasion designed for maximum effect on US public opinion. When the war ended there was great sympathy for the Soviet Union among Americans. In fact, British imperialism was still considered by many to be the greatest danger in the post-war world. Soviet behaviour in the first post-war years had done little to dissipate this goodwill. While inside the government there was a growing feeling that Stalinism was a serious threat, Americans in general were still well disposed towards the Soviet Union. Hence the limelight directed on Fulton on 5 March 1946. Here was the West's greatest orator and most respected statesman giving a public warning of danger in the East.

Churchill was most concerned with the situation in Eastern Europe. Having negotiated with Stalin during the war over the fate of the Polish government, he had a particular interest in Poland, where 1946 witnessed the persecution of the party of Mikolajczyk (a former member of the 'London' government, whose participation in the post-war, Soviet-sponsored, Polish government Churchill had negotiated). The Communist takeovers in Poland, Hungary, Bulgaria, Albania and Rumania were all following the same pattern, though at different speeds. In 1945 genuine coalition governments had been formed in which the Communists were only one of several parties. These governments carried out an agreed programme of land reform, anti-fascist purges and friendly relations with both East and West. But the offices in the new governments were allocated so that Communists were in charge of the key ministries: interior, information and defence. Thus propaganda, police and justice and the armed forces were in the hands of the one party, which filled important posts with its own nominees. Soon the genuine coalitions were replaced by apparent coalitions, in which the non-Communist members were chosen not by the parties, but by the Communists. Life was then made difficult for the more independent non-Communists: Communist control of the interior meant that their meetings might be broken up, or they might even be murdered, without those responsible being hindered or apprehended by the police; their newspapers were denied the means of production; and those who were most dangerous to the Communists could be branded as fascists or collaborators and dealt with accordingly. In the final stages all non-Communist political parties were suppressed, and police-supervised elections would give the Communists an overwhelming number of votes. By this time the government establishment would be well on the way to becoming a copy of the Soviet model.

This complete Communist takeover was probably not deliberately planned. Each stage was taken experimentally and was only made the foundation for the next stage when circumstances seemed to warrant it. (These circumstances were the desirability of consolidating Soviet power still further, and the expected acquiescence of the West.) The Soviet government was probably quite sincere in 1944 and 1945 when it assured east Europeans (King Michael of Rumania among them) that the entry of the Red Army did not mean a change in the social order. Yet it was the presence or the shadow of the Red Army which enabled the Communists in each country to take the offensive.

In three of the countries—Finland, Yugoslavia and Czecho-slovakia—which the wartime allies had agreed should fall in the Russian sphere of influence, events differed from what happened in Poland, Albania, Hungary, Bulgaria, Rumania and (to some extent) East Germany. One of the underlying reasons for the East-West conflict over Eastern Europe was that while the West had agreed that this region should be in the Soviet sphere it had secured agreement that democratic governments should be installed. But by democratic the West envisaged its own multi-party systems, whereas Stalin visualised the USSR's 1936 Constitution. In Finland, however, Stalin accepted a situation which was exactly that which western statesmen had anticipated for the entire Soviet sphere of influence: a government friendly to the USSR but having a genuine parliamentary regime and following its own, non-communist, policies. A completely different situation existed in Yugoslavia. Here the Communist grasp for power was almost complete at the end of the war. Tito's partisans had more or less liberated the country with little direct assistance from the Red Army. Although for a few months there was a coalition government in Belgrade, by the end of 1945 a fully fledged Communist government, 'confirmed' by 96 per cent of the votes in an election, was in power and a few months later was strong enough to execute for treason Mikhailovic, who had been the royalist leader of the non-Titoist partisans. Despite the fraudulence of the elections there is little doubt that Tito and his ex-partisans had strong support among the Yugoslavs. In this Yugoslavia differed from the other peoples' democracies and from East Germany, and resembled Czechoslovakia. This latter nation had been taught by Munich that alliance with the West was risky, and probably a majority of Czechs favoured a close relationship with their fellow Slavs in the USSR. Thus in free elections in 1946 the Czech Communist Party received no less than 38 per cent of the votes. Probably because of this success, the likelihood of the Party improving its electoral position, and the absence of the Red Army, there was no immediate attempt at forcible conversion into a 'Peoples' Democracy'. In any case the Communist ministers in the government held the key posts of Interior, General Staff and Information, while the Communist Gottwald was Prime Minister.

The Fulton speech produced a violent reaction in the USSR, Stalin describing Churchill as the instigator of the Third World War. Nine months later General Marshall became US Secretary of State and his appointment coincided with the containment policy towards the Soviet Union. This implied resistance to all further Russian advances. Early in 1947 the Marshall Plan, offering generous financial aid to war-ravaged countries, was introduced. While its aim was the restoration of economic health, it evidently had anti-Communist overtones, for its proponents believed that, since Communism had a special appeal to the poverty-stricken, US-induced prosperity would check the Soviet advance. Molotov and a strong Soviet delegation attended the initial talks on Marshall Aid but after some days of stone-walling walked out. The refusal of the USSR to accept Marshall Aid and its persuasion of East Europe (including Czechoslovakia) to do likewise, marked the final decision to take a totally uncompromising attitude in foreign relations.

The intellectual framework for the new hard line was presented to an international Communist congress by Zhdanov in September 1947. Zhdanov was himself probably the originator of the new policy. He had long been an advocate of an agressive foreign policy and no doubt the worsening international situation—that is, the stiffening American attitude—led Stalin to take his advice. Zhdanov now maintained that the world was split into two camps, one of which was led by the aggression-planning USA, the other by the peace-loving USSR. In this situation, said Zhdanov, the 'peace camp' must be solidified and strengthened. One move in this direction was the immediate establishment of the Communist Information Bureau (Cominform) to replace the defunct Comintern. Unlike the latter, its membership was confined to the Communist parties of the USSR,

East Europe, and France and Italy. Its purpose was to improve Soviet control over the different parties and to help establish Communist regimes in Czechoslovakia, France and Italy.

The new gospel was put into effect by all Communist parties. In France and Italy the powerful Communist parties, which hitherto on Soviet instructions had remained relatively dormant, embarked on a programme of strikes, disturbances and sabotage (including the derailment of passenger trains). This was carried out with so much gusto that the Communists lost much of their support among the electorate, especially in France. But chaos never developed to a degree sufficient to launch a successful coup.

In Germany the reunification of the western and Russian occupation zones became even more unlikely. At the close of 1947, a Foreign Ministers' Council broke up after Marshall had again refused Russian proposals on German reparations, and in March 1948 the Soviet representative walked out of the Allied Control Council in Berlin. This meant that the four-power administration of Germany had finally disintegrated. Also in early 1948 the three western zones of Germany were unified and their currency reorganised; the new western Deutschemark when introduced in West Berlin was a serious embarrassment to the East German financial system. In June 1948 leaders of the Communist countries met in Warsaw and were persuaded to promote an East German Democratic Republic. Concurrently there was a limited rearmament of East Germany with infantry-style forces euphemistically called 'Peoples' Police'. About the same time the gradual demobilisation of the Red Army was halted. Then, in mid-1948, the road and rail access between West Berlin and the western zones of Germany was closed. The western sectors of Berlin were thus blockaded.

Whether the Russian intention was to force the West out of Berlin, or to exact concessions in exchange for the lifting of the blockade, was never determined, for the blockade failed. Perhaps influenced by Hitler's failure to maintain his surrounded Stalingrad forces by airlift in the 1942 winter, Stalin and Zhdanov believed that the supply of a city of more than two million people by air through the 1948–49 winter would be impossible. In this they were wrong: despite the expense and the physical problems the western airlift was successful. Mock attacks by Soviet fighters (on one occasion causing the fatal crash of a British civil airliner) only stiffened western determination. Aided by co-operation from the West Berliners the blockade was overcome, and after 11 months it was called off.

The Berlin blockade prompted the West finally to create out of the French, US and British occupation zones the German Federal Republic, with its capital at Bonn. Another reaction was the North Atlantic Pact, involving the NATO alliance to co-ordinate the defence of Western Europe. Meanwhile the German Democratic Republic was established in the Russian zone, headed by the two Communists Grotewohl and Pieck. In subsequent years there were occasional meetings, discussions and proposals to solve the German problem and reunify the country, but both East and West could only make suggestions known to be unacceptable to the other. In fact the USSR and France and Britain, despite their protestations, preferred a divided Germany—and for similar reasons. As the years passed the limited rearmament of both halves of Germany took place, there was a growing divergence between West German prosperity and relative freedom and East German impoverishment and relative repression. An increasing number of illegal emigrants flowed from East to West Germany.

In the peoples' democracies the Communist governments modelled their policies after the pre-war Soviet experience, frequently causing extra trouble for themselves by a refusal to acknowledge that some pre-war Soviet policies were self-defeating. Collectivisation was undertaken at varying speeds and in some countries the peasants became as resentful as the Russian peasantry. Five Year or Six Year Plans were adopted, but the internal economy suffered from Soviet exploitation. This took two, connected, forms. Former German industrial enterprises in these countries were appropriated by the USSR as reparations (even though the property in most cases rightfully belonged to local owners, having earlier been confiscated by the Germans). These enterprises—nominally joint-stock corporations with a Soviet shareholding—used local labour and material but sent their output to the USSR and were administered by a department of the USSR Ministry of Trade. (There was a subversive joke current in Warsaw about a new kind of animal which the Russians had created by crossing a cow with a giraffe, and which grazed in Poland but was milked in the USSR.) The other instrument of Soviet exploitation was the commercial agreement. Agreements which the separate peoples' democracies made with the USSR reduced the former to a colonial status: the prices of their exports to the USSR were fixed well below world prices, while the items received in exchange were priced at a level several times higher than their real value. Thus the working populations of these countries were labouring long hours in arduous conditions and in exchange received a bare subsistence wage, the difference between what they contributed to the economy and what they received from the economy being taken by the Soviet Union. The anti-Russian feeling which this engendered was aggravated by the presence of the Red Army and by the existence in each peoples' democracy of a Soviet-controlled internal security network. The latter maintained informers everywhere, and its task included reporting the activities of the Communist leadership. Stalin did not trust even the Communist governments which he had himself helped to install.

While the impoverishment and repression of the East European populations was much commiserated in the West, it was perhaps the Communist leaders in these countries who deserved the most sympathy. These were people who had devoted their lives to improving the lot of their fellow-countrymen. They had fought genuine wrongs, had often spent years in prison or exile and seen their friends executed. In 1945 it seemed that at last they were to have the chance to show what they could do. Instead, being dependent in the first place on Soviet power for their attainment of office, and feeling deep loyalty towards the USSR, they were forced into the role of puppets. Far from freeing and enriching their peoples they had to repress them and to devote their resources to satisfying the economic demands of the Soviet Union. Their policies had to follow the Soviet example—for any improvement would imply that the Soviet practice was less than perfect. And to ensure that they did conform there was a net of informers and 'experts' placed in key positions by the USSR and owing allegiance only to the USSR. In Poland even the army was under the command of a Red Army officer, Marshal Rokossovsky.

One Communist leader—Tito—was able to reject all this, to refuse to sacrifice the welfare of his country to satisfy unreasonable Soviet requirements. Tito had not owed his success to the Red Army, and the Red Army was not stationed in Yugoslavia. Relations between Belgrade and Moscow worsened in 1947 when it became evident that Tito would not admit that the Russian 'road to socialism' was the only possible way. This was the basic cause of the 1948 break, although the ostensible issues were alleged rudeness towards Soviet advisers in Yugoslavia and allegations by Yugoslavia that Cominform (i.e. Russian) agents were conspiring against Tito (allegations which were true: the Cominform's aim was to support anti-Tito and pro-Soviet leaders inside the Yugoslav Communist Party). The USSR in turn alleged that Yugoslav agents were spying on Soviet representatives in Belgrade (which also was probably true).

In June 1948 the Cominform (whose headquarters had meanwhile been transferred from Belgrade to Rumania) passed a resolution expelling the Yugoslav Party, accusing Tito of taking an 'anti-Marxist and anti-Soviet' line, 'currying favour with the imperialists', describing his government as a 'shameful, quite Turkish and terroristic regime' and calling on good Yugoslav Communists to compel their leaders to change course. In later months more vituperative language was used, Tito duly taking his place in the rogues' gallery of 'fascist hyenas'. But Tito, much to Stalin's surprise and disgust, had the support of almost all his Party, withstood Soviet threats, and accepted economic (and later military) aid from the West—all this without abandoning his Communist principles and policies. For the first time, Russian Communism was shown to be not the only Communism. In the orthodox Communist world 'Titoism' ranked with 'Trotskyism' as the most degenerate, but dangerous, of heresies.

Trouble with Tito (which had led to the isolation and defeat of the Communist rebels in Greece) and the stiffening attitude of the West caused further Soviet pressure on Eastern Europe. In Czechoslovakia the mainly, but not entirely, Communist government was not considered an adequate guarantee of Czech friendship, so a coup was carried out in February 1948, by which the Communists gained sole control. A few weeks after the coup Masaryck, the highly respected and popular, but non-Communist statesman, was found dead beneath a high window. In the older peoples' democracies purges of the leadership were carried out with the aid of the Soviet informer network. Leading Communists who were suspected of sympathising with Tito's stand were arrested and tried on fantastic, Vyshinsky-style, charges. Many were executed but a few (including the former Hungarian premier Nagy and the former Polish Party Secretary Gomulka) were merely incarcerated. Czechoslovakia, being the last country to become a peoples' democracy, was the last to be purged. Two stalwarts of the Czech Communist Party, Clementis and Slansky, were among those executed. The crimes of which they were convicted included spying for the British and consorting with Zionism.

A peculiarity of 1949 was the beginning of the 'Peace Campaign'. The Peace Campaign, its World Peace Council, and various national Peace Congresses were largely sponsored by local Communist parties and the aim was to amass signatures under petitions 'against war'. This was not difficult as few people were against peace. But the appeals against war had an anti-American and pro-Russian slant, whereas in countries with a non-Communist press people were aware that, for example, the USSR maintained the world's largest army. There was also something illogical in the allegation that the USA was seeking war against the USSR; if this was the case it was difficult to understand why in fact the USA had not already attacked, for it had a virtual monopoly of atomic weapons. Although people of goodwill in their millions signed the Stockholm Peace Appeal in 1950, its effect was negligible. This was partly because although many well-known people signed, others did not, claiming that the petition was hypocritical and anti-American. One of those who refused was J. B. Priestley, who was then denounced as a warmonger, while his novels, previously highly praised in the USSR, were condemned in lurid phrases. The Korean war further discredited the Peace Campaign. Its only lasting achievement was to make 'peace' a suspect word, and to embarrass genuine pacifists.

In the Far East the Chinese Communists, to Stalin's surprise, finally overcame the Kuomintang and established the Chinese Peoples' Republic in 1949. In 1950, after the USA had withdrawn its troops and had seemed to indicate that it did not regard South Korea as important, troops of Communist North Korea invaded the South. Thanks to a Soviet walk-out at the United Nations, the USA was able to secure a United Nations resolution treating this attack as aggression and organising a UN force to meet it. This force was provided mainly by the USA but contained units from many other nations. Soviet material support of North Korea proving insufficient, China, at this time heavily dependent on Russian goodwill, was induced to send troops. There developed a military stalemate, the USA being unwilling to use atomic weapons or attack Chinese forces outside Korea. Negotiations were started for a truce but only after Stalin's death was an armistice signed, restoring the previous situation.

Although the victory of Mao Tse-tung seemed, and was publicised as, a great victory for Communism, in fact Stalin was probably not overjoyed to receive into his fold a country with three times as many people as the USSR and whose Communist government had achieved power without the help, in fact in spite of, the Soviet Union. However, the USSR gave the new China considerable economic, technical and military assistance, but with the usual informing and supervisory arrangements.

At the United Nations the USSR never abandoned its wartime concept of what this organisation should be—an aid to the management of the world by the victorious big powers. Hence frequent use of the veto and occasional walk-outs were a logical reaction to the 'one nation, one vote' system whereby a collection of small nations could out-vote the USSR. After the death of Zhdanov, Molotov was replaced as Foreign Minister by Vyshinsky, who represented the USSR at the United Nations. Vyshinsky's mastery of unconstructive vituperation made him an ideal representative in an organisation which Stalin had come to regard as useful only as a propaganda outlet. Soviet behaviour at the UN, however, aroused the resentment of the smaller nations which had placed great hopes in this body.

Soviet foreign policy in the post-war Stalin years is a good example of the self-fulfilling suspicion. In 1945 the USSR had the goodwill of the USA, of the British socialist government and of most other governments and peoples. In Eastern Europe pro-Russian governments were in power or about to take power. Yet the Soviet government chose to insist that it was surrounded by hostility, that the old capitalist encirclement still existed, and that the USA was an implacable enemy. Soviet policy succeeded in transforming these fantasies into reality. By 1953 the West was rearmed and united in NATO, two of whose members—Turkey and Norway—bordered the USSR. The Communist and pro-Soviet members of the British House of Commons lost their seats in the 1950 election. The peoples of East Europe resented the Soviet Union and their original Communist leaders had been executed or imprisoned—except Tito, who was defiantly preaching that the Russian road to Communism was a dead end. West Germany prospered while East Germany stagnated and thousands of East Germans, together with Red Army deserters, were voting with their feet against the Soviet system. An unsuccessful war in Korea had been fought and had lost goodwill among Chinese Communists. The USA despite Soviet protests had successfully arranged a Japanese peace treaty by which Japan would prosper and remain in the American sphere of influence. Such was the situation inherited by Stalin's successors.

The Economy

Both industry and agriculture were in a sorry state by 1945, but recovery was faster than expected. In 1946 the Fourth Five Year Plan (1946–50) was approved, and this had as its aim the restoration of production to the pre-war level. In fact, for the key branches of industry the 1941 levels were regained within the first two or three years of the Plan.

Among the factors responsible for this quick recovery was the centralised planning system, which was specially suited to deal with this kind of crisis. Then there was the superficial nature of much of the destruction wreaked by the Germans: when the rubble had been cleared away, there usually remained more than the foundations of the old structures on which to build anew. Also, these elementary clearing and rebuilding tasks did not demand skilled labour: it was work suitable for forced labour (such as war prisoners) and for women. Moreover, much of the factory equipment had been safely evacuated to the east. After the war this tended to remain in the east, so as not to interrupt production, and new plant was gradually installed in the old factories. There was at first considerable assistance from abroad. Britain, Sweden and UNRRA provided some key raw materials and plant. More significant were reparation payments and, later, highly advantageous trade agreements with the peoples' democracies. The Russian-occupied zone of Germany contained more than a third of that country's industry—and Germany was a leading industrial power. Those factories and specialists not transferred bodily to the USSR were working on behalf of the Soviet Union. Rumania, Hungary and Finland were also contributing heavily. Inside the Soviet Union labour discipline was strict, real wages were kept to a subsistence level so as to make available more resources for new investment, and the nominal 48-hour working week remained in force. Personal savings accumulated by wartime hard work (or by Black Market operations) were liquidated in the 1947 currency reform. Although housing was not neglected in the Plan shortage of living space remained acute especially in the towns, where several families might share a single room.

A number of gradiose construction projects were commenced. These included the Volga–Don ship canal and huge hydro-electric stations at Kuibyshev and Stalingrad whose dams created vast artificial lakes. All these were a serious mis-allocation of scarce resources: the Volga–Don canal even ten years after its completion in 1952 was carrying little traffic, and the power stations were so enormous that they took years to finish, which meant that the investment of labour and material long remained unproductive. The various works were known as 'Stalin's Grandiose Projects of Communism'. Economics had been sacrificed in favour of propaganda.

Agriculture, as always, lagged behind industry. There was a poor harvest in 1946 and the food distribution system broke down in places, so that there were famines in 1947. Because the MVD internal security system had not recovered from the relaxations of the war, and as the population was less ready to accept painful bureaucratic failures once the Germans were defeated, the food shortages led to some disturbances, the most serious of which appear to have been the Kharkov riots.

During the war, when the collective farms were manned by women and old men, discipline and organisation had deteriorated. In particular, land belonging to the collective had been appropriated by the peasants and added to their private plots. Also, the system whereby the work was done by small groups ('links') was unsatisfactory because the members of each link, being of the same family or close friends, could exploit the absence of supervision. As the tractor factories had been making tanks for about five years, and most of the horses had been taken by the army or eaten, there was a crippling shortage of tractive power; in places ploughing was done with spades, or by women harnessed to a plough.

A fundamental problem on the farms was the weakness of Party representation. It was difficult to find recruits among the peasants; those who were not resentful were usually of unsuitable character or education. Without Party members to keep the local authorities informed, and to act as ginger groups inside the farms, all kinds of abuses occurred. Not only land but also implements were purloined by the peasants for their private use; farm chairmen appointed friends and relatives to soft jobs on inflated farm administrations. As a reaction to this, the Party and government local authorities appointed and dismissed farm chairmen without even informing the peasants concerned.

When Khrushchev, who fancied himself as an agricultural expert, arrived in Moscow, one of his first ideas was the amalgamation of the collective farms. This helped to ensure that almost every farm would be big enough to organise its own Party cell, and it also made better use of agricultural specialists. By the end of 1952 the new enlarged collectives totalled about 95,000, compared to the 250,000 smaller farms of 1950, and about three-quarters of the 1952 farms had Party cells. Khrushchev advocated a further advance, towards 'agrotowns'. These were to be even bigger amalgamations and would centre on specially built new towns which would house, administer, service and entertain the peasants. Private plots would be moved to the outskirts of the agrotowns. This idea, after some discussion, aroused so much opposition inside and outside the Politburo that it was never carried out.

By the end of the Plan, agricultural production was said to have regained the pre-war level, but this is doubtful. Certainly food production was well below requirements: malnutrition could be observed even on the farms. Meat and dairy products were particularly scarce.

Intellectual Life

In 1945 it seemed that the outgoing atmosphere of the war years might be perpetuated in the arts and sciences, with a useful cross-fertilisation of western and eastern experience and concepts, free imports of western literature, and free movement across frontiers for creative artists. But this feeling of kinship did not last long. Possibly the effect on Red soldiers of acquaintance with the capitalist world in liberated Europe—where life was immeasurably better than propaganda had painted it—was one of the reasons for the decision to vilify everything western and elevate everything Russian. This decision naturally affected most of all the intellectuals with a mass audience: novelists, dramatists, poets, historians, film-makers, artists, philosophers, musicians and editors.

The decisive blow against freedom for the arts came in 1946 when Zhdanov demanded a purge of two Leningrad literary journals. These had published work by the satirist Zoshchenko and by the old-established and respected poetess Akhmatova. Zoshchenko's had been *The Adventures of a Monkey* in which, according to Zhdanov, the monkey was anti-Soviet, mouthing 'vile and poisonous' statements implying that in the USSR life in a zoo was better than life outside. Akhmatova was described by Zhdanov as half-way between a nun and a prostitute, whose poetry was depressing and poisonous. The editorial staff of the unfortunate journals was purged. Zoshchenko and Akhmatova were loudly reviled by the more conformist of their fellow writers and were unable to get further work published either by the journals or by the state publishing houses.

This purge had wide repercussions. The staff of the newspaper *Literary Gazette* was condemned for printing a portrait of Akhmatova the previous year. Pasternak, the greatest of all living Russian poets, was condemned for his 'apolitical' poems.

This repression of art, and the distortion of art to serve narrow political dogmas continued for many years, although in Khrushchev's ascendancy much of the pressure was relaxed. Mediocre writers probably welcomed it, for it reduced the genuine artists to their own level, that of copywriters working for the Party and state. Zhdanov appeared to have two aims: to root out western sympathies, and to elevate all things Russian. The composer Shostakovich was accused of 'rootless cosmopolitanism'. The economist Varga was condemned for doubting the official theory that the USA was on the brink of economic depression. Eisenstein was criticised because his film *Ivan the Terrible* portrayed the tsar's bodyguards as the thugs they were, rather than as a 'progressive army'. Eisenstein duly denounced himself, like many other creative artists who knew that unless they acknowledged their transgressions they would not again be allowed to reach a mass audience. (This process of public accusations followed by self-denunciation and recantation became known as 'criticism and self-criticism' and was applied, sometimes usefully, in all spheres of Soviet society.) In literature scholars were condemned for claiming that Rousseau had had an effect on Russian literature, or that Pushkin was essentially a European poet, or, in general, that any European influence had had any effect on any Russian literature. One of the classic Russian novelists, Dostoevsky, disappeared from the bookstores, the disturbed psychology of his heroes being considered harmful to the reader. Novels and plays and films appeared showing Americans to be gum-chewing slobs, busily making profits and germbombs. One novel portrayed US tanks, going into action during the war, painted with soap advertisements, and American officers distributing price-lists at the front, or making an attack with gun in one hand, commercial samples in the other. Nor did the British war effort escape denunciation: Dunkirk was described as an arrangement between Hitler and Churchill whereby in exchange for sparing the British army Hitler would be given a free hand against the USSR. In one play British officers in a displaced persons' camp were shown terrorising Russian children who wished to return to the Soviet Union. A film showed Churchill revealing to Hitler the details of a planned Red Army offensive. Western authors formerly popular in the USSR were described as putrid, lecherous, anti-human and degenerate.

The other side of the coin was the production of new works extolling both Russia and Stalin. Historians devoted their energies to proving that the radio, telephone, aeroplane, tank, tractor, printing press—in fact almost everything—were Russian inventions. Or that, for example, Lord Nelson was taught by a Russian admiral. Novelists and playwrights were careful to put into the mouths of their heroes a modicum of praise for Stalin, and older Soviet novels were reissued with appropriate paragraphs inserted. In films, Stalin was shown in heroic Civil War poses, and making, alone, all the correct decisions in the Second World War.

The establishment of Israel introduced a fresh complexity, because it implied that Russia's many Jews might now have sympathies with a foreign state. In fact the term 'cosmopolitanism' seemed at times a euphemism for Jewish national feeling. Although anti-semitism was never officially approved, anti-Zionism was respectable. In 1949 many Jewish drama and literary critics disappeared, and the last Jewish newspaper was closed down. The more conformist Soviet journalists, who had never quite managed to exclude mention of America in describing the war against Japan, did achieve a similar feat: portrayal of Nazi atrocities without mentioning the Jews.

In academic life, formalism and objectivism were condemned: that is, research which brought no benefit to the socialist state, or which contained judgements which were independent and not related to the needs of socialism. At the same time, truth was subject to pronouncements by the Party. This was particularly marked in biology. The Russian botanist Michurin had done world-acclaimed work on controlling the heredity of plants, and Lysenko, a self-educated peasant, had in the 1920s continued his work, successfully developing quick-ripening grain which could be grown in regions with short summers. Lysenko subsequently elaborated theories purporting to show the possibility of not only modifying, but completely changing, the heredity of plants. Lysenko's theories were attacked before the war by many Soviet scholars, some of whom were arrested. In 1948 Zhdanov announced his support of Lysenko, who now claimed that his critics were western-inspired. Those scholars who would not conform to the officially proclaimed truth of Lysenko's theories were replaced by his protégés. In linguistics the theories of the Soviet scholar Marr had been accepted since the thirties. Marr had proclaimed that a people's language is a superstructure arising out of the social structure. Therefore a change in the social structure (for example, a socialist revolution) would gradually lead to a new language. This theory became a dogma and then a battleground after the war, until in 1950 Stalin published *his* opinions on the linguistic question. In these he rejected Marr and asserted that language was independent of the social structure; when different languages confront one another they do not merge, but the strongest drives out the others. Hence after the victory of socialism there would not develop a new socialist world language. Instead, it was implied, Russian would prevail. After this pronouncement the influence of the entrenched Marrist scholars was shaken in the universities, there was more freedom for linguistic research, and Russian began to be regarded as a future common language. It became the official language at political events, and in the peoples' democracies it became compulsory in schools. In 1952 came Stalin's last theoretical contribution. In his *Economic Problems of Socialism* he freed economic science from some of its more extreme dogmas, notably the assertion that basic economic laws could be changed by merely political action. This implied that future policies should be based on economic reality.

Intellectual repression was helped by a complete blocking of western influence. Not only were non-Communist foreign newspapers unobtainable, but foreign radio transmissions were jammed, only a few approved foreign books were translated into Russian (and these were sometimes abridged), only the most pro-Soviet foreign writers and artists were allowed to visit the USSR, and very few Soviet citizens could visit the West. Thus Soviet newspapers, books and radio were able to publish ludicrous 'truths' about the West without fear of contradiction. For example, in the *Great Soviet Encyclopedia* (published in 1951, still a standard work in 1964, and quite typical of the fabrications of the Stalin period), the photographs illustrating London, apart from conventional architectural and landscape views, comprised two pictures which claimed to show troops and police repressing strikers, two peace meetings, a picture of sheets drying on a line, entitled 'London's Slums', a photograph of workers cycling through a gate and labelled 'Strike at a power station', a picture of a queue outside a shop advertising 'Horseflesh for human consumption', and a photograph of American troops marching down a road, over the caption 'American soldiers on manœuvres in Kensington Gardens'.

Party and Government

The need during the war to broaden the Party's base among the people had led to an almost unrestricted acceptance of new members. Especially in the army were new members found; the pre-war preference for intellectual or administrative workers disappeared. In 1942 no less than two million new members were accepted and by the end of the war there was a total of nearly six million. Recruitment then slackened, but by 1952 there were nearly seven million members. A similar expansion occurred with the Komsomol, which had about 16 million members by 1952. So far as the Party was concerned there was after the war a renewed emphasis on administrative and supervisory employees, rather than manual workers or peasants, although it was still possible to claim that the majority of members came from worker or peasant families. While at the top of the Party the older generations were firmly in command it was possible for the new young members to attain responsible local positions.

But as the Party grew its influence diminished. The main reason for this was Stalin's increasing use of direct, centralised authority. Stalin still combined the position of head of government and head of Party, and he relied more and more on his private secretariat (still under Poskrebyshev). Thus the Party and government organs, which were theoretically supposed to develop and execute policy, were in fact bypassed. For example, the Party Congress, which according to the *Rules* was to be held every three years to discuss and approve the Party Programme, was in fact not held once between 1939 and 1952. Even the Politburo was disused. The fact that the government organs were as much Stalin's business as the Party organs meant that the latter no longer had real supervisory authority over the former.

Stalin was the undisputed leader and was portrayed as the world's greatest living genius, the saviour of Russia, Lenin's indispensable assistant, the leading Marxist theoretician, strategist, philosopher, linguist and economist. But below Stalin among the Politburo members there was conflict about policies linked with rivalry of ambitions. During the war it was Malenkov who became Stalin's confidant and principal aide, and in 1945 he seemed to be the obvious successor. But in 1945 another of Stalin's old supporters, the well-educated Zhdanov, returned from his Leningrad stronghold to the Party Secretariat in Moscow, immediately becoming a rival of Malenkov. The latter at the time was in charge of German reparations, and his policy of removing plant from Germany to Russia had led to waste and abuses. Zhdanov, supported by his protégé Voznesensky (an economic specialist and candidate member of the Politburo) attacked Malenkov's policies, and a consequent investigation headed by Mikoyan condemned the dismantling policy. Although Malenkov was defended by Kaganovich and Beria (both of whom had received for their own departments much plant and material from Germany), by 1946 he had lost his position as Party Secretary. Zhdanov, with his uncompromising foreign and cultural policies, was now Stalin's close adviser. Voznesensky became a full member of the Politburo and subsequently received a Stalin Prize for his book on the Soviet wartime economy.

But 1948 was a bad year for Zhdanov and his supporters. The failure of the Berlin blockade and the defection of Tito strengthened those of the Politburo, like Malenkov and Beria, who had favoured a more moderate foreign policy. In July Malenkov regained his position in the Party Secretariat. Then, in August, Zhdanov died and there followed what became known as the 'Leningrad Case'.

Zhdanov had risen to influence as Secretary of the Leningrad Party, perhaps the most important of the local Party organisations, and in his rise he elevated his friends and supporters from Leningrad. The most important of these was Voznesensky. Others were Rodionov (who became Premier of the Russian republic), Kuznetsov (who became a Party Secretary and for a time was entrusted with internal security) Kosygin and Popkov. Following the death of Zhdanov false evidence was prepared by the MVD, probably with the connivance of Stalin, certainly with the assistance of Beria, and the acquiescence (at least) of Malenkov. Stalin may have feared a manifestation of Titoism, for the Leningrad Party had always maintained a subtle suggestion of independence. On the basis of the false evidence the Zhdanov protégés disappeared from their posts and it was revealed after Stalin's death that Voznesensky, Kuznetsov, Rodionov and Popkov had been quietly executed (Kosygin survived). Within a few months Malenkov regained his former status in the Party as first after Stalin.

In 1952 a Party Congress was at last called. Stalin was present but entrusted the speech-making to his assistants. Malenkov presented the main report and Khrushchev the report on the new Party *Rules*. Khrushchev had arrived in 1949 from the Ukraine, where he had been both premier and Party Secretary. He had made his mark as an agricultural specialist, probably playing a part in the demotion of Andreyev, who had been the previous farming expert. Although his 'agrotown' proposals had been rejected he had nevertheless built a strong position for himself. He was a Party Secretary and had contrived to fill many posts with his protégés, including old comrades from the Ukraine Party organisation.

The changes in the Party *Rules* involved the abolition of the Politburo and the Orgburo. Instead there was to be an enlarged Presidium in which new, younger, men could be groomed for future responsibility. The replacement of the older leaders may also have been the motive behind the 'Doctors' Plot' of late 1952. This new conspiracy was first 'discovered' when one Lydia Timashuk, a woman doctor who was also a part-time MVD informer, wrote a letter to Stalin accusing nine highly placed medical specialists of using improper methods. Stalin thereupon ordered the arrest of the doctors and threatened the Minister of State Security (Ignatiev) with execution if he failed to obtain confessions from the accused. The confessions were duly composed (including among other things an admission of killing Zhdanov) and signed by the accused. Stalin died before the executions took place and the new government re-examined the case. The doctors were freed (except two, who may have died during torture), Lydia Timashuk was requested to hand back the Order of Lenin awarded for her vigilance, and some members of the MVD (though not Ignatiev) were executed for their part in the framing. There is a strong possibility that if Stalin had not died the doctors' confessions would have been the launching pad for a new and extensive purge. Beria (who apparently had no role in the Doctors' Plot), Mikoyan, Molotov and Kaganovich may well have been intended victims.

The Cult of the Individual

Stalin had always shown signs of eccentricity, and it has been suggested that his paranoid psychology deteriorated even further after a mild stroke in 1946. In his later years he was elevated into a god-like figure by all possible means: newspapers, books, plays, films, paintings, radio and speeches. As soon as the war was over Marshal Zhukov, who more than anybody else could claim to be the architect of victory, was relegated to an unimportant army post at Odessa, and Stalin's portrayal as the great strategist was intensified: the disastrous retreat of 1941 was described as 'active defence' planned by Stalin, who had forecast the invasion long before. All the subsequent victories were shown to be single-handed Stalin victories. In 1948 appeared a standard biography of Stalin, written with the subject's own participation. In this he was shown as a modern Lenin and world-shaking genius. The earlier *History of the Communist Party of the Soviet Union (Bolsheviks)*, the standard text-book for political instruction, was also largely written by Stalin and accorded him a leading role in every success. Monuments of Stalin, some enormous, grew like mushrooms all over the post-war USSR: special workshops produced the standard models, valuable materials like copper were used in the de-luxe versions. The Prague skyline was ruined by one of the latter. As a reply to the western Nobel Prizes, Stalin Prizes were established for highly approved artistic or scientific work. Khrushchev later remarked that even the tsars did not name prizes after themselves. Various cities and institutions were already named after Stalin (Stalingrad, Stalino, Stalinsk, Stalinabad, and so on, *ad nauseam*).

At the same time Stalin was portrayed as a man of the people, even though in the last quarter-century of his life he never visited a village or collective farm. His knowledge of the USSR was obtained from films and the written word, neither of which revealed the truth: he was thus, to a large extent, misled by his own propagandists.

It became customary for at least the first and last paragraphs of any serious article or book to be devoted to Stalin's interest or genius in that particular subject, even if it was poultry breeding or sewage disposal. On the occasion of his seventieth birthday the Soviet newspapers devoted almost their entire space to the event. A popular weekly magazine had as its cover a picture of Red Square as it was on the night of his birthday with, suspended in the sky above, a giant portrait illuminated by a halo of searchlights.

He died in 1953. The Soviet Union which he bequeathed to his successors was a nation politically demoralised, but also the world's second greatest military and industrial power.

VII

Khrushchev's Decade

The Death of Stalin

What exactly happened in Stalin's last days of activity at the end of February in 1953 is uncertain. On the 17th Stalin received the Indian ambassador, the last foreigner to see him alive, and made some pregnant remarks about the need to exterminate wolves. On the 25th the vigilance campaign in the press, which had been heralded by the Doctors' Plot and was obviously the prelude to large-scale purges, was unaccountably suspended. On 4 March Moscow Radio announced that Stalin had suffered a serious stroke during the night of 1–2 March. Later, on the 4th, the radio for a time went through the motions of mourning (a 20-minute silence followed by sombre music) but the following day spoke merely of a further deterioration in Stalin's condition. Finally, on the 6th, the radio announced that Stalin had died on the 5th. Later the same day the Party Central Committee and the Council of Ministers jointly appealed for unity and the avoidance of panic, and that night MVD troops moved into the capital and closed certain strategic streets.

Although press and radio were in full mourning, the Russian people were apprehensive rather than sorry: they feared that Stalin might be followed by something worse. Few could have failed to notice the deliberately short lying-in-state, or the absence in the press of valedictory articles by the Party leaders. On 9 March the eight most powerful political leaders—Malenkov, Molotov, Beria, Khrushchev, Kaganovich, Voroshilov, Mikoyan and Bulganin—carried Stalin's coffin to the Mausoleum, where the embalmed body was to lie under glass alongside Lenin.

The Rise of Khrushchev

Delay in reporting Stalin's end to the public was presumably due to the leaders' wish to thrash out the problems of succession first. Probably all realised that Stalin's methods could not be continued, but undoubtedly there were some, like Molotov and Kaganovich, who would have liked to continue the old policies, while eliminating the grosser abuses. The new leadership, established on 6 March, gave Malenkov the leading roles in both Party and government: Secretary of the Party's Central Committee and Chairman (i.e. Premier) of the Council of Ministers. Notable also was the resurrection of Marshal Zhukov, who became Deputy Minister of Defence; evidently the sympathy of the Red Army was sought. But within a few days those who resented so much power in Malenkov's hands had marshalled enough support to persuade the latter to give up his Party supremacy and concentrate on his work as head of government. What emerged from this was collective leadership, and the Party was again equal, if not yet quite superior, to the government.

Malenkov's post as First Secretary of the Central Committee was taken by Khrushchev, and it was these two, with Beria, who formed the nucleus of the collective leadership. Almost immediately Khrushchev began to appoint his protégés to important Party posts: Kozlov became head of the Leningrad Party organisation, replacing one of Malenkov's supporters. Beria was still in charge of the Ministry of the Interior (MVD) with its police, private army and informer network. This was no doubt considered a threat by his colleagues, and in June 1953 he was 'arrested'. He was accused of all manner of crimes, some true and some fantastic (one charge was that he had spied for the British for several decades). There was an anti-Beria campaign conducted through the press and public meetings; subscribers to the *Great Soviet Encyclopedia* were asked to remove the pages devoted to Beria and were supplied with neatly tailored replacement pages about the Bering Sea. In December it was announced that he had been tried and shot. Many of his supporters in the USSR and peoples' democracies were also purged, some being executed. Subsequently he was made the scapegoat for various unpopular or unsuccessful policies.

Within the remainder of the leading group there were several differences of opinion and attitude: Molotov was against making concessions to Tito and, like Kaganovich, opposed many of the conciliatory policies favoured by the others. There were differences over coexistence, agricultural policy and the relative importance of heavy and light industry. Above all, there was the role of the Party: Malenkov seemed to attach most importance to the governmental organs while Khrushchev, being the Party leader, wished to restore the Party to the unquestioned leading position it occupied in the twenties. From 1953 to 1958 policy differences and the distribution of leadership reacted on each other as Khrushchev eliminated first one rival and then another, modifying his policies when necessary to gain supporters.

In February 1955 came the first big success. Malenkov was induced to resign as Prime Minister, admitting that he was inadequate for the job, and became Minister for Power Stations. (This in itself was an innovation: no longer, it seemed, were ousted leaders to be liquidated.) He was succeeded by Bulganin and for a time the latter and Khrushchev became the joint leaders of the USSR, perambulating together in all parts of the world. Khrushchev was now first among equals, but his flamboyance and subsequent policies (like the manner and consequences of his criticism of Stalin and his reorganisation of Party and economic administration) began to create an undercurrent of hostility.

In June 1957, while the ruling pair were visiting Finland, other leaders planned the dismissal of Khrushchev and his supporters in the Central Committee's Secretariat. On his return Khrushchev was attacked in the Party Presidium for his ideological adventures, and his alleged encouragement of a 'Khrushchev cult'. His dismissal was demanded by a majority of the eleven members of the Presidium. However, he was able to demand that his future should be decided not by the Presidium, but by the larger Central Committee. Then, with the aid of military aircraft arranged by Zhukov he was able to rout his opponents by bringing into Moscow those Central Committee members favourable to himself. Zhukov spoke against Khrushchev's opponents (Malenkov, Molotov, Kaganovich) and accused them of participation in the purges of the thirties. Outvoted, the opposition found itself called the 'anti-Party Group' and accused of conservatism. (Molotov was criticised especially for his anti-Titoism, Kaganovich for softness towards reactionary railway steam locomotives.) The trio, plus Shepilov (a Khrushchev protégé who had changed sides after mistakenly thinking that his patron would be defeated) were expelled from the Central Committee, although they remained (until 1964) Party members. Molotov became ambassador to Mongolia, Kaganovich a factory manager in the Urals and Malenkov a power station director in Central Asia. Marshal Zhukov and several others were rewarded with full membership of the Party Presidium.

After this victory Khrushchev felt strong enough to put the Red Army back in place. Hitherto the army leaders had been among the most ardent de-Stalinisers, often demanding more than the Party was willing to concede. Notably, the military had taken advantage of their position by downgrading the role of political commissars in the army. Marshal Zhukov was foremost among the officers and was popular in the army and among the public. In late October *Pravda* appeared with a front-page article on Zhukov's return from a triumphal tour of Yugoslavia and Albania and with a back-page announcement of his dismissal. He was succeeded by Marshal Malinovsky while another of his former colleagues, Marshal Koniev, led the propaganda campaign against him, accusing him not only of hindering Party work in the army, but also sharing responsibility with Stalin for the defeats of 1941, and of starting his own personality cult.

There only remained Bulganin, and in March 1958 he duly resigned the premiership, being replaced by Khrushchev. Thus the supreme Party post of General Secretary and the supreme government post of Prime Minister were once more combined in one person: Khrushchev. As for Bulganin, he was sent to the Caucasus in a minor capacity, then returned to Moscow to do a self-criticism before the Central Committee. In this he confessed that in 1957 he had encouraged the anti-Party Group. This self-criticism was condemned as too superficial, and the unfortunate ex-Premier was abused by various members before being allowed to slip away into obscurity.

Party membership expanded in line with the increase of the Party's influence after 1953. By 1961 membership was around ten million, or two per cent of the total population, plus about twelve million Komsomol members. But the paring down of the bureaucracy under Khrushchev did not exclude a reduction in the Party's *Apparat* of full-time executives. Between 1952 and 1961 these fell from three and a half per cent of the total membership to less than two per cent.

De-Stalinisation

Perceptive Russians no doubt drew the correct conclusions from the virtual disappearance from the newspapers of the habitual worship of Stalin. Those who did not must have realised at the end of March (when the 'doctor plotters' were released) that things were changing. Then, between 1953 and 1956 although there was never any direct criticism of the late leader the condemnation of the personality cult and the reversal of Stalinist policies left no doubt about the new leaders' intentions. Among the innovations were the restoration of relations with Yugoslavia; the arrest of Beria and consequent restraint on the security service, together with insistence on socialist legality; condemnation of the ponderous pseudo-heroic architectural styles of the formerly high-praised Moscow Metro and Volga-Don Canal; greater emphasis on light industry, on consumer goods production, on trade, and on financial incentives for the peasants; the opening of the Kremlin to the public and the abandonment of the practice whereby ministers were whisked from the Kremlin to their country houses along specially reserved and heavily guarded traffic lanes; the visits of the leaders to different countries and (no less novel) to town and country in the USSR; the dissolution of many forced labour camps; the acceptance of foreign tourists in addition to carefully chosen delegations; permission for those Russian wives who had married Allied servicemen during the war to rejoin their husbands (that is, those whom pressure and threats had not driven to divorce): the rehabilitation of a few victims of the Georgia purge of 1937; the publication of new novels expressing criticism of the bureaucracy, and the reprinting of Dostoevsky; renewed interest in foreign technology and methods; and, not least, the demotion of Molotov and Kaganovich.

Then, in February 1956, the 20th Congress of the Communist Party of the Soviet Union was held, with about 1,400 delegates representing the various Party organisations of the USSR and with delegations from foreign Communist Parties. Early in the proceedings it was evident that Stalin could now be openly attacked by name. Malenkov, Mikoyan, Khrushchev and others attacked various aspects of the late leader. The personality cult, the fantastically tendentious *History of the Communist Party of the Soviet Union* (*Bolsheviks*), Stalin's *Economic Problems of Socialism*, past agricultural policy, were condemned and, most notably, well-known Bolsheviks who had been purged before the war and became unmentionable were once again named and praised. The purge of the Polish Communist Party in 1938 was acknowledged to be quite unjustified. Gomulka, who had been purged since the war, was commended, and so was Bela Kun, the Hungarian Communist leader executed in the USSR in 1938. On 25 February the delegates attended a closed session to hear what was later to be known as 'Khrushchev's secret speech'. This speech was never published in the USSR, but Party and Komsomol members were later acquainted with it, and its main themes gradually percolated down to the masses. Copies (probably edited) were also sent to foreign Communist parties and it was one of these which was the source for the texts published in western newspapers (the authenticity of which was never denied by the Soviet government).

Khrushchev began his speech by describing how it had become necessary to explain 'the great harm caused by the violation of the principle of collective leadership and . . . the accumulation of immense and unlimited powers in the hands of one person', and recalled how in Lenin's day the Party's Central Committee had been genuinely consulted on policy issues. Then Khrushchev read out Lenin's last letters about Stalin, his testament, and his demand for an apology after Stalin had insulted his wife: '. . . I consider as directed against me that which is done against my wife'. These revelations apparently caused 'commotion in the hall'. Khrushchev continued by saying that when Stalin was in power anybody who differed with him was '. . . doomed to removal from the leading collective and to subsequent moral and physical annihilation'. Passing to 'the struggle against Trotskyites, Zinovievites and Bukharinites', Khrushchev affirmed that their defeat had been correct, but questioned whether it had been necessary to eliminate them physically after routing them ideologically.

The biggest part of the speech was devoted to 'crimes against the Party'. In Lenin's day, even at the most difficult times, Party congresses and meetings of the Central Committee were called regularly, but Stalin had ignored these organs. In 1937–38 70 per cent of the Central Committee members had been arrested and shot. Khrushchev then hinted that the murder of Kirov had been arranged by Stalin. Other important party functionaries had been liquidated and some of their pathetic appeals to Stalin (taken from the MVD archives) were read to the meeting: for example, that of the old Bolshevik Eikhe: '. . . not being able to suffer the tortures to which I was submitted by Ushakov and Nikolaev . . . who took advantage of the knowledge that my broken ribs have not properly mended and have caused me great pain, I have been forced to accuse myself and others. Most of my confession has been suggested or dictated by Ushakov. . . .'

Stalin's role in the war was surveyed, especial reference being made to his refusal to heed warnings of the 1941 invasion and his reluctance to countenance strategic retreats. The purge of officers in

1937–41 was put forward as one other reason for the defeats of 1941. The post-war purges were condemned, as was Stalin's later self-glorification. A bizarre detail was the revelation that Stalin, suspecting Voroshilov of being a British agent, had hidden microphones installed in his home. The speech concluded with a summons to repair the damage and to return to the spirit of Leninism.

The effect of this speech was enormous, and in the following years policy in all fields was changed radically. It is true that this change took the form of two steps forward, one step back, as over-eager de-Stalinisation gave way temporarily to a stabilising re-Stalinisation. But in the long term there was a significant shift of aims and attitudes, quite apart from the superficial changes like renaming Stalingrad Volgograd and razing the previous decades' crop of Stalin statues. But it was noticeable that Khrushchev had confined his condemnation to the harm Stalin had done to the Party in his later years: his general policies in the early thirties were not questioned. Nor were all the details of the Purge given. This was explicable because many of the 1956 leaders, including Khrushchev himself, had taken part in this, and not on the side of the angels.

The Peoples' Democracies

The most dramatic repercussions of Khrushchev's indictment of Stalin were in the peoples' democracies, in most of which the Stalinists were dismissed. Already in 1953 when Stalin died there had been a revolt in East Berlin and Saxony which, however, was easily suppressed and condemned as a capitalist plot (despite the fact that German workers were the main participants.) In Poland the demoralisation of the Party, faced with a wholesale reversal of previous 'truths', encouraged a decade's tension and resentment to explode in the Poznan riots of June 1956. Although the USSR again condemned these as an American-inspired conspiracy the Polish government (as well as the Yugoslav) acknowledged that they were a genuine and justified protest by the workers. Despite ominous manœuvring by Russian forces to accompany an emergency visit by Khrushchev and Molotov to Warsaw, the Poles succeeded in negotiating for themselves more freedom from Russian interference. Gomulka had been restored to power and Marshal Rokossovsky lost his place in the Polish Politburo. In the following years Poland restored its diplomatic, commercial and cultural ties with the West while maintaining its place in the socialist camp. In fact it was largely through Poland that western cultural influences began to permeate into Russia.

In Hungary the Stalinist Rakosi was ousted and this encouraged a mass movement led by intellectuals and students directed against the USSR and the local Communists. Despite some concessions by the new Nagy government this movement developed into a country-wide rebellion in October 1956. The government submitted to popular demand for an end of repression and of Russian occupation, while the Red Army garrisons showed unwillingness to shoot the insurgents, who were supported by the Hungarian army. However, more reliable Soviet troops were sent, Hungarian officers who had been invited to negotiate with the Russians were arrested by the latter, and Red Army tanks moved in to suppress the revolt. A new puppet government under Kadar was appointed. Many executions followed, including that of Nagy in 1958. Nevertheless, although the revolt failed fear of its repetition led to an easing of life in Hungary.

One of the factors contributing to disturbances in the peoples' democracies was the admission for the first time, at the Party Congress in February 1956, that there was more than one road to socialism— it was no longer demanded that all Socialist countries should imitate the USSR's policies. This admission was made as a concession to Yugoslavia. The existence of Tito's rival and more inviting brand of Communism was a serious embarrassment to the USSR and a repair of the break was one of the first concerns of the post-Stalin regime. Molotov had been unenthusiastic, however, and his patronising suggestion that the Soviet government was willing to forgive Tito pleased neither Tito nor Khrushchev. When in 1955 Khrushchev and Bulganin visited Belgrade it was clear that, although at the inter-state level relations were fully re-established, in the inter-Party sense there was still a great deal of frigidity. But after 1957, and especially after the beginning of Chinese vituperation, the Yugoslav Communist Party edged closer to the Soviet Communist Party. Tito still maintained his relationships with the West, and obviously differed with Moscow on several points, but Yugoslavia was once more generally acknowledged to be a member of the socialist camp. But not by Albania.

In the days when Tito was the degenerate heretic of the Communist world Albania had been his loudest and most savage critic. This, and the refusal of Albania's leaders to acknowledge Stalin's defects, caused a break in relations between that country and the USSR. Later a more serious rift appeared—between the USSR and China. The Chinese Communists had no reason to feel grateful to the USSR despite the economic and technical aid received in the early fifties. Moreover, after Stalin died Mao Tse-tung, who had far greater stature than Khrushchev (or in fact Stalin) as a revolutionary hero, ideological theorist, and man of culture—could hardly be expected to acknowledge the USSR's unadulterated leadership of the Communist world. Chinese innovations like the communes and the 'Great Leap Forward' were frowned upon by the Soviet Communist Party, as was the suggestion that China was already on the road to Communism. (The Soviet concept was that only the USSR had reached this stage: the younger Communist countries were still on the road to socialism.)

Open controversy began around 1960, although before then there had been some tension. Russian specialists were withdrawn, the USSR refused to support China in its border dispute with India, and China retaliated by helping Albania. At international Communist conferences the Chinese delegations began to condemn Soviet policies, although at this stage neither the Russians nor the Chinese named each other: the Chinese referred to the Soviet leadership by proxy, using the term 'Yugoslav revisionists', while the Russians meant 'China' when they said 'Albanian dogmatists'. But by March 1963 relations had become so bad that Khrushchev taunted the Chinese for tolerating colonies (Hong Kong and Macao) on their territory. The Chinese response was to hint that territorial revision in the future might well include territory taken from China by the tsars in the nineteenth century (including the Vladivostok region). Also, alleging that the USSR's retreat in the 1962 Cuba crisis was another Munich, China rejected peaceful coexistence and wooed the Communist parties in the underdeveloped countries: violent revolutions, not gradual transition, was the Chinese recommendation for the success of Communism.

In June 1963 a 60,000-word 'letter' set forth the Chinese side of the argument, and the Russians replied in another long letter. While the Russian arguments were published in China, the Russian people were never given a full opportunity to study the Chinese case. In fact Moscow expelled Chinese officials said to have distributed copies of the Chinese letter inside the USSR. Nor were the Chinese dining-car waiters on the Pekin–Moscow train considered a good security risk: these men, the Soviet government claimed, had been dropping copies of the Chinese letter from the train as it wended its way through the Russian countryside.

The existence of this dispute, and the need for the USSR to gain or keep support among other Communist parties, put the latter in a better bargaining position. Rumania in particular took a more independent line, signing a trade agreement with the USA (which did not however include a 'most-favoured nation' clause as enjoyed by Poland and Yugoslavia). The Soviet Communist Party was not able to obtain sufficient support to arrange an old-style international conference of Communist parties at which the Chinese Party would be unanimously condemned. In the non-Communist countries local parties split into pro-Chinese and pro-Russian factions.

In 1964 the Italian Communist leader Togliatti, whose moderate policies had gained much support among Italian voters, died in Yalta. His death was followed by the publication by the Italian Communist Party of his testament in which he criticised, directly and obliquely, Soviet attitudes towards other Communist countries. Although he opposed the Chinese ideological line, he felt that abuse and denunciation should be replaced by genuine argument, and that a formal split between the Chinese and Russian parties should be avoided. He asserted the importance of the autonomy of different national Communist parties, and criticised the slowness with which personal liberty was being restored in the Communist countries. He recommended that problems and policies should be openly debated by Party leaders, that non-Communist foreigners should not be regarded as enemy agents, and that Party propaganda should give a more accurate and less rosy picture of Communist reality.

Foreign Policy

Stalin's foreign policy having proved quite bankrupt, and wishing for a reduction of tension and armaments as a pre-requisite for raising the Russian standard of living, the post-Stalin government soon began to take action to reduce western hostility. These moves to relax the Cold War were made more difficult by the new US government, with Foster Dulles as its Secretary of State. Dulles had studied foreign affairs and had drawn from the post-war years the conclusion that only an uncompromising approach to the USSR would produce results, hence his brinkmanship and his hints about liberating Eastern Europe. Thus just as the Soviet Union adopted a soft policy the US State Department adopted a hard line. But despite this the period from 1953 onwards was marked by a cumulative if uneven process of relaxation.

The one problem which proved insoluble was the German question. The East German revolt was followed by a four-power foreign ministers' meeting in 1954 (the first for five years) but this was abortive, as were subsequent attempts to negotiate this matter. Berlin was a main issue: Khrushchev described it as a 'fishbone in the gullet'. German reunification became no more likely, while German rearmament and the possibility that one day Germany might reclaim her lost eastern territories (mainly in Poland) alarmed the countries of Eastern Europe as well as the USSR. The Warsaw Pact—a military alliance between these countries—was one consequence of this fear. Nevertheless, the USSR conceded diplomatic relations with Western Germany, and returned prisoners captured in the war (those few, that is, who had survived). But East Germans continued to flock to the West, especially through Berlin, and in 1961 the East German government built its notorious Berlin Wall to stop this (claiming that it was to prevent western infiltration). East Germans attempting to cross the frontier were shot at, although probably a majority of the Peoples' Police on these occasions deliberately missed their target. There were times when the Soviet government might have abandoned the East German regime (that is, agreed to free elections) in exchange for other concessions; certainly Ulbricht did not always receive as much Russian support as he would have liked.

At Geneva in the summer of 1954 the Korean and Indo-Chinese wars were finally ended. The following year the Austrian Peace Treaty was at last negotiated, and the Red Army left that country. Relations with Finland were improved by the dissolution of the Karelo-Finnish Republic (this became part of the Russian Republic) and the evacuation of Soviet forces from the Porkkala base in 1956. The Soviet leaders, especially Khrushchev and Bulganin, made official visits to many countries, gaining a first-hand knowledge of the outside world which Stalin had never troubled to acquire. In Britain the pair were photographed with the Queen but the effect was somewhat spoiled by a noisy difference of opinion between Khrushchev and the British socialist George Brown. (Attempts at this time to gain the support of European non-Communist socialists were usually unsuccessful; the latter were not willing to forget, or forgive, the liquidation of East European socialists in the preceding decade.) India was another country visited, and the Stalinist view of Gandhi as a friend of British imperialism was publicly rejected by Khrushchev. Most noteworthy of all was the visit of Khrushchev and a 100-strong entourage to the USA in 1959.

The official visits were paralleled by the development of foreign tourism, although western citizens visiting the USSR far outnumbered Russian tourists in the West. There were trade and cultural agreements: American films were shown in the USSR and Russian universities were attended by selected British and US students. Notable also was the end of jamming of BBC Russian-language broadcasts (although these were fairly innocuous from the ideological point of view). In 1957 the Cominform was dissolved, to the relief of the non-Soviet Communist parties which had in the past suffered from its interference.

The thaw in foreign policy was temporarily reversed from time to time. After the Hungarian revolt (which was portrayed as an imperialist plot carried out with the connivance of Tito) there was more tension, particularly with Yugoslavia. (This was renewed in 1957–58 when Yugoslav 'revisionism', as expressed in the Yugoslav Party Programme, was savagely condemned.) Another minor crisis occurred in 1960 when, on the eve of a Paris meeting between Eisenhower, Macmillan, Khrushchev and de Gaulle, an American U2 photographic reconnaissance aircraft was shot down over the USSR. After the US President had failed to apologise for this, Khrushchev wrecked the talks and returned to Moscow, even though he had been aware of the American flights long before this incident. A much more serious crisis occurred at the end of October in 1962. In 1961 Castro, the leader of the successful Cuban revolution, declared himself a Marxist-Leninist, an American-inspired invasion of Cuba failed, and Cuba became dependent on the USSR for the sale of its sugar crop. In addition to this, there was Soviet investment and technical advice including military aid. In October 1962 President Kennedy announced that missile installations of a nuclear and offensive nature (i.e. surface-to-surface medium range) were being prepared in Cuba and that rockets were coming from the USSR. The President ordered a selective blockade of Cuba: all ships carrying missile equipment would be turned back. Furthermore, Kennedy stated that any missile directed from Cuba against any country in the western hemisphere would be treated as an attack by the USSR against the USA. There was a limited mobilisation and American forces began to concentrate in Florida: Kennedy had implied that unless the offensive (as distinct from defensive) missiles were removed they would be destroyed either by bombing or by an invasion of Cuba. This ultimatum meant, in effect, either a Soviet withdrawal of these missiles or war. In the first few days, at the UN and elsewhere, the Soviet response was to denounce American 'piracy', to refuse to admit that offensive missiles had been supplied to Cuba, and to accelerate the preparation of launching sites. However, Soviet ships en route to Cuba and carrying missiles were slowed down; other Soviet ships were allowed to pass through the ring of US warships. Later when it became clear that US intentions were inflexible a series of messages between Khrushchev and Kennedy (not all of which were published) evolved an agreement: offensive missiles, together with their Red Army specialists, would be withdrawn from Cuba and the USA could verify the removal. The agreement, which was formalised through the UN, was reached without the participation of Castro and this disregard of the Cubans on the part of the USSR was resented by the former and used as a propaganda theme by the Chinese: Khrushchev was accused of deserting true revolutionaries for the sake of placating the imperialists.

The Cuban crisis evidently had a profound psychological effect on both Khrushchev and Kennedy. Both had been brought to the brink of a Third World War, and had helped each other to draw back: Khrushchev by withdrawing his missiles, Kennedy by giving in exchange for this a return concession: a promise not to invade Cuba. The correspondence between the two leaders at this time was pervaded by a mutual but unspoken sympathy, a realisation that in the confrontation between the USSR and USA each leader was compelled to do what he could to put his opponent at a disadvantage but that if one overstepped the mark the other's duty was to help him extricate himself, not to offer the choice of humiliation or war. It is ironic that just as Khrushchev was agreeing to withdraw his missiles street-marchers in the West were denying the existence of these same missiles and portraying the crisis as an American aggression against Cuba. It is ironic too that the Cubans, who were the only people to be humiliated by the affair, were fully informed of the situation, whereas the Russians, whose government had reacted responsibly, were never given a full account.

Correspondence continued privately between Khrushchev and Kennedy right up to the death of the latter and doubtless it was these letters which were the essential element in US-USSR relations during this period, not the façade of meetings, conferences, diplomatic notes and UN addresses which filled the newspapers and wavebands. The two men had met at Vienna in 1961, but this encounter was chilly. Their post-Cuba relationship was closer and warmer and it was probably this which enabled two tension-reducing agreements to be made.

One of these concerned the 'hot line', a direct and exclusive telephone link between the White House and the Kremlin, for use in crises. This was aimed at preventing an accidental war which might be provoked by unsatisfactory communications leading the leaders into misunderstanding each other's intentions. The other was an agreement to halt the testing of nuclear devices in the atmosphere. (US doubts whether in the absence of on-the-spot verification—in general opposed by the USSR—underground tests could be detected was the reason why an agreement to ban all tests could not be reached.) Many other countries (but not France or China) signed this agreement, which, although it came too late to prevent an unhealthy scale of radio-active pollution, did at least mitigate that pollution. The agreement also encouraged the hope that further accords would be reached, and could thus be presented as a justification of Khrushchev's policy of 'peaceful coexistence'.

Coexistence as an alternative to the Cold War was not originally a Khrushchev concept. As early as 1954 Malenkov, impressed by the catastrophic power of nuclear arms, had publicly forecast that a new war would be the end of world civilisation. Soon after, he was persuaded to modify this, and claimed merely that an atomic war would be the end of the capitalist form of civilisation. However, Khrushchev in later years adopted the view that war would be disastrous for the Communist as well as the capitalist world. This, and the desire to learn from the West, was the reason for the theory of competitive coexistence without war. Unlike Pekin, Moscow regarded peaceful coexistence as a long-term policy even though eventually capitalism would be routed by Communism. Khrushchev went as far as modifying Lenin's opinions on this subject: Lenin had stated that war was inevitable between the imperialists and Communists, and that such a war would lead to the final defeat of capitalism, but Khrushchev pointed out that conditions had changed enormously since Lenin's time and the latter's view, correct at the time, could not apply in the nuclear era. Moreover, the Communist countries had become strong enough to deter the unleashing of an imperialists' war. Thus it happened in 1960 that on Lenin's birthday Pekin quoted his views about the inevitability of war to show that coexistence was anti-Leninist, while in Moscow his other writings about the brotherhood of men were quoted to show that coexistence was truly Leninist.

Coexistence also entailed the support of non-Communist but anti-imperialist regimes in the colonial and ex-colonial countries, even though these regimes might be of a bourgeois nature. Moscow believed that nationalist movements would eventually give way, or be transformed, to Communist movements. In Cuba this in fact happened. In other countries the USSR found itself aiding governments of countries like Egypt and India which repressed the local Communist parties. In the Middle East this policy paid quick dividends: the supply of arms to Egypt, hitherto a western preserve, caused the various weaknesses and ineptitudes of the US, British and French governments to result in the 1956 Anglo-French-Israeli invasion of Egypt. While quiet US threats forced Britain and France to abandon this campaign, Soviet threats of using rockets against London and Paris were believed by most Arabs to have been the deciding factor. Further Soviet diplomatic and propaganda successes followed in the Middle East.

Implied also by the coexistence concept was the possibility of Communist regimes attaining power by normal parliamentary means. This was especially gratifying to the Italian Communist Party, whose comparative moderation had earned it enormous electoral support in the post-war years. But the possibility of Communism without revolution was, to the Chinese, another 'revision' of Leninism.

From time to time, to mollify home critics or the Chinese, or in response to international tension, Khrushchev seemed to abandon coexistence. But in any case he had never pretended that ideological hostility should be relaxed. Coexistence was to him simply the best way, in the circumstances of the time, to 'wage the class war'. Ideological coexistence, said Khrushchev in his habitual folksy language, would not come about 'until shrimps learn to whistle'. There were signs, too, that opponents of coexistence inside the USSR were not entirely powerless. The U2 incident may well have been exploited by these opponents, and certain actions which almost certainly were planned by the MVD also probably had as their aim the embarrassment of Khrushchev's diplomacy. In 1963 a Yale professor studying in the USSR was held for trial after incriminating documents had been foisted on him, and released only after a strong protest by President Kennedy. Other western scholars innocently pursuing their researches were mistreated from time to time. In 1964, just as a visit by Khrushchev to Western Germany seemed imminent, a near-fatal mustard gas attack was made on a member of the German Moscow Embassy's staff. Yet it was evident that the people of the Soviet Union as a whole supported the new foreign policies.

Industry

The sacrifice of the individual consumer and of the peasantry in favour of heavy industry, which had typified economic policy under Stalin, was partially repudiated by his successors. Presumably with the support of Mikoyan (the expert on trade) and Kosygin (the specialist on light industry), Malenkov announced a drive to increase consumer goods production and develop retail trade. In effect the new policy, while not going so far as to minimise the role of heavy industry, implied that light industry would henceforth have equal priority. Since food production and many raw materials for light industry depended on agriculture, measures to improve farm production were taken at the same time.

But the Fifth Five Year Plan (1951–55) was still in force and prescribed the usual Stalinist emphasis on heavy industry. The various economic ministries, and the industries under them, found themselves unable to satisfy both the requirements of the Plan and the new targets announced by Malenkov. Also, it became evident that the extra incentives granted to the peasantry were not resulting in the expected increase of agricultural production. Hence by mid-1954 it became evident that the promised flow of goods into the shops would not take place. The situation was made worse by the opposition of many functionaries who could not easily throw off the indoctrination of the Stalinist years and accept that consumer goods were important. The decision to solve agricultural problems by developing the 'virgin lands', which meant increased investment in agricultural machinery, and the promise to aid China's development of heavy industry, also proved burdensome. Opposition inside the Party leadership to the programme for light industry, probably headed by Khrushchev, led to the almost simultaneous abandonment of this programme and the resignation of Malenkov in early 1955. But the goals of the Sixth Five Year Plan (1956–60) proved far too optimistic, and this Plan was repealed after two years. A new and somewhat more modest Seven Year Plan (1959–65) replaced it. In the late fifties, despite setbacks, there was a definite improvement in consumer goods supplies. In shoe production, for example, the 1940 production of about one pair per person per year had not been improved by 1953, but by 1959 had risen to about one-and-a-half pairs. Production of television receivers (very small in 1953) had risen to one-and-a-quarter million per annum by 1959. Over the same six-year period production of energy (coal, electricity, oil) about doubled.

Consumer goods imported from abroad also began to trickle in, and were usually sold out within minutes of their appearance in the shops. Foreign trade increased in the late fifties for both political and economic reasons: trade relations were expected to lead to better foreign relations, and foreign industry could supply wants which were not satisfied by home production. Thus Soviet foreign trade (which remained very small if calculated on a *per capita* basis) was designed to obtain goods which were unavailable, perhaps temporarily, at home, rather than to exchange products best made in the USSR for products which could be made best or more cheaply abroad. Soviet foreign trade was also rather inflexible because it relied on bilateral barter agreements rather than on multilateral trading. The rouble was not freely convertible into other currencies.

There was a limited effort to trade with the European Peoples' Democracies on a basis of cost advantage. This took the form of co-ordinating the economies of these nations so that a given country would be responsible for supplying certain items to the whole bloc. For example, Czechoslovakia supplied electric passenger locomotives to the USSR and other Peoples' Democracies; the USSR sent oil to Central and Eastern Europe via a new pipeline. These co-ordinating moves were arranged by the Council for Mutual Economic Assistance (known in the West as Comecon). This had been founded in 1949, mainly as an instrument for Soviet exploitation of the Peoples' Democracies. But in 1954 it became a more equitable organisation. However, it never succeeded in organising extensive co-ordination, for this would have meant that some countries would have had to abandon industries which could operate elsewhere more cheaply. These countries, and notably Rumania, would not agree to this.

Meanwhile another characteristic of the Stalin years—the centralisation in Moscow of economic management—was being changed. The system whereby 30–40 different ministries administered and planned the various industries of the USSR was becoming more and more unsatisfactory. The directors of factories were inundated with directives and questions from Moscow, and had little chance to use their own judgement: the nature and volume of their production, and of their input, were fixed for them by Moscow officials who often had little knowledge of the local circumstances. Directors could not make adjustments in their budgets without ministerial sanction, which meant very often that the funds available to an enterprise were not used in the best possible way. Managements were judged by their fulfilment of the production plan and used all kinds of devices to ensure that they would not fail in this respect: they forwarded to their ministry deliberate under-estimates of their productive capacity so that the target set for them would be moderate; to safeguard themselves against non-delivery of necessary materials they maintained excessive stocks and employed so-called 'pushers' who in exchange for high rewards would negotiate through illegal channels for unplanned allocations; they would infringe the laws on working hours and working conditions (the trade union organisations did not protect the workers against this); and in the last resort they would falsify their statistics. Since the local Party organisation was also judged by how well the production targets were met, these misdemeanours often enjoyed the acquiescence, and sometimes the connivance, of Party officials.

This situation was caused by the clumsiness of the central planning system, and worsened as the economy developed and became more complex. When a factory needed to buy thousands of different components from all over the USSR, the channelling of orders through the ministry in charge of that factory via the different ministries supervising supplying factories was a long and cumbersome process which frequently broke down. Inefficiency was the keynote: for example, an enterprise requiring cement would not ask the nearest cement works for supplies; the ministries would make the arrangements and some months later the cement might be shipped from some remote works thousands of miles away.

During the Malenkov regime some tentative steps were taken towards increasing the powers of directors, and improving the quality of production by learning from western practices. After Khrushchev attained power he introduced further-reaching reforms. In early 1957, after a good deal of argument, the USSR was divided between regional economic councils, which were to administer and plan the industries of their own particular territory. The majority of the industrial ministries were dissolved. (Some, like railways and electricity, survived, and later some 'State Committees' were set up to provide central supervision of certain key industries like civil aviation.) The number of economic regions was greater than efficiency demanded: Khrushchev was compelled to establish them with boundaries similar to the Party's regional organisations, in order to keep the support of the latter. But in 1962 they were reduced from about 100 to less than

50. At the same time the planning system was reorganised, but apparently with disappointing effect for in 1962 there was a further reform by which the State Planning Committee was given the responsibility for long-term planning while a National Economic Council checked the fulfilment of the plans year by year.

The decentralisation of management did result in increased efficiency, for the regional economic councils had a good knowledge of their local circumstances, unlike the Moscow ministries which they replaced. But there were defects also. The number of regions was larger than economic and geographic conditions warranted (a partial remedy for this was the creation of 'super-regions'). The regional councils usually gave preference to industries in their own area so that, for example, if a factory failed to produce its quota local clients would receive the bulk of their requirements while outside customers would be rationed. Most important was the fact that despite its faults the old centralised bureaucracy did play a role which in the absence of a free market economy was not easily dispensible.

In a western-style economy resources and products are allocated roughly where they are required by the fact that where the need is greatest profits should be highest, and suppliers naturally send their goods where they sell most profitably. If a system of planned production and distribution is substituted for the market economy, as happened in the USSR, arriving at the best pattern of priorities depends on the central planning authorities, that is, on people sitting at desks studying statistics. This has a certain advantage in conditions of crisis when only a small number of commodities are involved, for the central planners are in a position to evaluate the needs of the country as a whole. But as the Soviet economy became more complex the minute details of each and every exchange and its interactions could not be efficiently prescribed. The individuals directly concerned were more likely to arrive at the most satisfactory arrangement, but from a national point of view their decisions did not necessarily guarantee the most efficient use of resources, because prices did not reflect the true relationships between the values of the various commodities.

Thus the USSR was faced with the need to use the price system as regulator of the economy. This had long been resisted on ideological grounds because the concept of prices reflecting supply and demand was regarded as a distinguishing feature of capitalism. Nevertheless, in August 1962 a Professor Liberman published an article advocating the reintroduction of a genuine profit incentive in economic life. In particular he suggested that factory directors should be allowed to decide by what means their production targets should be met and if they succeeded in making a profit should be allowed to use that profit in the way they considered most beneficial. These proposals appeared to have the approval of Khrushchev, who took care to explain that, whereas in capitalism profit was the aim of production, in the USSR it needed only to be an index.

A limited experiment was begun in 1963 in the clothing trade. Despite Khrushchev's earlier rejection of Malenkov's consumer goods programme, after 1958 he had continued to produce more for the shops. But the structure of trade, whereby the goods were allocated to the shops according to plans which did not take into account what the shops required, led to an immense pile-up of unwanted goods in the stores: as supplies became more plentiful, people refused to buy products of poor design or quality. The experiment of 1963, which proved very successful, was extended to allow certain clothing stores actually to order merchandise of their own choice from the factories. With the influence of the profit motive this meant that the stores ordered what could most profitably be sold (that is, what the customers most needed), while the factories produced not what was easiest, but what the stores wanted.

Technology

'Catch up and overtake American *per capita* output by 1970' was one of Khrushchev's favourite economic slogans. Its attainment always seemed doubtful, for, although Soviet rates of growth in conventional products were higher than American, in the USA the increase in well-being took the form not so much of conventional commodities (which already in many fields were more than required) but of improvements in amenities and services and the production of entirely new commodities. Nevertheless, it was realised that the old preoccupation with staples like coal and steel had caused the Soviet planners to ignore certain key industries which were already highly developed in the West.

Notable among these was the chemical industry, and under Khrushchev this was expanded, especially in the sectors of plastics and artificial fertilisers. In many cases western firms built the new factories, thus sharing with the USSR their technical experience.

The death of Stalin likewise permitted the modernisation of transport, which had been held back by conservatism. The railways ceased building steam locomotives in 1956, and Aeroflot was re-equipped with jet aircraft: for a time the TU104 was the world's only jet airliner in operation. To support the USSR's new policy of trading with all parts of the world, especially the developing nations, a fleet of modern freighters was bought from the shipyards of Eastern Europe.

Rocketry was another technology which received high priority. Like the USA, the USSR benefited from German experience and developed missiles to carry nuclear warheads. In the mid-fifties it seems probable that a decision was taken to replace the conventional bomber by missiles. At the same time, by flying the few prototypes of a new bomber design in a Moscow air display, it may have been hoped to mislead the USA into believing that a new Soviet bomber fleet was in the making. US resources, however, were capable of simultaneously building a matching bomber arm as well as developing missiles, and in any case American espionage soon revealed the Russian concentration on missiles.

The advantage of the USSR in conventional espionage at this time was compensated by the technical excellence of US devices. For some years up to 1960 the U2 high-altitude reconnaissance aircraft had from time to time flown on selected routes over the Soviet Union, and the virtuosity of its photographic equipment resulted in finely detailed photographs of key Soviet installations. At the same time, a high-power radar station in the mountains of Turkey surveyed experimental rocket launchings east of Stalingrad. Thus the USA knew much more about Soviet strength than the Soviet government realised. In the end, this Soviet effort to achieve missile supremacy may have alarmed the US press (and given Kennedy an effective election issue) but it proved expensive; the goal was never achieved and the liquid-fuelled rocket which had been standardised was unsophisticated and cumbersome.

There was however a useful by-product. Although the Soviet missile was much bigger than was needed to carry a nuclear warhead, it was ideal for space research, and in October 1957 the world's first artificial earth satellite, or *sputnik*, was launched by the USSR. This was followed in 1961 by the world's first human flight into space by Major Gagarin of the Red Air Force, the first female cosmonaut in 1963, and the first three-man venture into space in 1964. In terms of spectacular achievement (though not necessarily in volume of research) the USSR was ahead of the USA. Both the USA and USSR began to send photographic reconnaissance satellites over each other's territory.

Although the USSR had devoted to its space programme scarce resources which might have been used better elsewhere, the psychological effects of these successes were enormous. Inside the USSR both the Party's and the people's self-confidence was enhanced; for the first time the USSR had a technological 'first' which was clearly not a propagandist's invention. In the West the consternation of 1957 gave way to a wholly beneficial reappraisal of national goals and the place of education. In other countries the USA could no longer be regarded as the unquestioned leader in technology.

Agriculture

Soon after Stalin died it was openly admitted that what western specialists had long been alleging about Soviet harvest statistics was true—that in fact the figures for grain production had been systematically inflated. Agriculture remained the weakest sector of the economy and only a radical improvement could ensure sufficient food, especially animal products, for a growing urban population.

Even during the premiership of Malenkov it was Khrushchev who played the leading role in agricultural policy. In these first post-Stalin years the procurement prices of farm products were raised on the assumption (only partly realised) that higher prices would encourage greater production. Taxes and compulsory deliveries from the peasants' private plots were reduced. At the same time agricultural specialists hitherto enjoying administrative jobs in Moscow and other centres were sent into the countryside for on-the-spot work at farms and tractor stations. Moscow-dictated plans were limited to the amount and type of product to be delivered by each farm; the farms could thus choose their own methods of attaining the targets. Party officials were sent to the farms to inspect and reorganise. In 1954 there also began the ploughing of the 'virgin lands', an area in southern Siberia and northern Kazakhstan hitherto untilled. Criminal proceedings against peasants failing to fulfil delivery requirements were dropped, and arrears cancelled.

In 1958 the Machine and Tractor Stations, which had hitherto provided an element of control over the collective farms they served, were transformed into repair stations, while their equipment was offered for sale to the farms. This decision was greeted by celebratory orgies on the farms and long faces in the MTS, whose employees were demoted from virtual masters to virtual employees of the collective farms.

About the same time the complicated procurement system was simplified, releasing thousands of bureaucrats for more productive work and making life easier on the farms. Compulsory deliveries and payments in kind were abolished, being replaced by state purchase at fairer prices. Collective farms were given the same priority as state farms in the supply of implements and fuel.

But the inherent contradiction of Soviet agriculture remained: the fact that the yield per acre of the predominant socialist sector (that is, the state and collective farm lands) remained far below that of the 'private' sector (the peasants' individually owned plots). Measures to increase production, particularly of animal products, often had the side-effect of enlarging 'private' output without affecting 'socialist' output. Already by 1958 Khrushchev was complaining that private cows were multiplying while socialist cows were not. From time to time restrictive measures were adopted against the private plots but were probably not strictly enforced. Meanwhile, the virgin lands programme was beset by difficulties. The youth volunteers sent from European Russia to provide labour found inadequate accommodation awaiting them and mismanagement of all kinds. The planned output of these lands was far from being fulfilled. Nevertheless, the USSR's agricultural targets were raised again in 1959, Khrushchev hoping that this was justified by his continuing dismissals of agricultural bureaucrats, his advocacy of maize as a high-yield crop on which cattle-raising could be based, and the extension of his virgin lands scheme.

The following years witnessed an increase of grain production, but mainly through the extension of the cultivated area rather than an increase of productivity per acre or per peasant. Although the proportion of collective farm acreage declined (because the virgin lands were exploited by state farms) the ideological problem of the high-yielding private plots remained. In these years there was a continuing rotation of officials as one dismissed administrator took the place of another. Ministers of agriculture and premiers of Kazakhstan changed rapidly as scapegoats were sought for disappointments. Khrushchev's current theories were often slavishly adopted without considering the variations of local conditions.

Although in 1962 Kazakhstan was producing less than two-thirds of its grain target, and elsewhere in the USSR there were other failures, nevertheless that year had a record harvest, with over 140 million tons of grain. But 1963 was disastrous. Bad weather, together with the exhaustion of the under-fertilised virgin lands, meant that only about 110 million tons were harvested. The shortage of fodder caused a serious setback to the struggling animal production programme, there were local bread shortages, and the Soviet Union was forced to buy about 12 million tons of Canadian and US wheat. The 1964 harvest was slightly better, but the crash programme introduced late in 1963 for the production and extended use of artificial fertilisers only promised a long-term improvement.

It seemed inevitable that sooner or later some of the basic concepts of Soviet agricultural policy, particularly of collectivisation, would be revised, however delicate this might be ideologically. At least a third of the labour force was agricultural, yet the demand for agriculture produce was not being met. (In the USA, where admittedly geography is slightly more favourable, the eight per cent of the labour force employed on the land was consistently producing a surplus for export and reserve.) At the same time, the lag in agricultural production and the eclipse of the virgin lands was not as clear-cut a failure as was sometimes alleged. After all, the population was rising (it reached 225 million in mid-1963) and the ratio of town-dwellers (mainly food-consumers) to country-dwellers (mainly food-producers) had risen to 52:48. The virgin lands for a few crucial years did bridge the gap between supply and rising demand.

Social Policy

The end of Beria and the limitation of MVD activities was followed in late 1958 by changes in the law. These changes formalised the reforms which had in fact been made in practice since 1953. The MVD, apart from losing Beria and his associates, had also suffered from the executions following the reopening of the 'Georgian Case' of 1951 and the 'Leningrad Case'. The dissolution of most workcamps (sometimes after strikes of their inmates) had stripped the MVD of its private industries, and its military tribunals had been dissolved in 1953. By 1957 only about two per cent of the Soviet prison population were political prisoners. In 1956 surviving labour camps were transformed into labour colonies and their inmates were administered more sympathetically. In 1954 internal security was transferred from the MVD to the KGB, and to emphasise the Party's interest

Shelepin, hitherto head of the Komsomol, was subsequently appointed chairman of this body.

The new criminal code specified that only those who had actually committed a crime were to be sentenced. Only the courts could pronounce sentence and confessions alone would no longer be sufficient to convict. Defence lawyers were to receive more information about their cases. The age of criminal responsibility was raised to 16 from the 12 years to which it had been reduced in 1935. These reforms were a step forward, but the situation was still far removed from the western concept of justice. Anti-state activity, which included calumny against the Soviet state (that is, grumbling) could still warrant imprisonment. The so-called 'Parasites Law', whereby persons who were fit for work but were not (officially) employed could be banished by meetings of the inhabitants of a given block of flats or street, was a virtual invitation to denounce unpopular or nonconformist citizens. Equally arbitrary were the *druzhiniki*, young volunteers with red armbands who formed a kind of part-time auxiliary police. At their best the druzhiniki were represented by young men clearing the streets of drunks, at their worst by young prigs detaining innocent citizens who happened to have left their identity papers at home, or by pimply-faced maidens humiliating young couples suspected of exchanging a surreptitious kiss in public.

The end of Stalinist repression was followed by an upsurge of lawlessness and hooliganism. There was also, apparently, an increase in illegal commercial activity. In 1961 and 1962 therefore the death penalty was introduced for a wide range of crimes: bribe-taking, embezzlement of state property, currency speculation, second-offence rapes, and attacks on police or druzhiniki. In the number of misdemeanours warranting execution the USSR had caught up with and overtaken most other countries.

Many executions were carried out and publicised. Because the published names of apprehended 'speculators' contained a very high proportion of Jewish names it was sometimes alleged that anti-semitism was at work. Probably a more valid criticism would have been to question the ethics of these penalties. Speculation often meant that an essential service overlooked by the planners was being supplied (illegally and for a good profit) by private enterprise. For example, as late as 1964 a Soviet citizen requiring new spectacle lenses might have to wait a year or more (because the lens-makers found it easier to fulfil their production plan, fixed by number or weight of lenses, by concentrating on one particular formula: anyone not requiring that prescription was unlucky). Thus an individual establishing an illegal private enterprise to supply this deficiency was providing an essential service to the citizens and indirectly to the state as well. And if he used purloined optical glass it was only because legal supply channels were closed to him.

In the arts liberalisation resulted in the production of a few works which for the first time criticised previously sacrosanct phenomena, and in so doing took de-Stalinsation a stage further. In Stalin's time the task of literature had been to show the reader what to think and how to behave in the new society which the Party was creating, but after 1953 there was a partial return to the critical tradition of Russian literature. At the same time the majority of writers, who were careful not to go further than the Party would wish, played an important role in bringing the re-appraisal of the Stalin years into the consciousness of the masses. From time to time Khrushchev called the more adventurous writers to heel; on other occasions he overrode the censors of the state publishing house to ensure the printing of radical works. Ehrenburg's *The Thaw* was one of the first novels hinting at the need to de-Stalinise. Ovechkin's fiction ridiculed the stupidities of collective farm administration. Dudintsev in *Not by Bread Alone*, portrayed the deadening effect of a greedy, domineering, bureaucratic factory manager on his more enterprising subordinates. *One Day in the Life of Ivan Denisovich*, which first appeared in 1963 (and was sold out within minutes) was about concentration camp life, written by a former inmate. The young poet Yevtushenko's *Baby Yar*, about the Nazi massacre of Kievan Jews, hinted that anti-semitism still existed in the USSR. Parallel with these developments in literature were changes in the kind of films, plays and painting produced by Soviet artists. There was even an exhibition of modern art, hitherto regarded as decadent, at which Khrushchev made homely remarks about what kind of picture a donkey could paint with its tail. There was some resistance to the new look in the arts, mainly from those whose lack of talent had had full opportunity to express itself in Stalin's day. These critics and writers made a brief reappearance in the Pasternak affair. In 1958 this poet innocently sent the manuscript of his novel *Doctor Zhivago* for publication abroad just before it was condemned as unfit for publication by the editors of *Novy Mir*, a literary journal specialising in serialisation of outstanding novels. *Doctor Zhivago* was a sympathetic study of a patriotic Russian intellectual who could not accept the results of the 1917 Revolution. Thus the novel presented an unpublishable anti-Soviet view and, to make things worse, in its style and language was worthy of comparison with the classics of nineteenth-century Russian literature. Abroad Pasternak was in fact awarded the Nobel Prize; at home, a denigration campaign began. The unfortunate author was called a 'pig' and a 'weed', by untalented (and probably envious) fellow-writers. He was threatened with banishment from the USSR, but after writing contrite letters to Khrushchev and *Pravda*, and rejecting the Nobel Prize, was allowed to die a natural death soon afterwards. After he died his friend, after whom had been modelled the heroine of *Doctor Zhivago*, was sent to a labour colony.

During the post-Stalin decade some measures were taken in favour of various depressed classes. The wartime nationalities policy, with its elevation of everything Russian at the expense of the national feelings of other peoples of the USSR, was partially reversed. In Latvia and the Ukraine many Russian Party officials were replaced by natives. Former national heroes (like the Caucasian patriot Shamil, depicted in 1950 as a British agent) were rehabilitated, and the tendency to justify tsarist empire-building ceased. On the other hand, a subsequent educational change strengthened the role of the Russian language in the non-Russian schools.

The wages of the lowest-paid workers were the first to be raised, and trade unions were exhorted to be more active. However, the latter, although they more frequently resisted abuses by managements, still served the government rather than the workers.

By 1960 there was a 42-hour working week for most, and workers no longer needed their management's permission to change jobs. A start was made at extending social services like pensions to the peasantry: hitherto this half of the USSR's population had been excluded. An educational reform, strongly advocated by Khrushchev, interposed a period of work in industry or agriculture between leaving school and entering university. This was partly directed against 'the white-handed people'—generally children of the intelligentsia who, not always by fair means, easily entered university and avoided any experience of manual work.

The Church under Khrushchev

Renewed attacks on religion began about 1958. Possibly these were due to the absence of Stalin, who in his last years became almost a protector of the Orthodox Church. Possibly also by 1958 it had become evident that the faith in secular and atheistic education had not been justified: despite the educational system many young people continued to be churchgoers. Although there were no violent anti-religious campaigns as in the first decades of Soviet power, constant administrative and fiscal harassment succeeded in closing about half of the 20,000 Russian Orthodox churches and three of the six seminaries. In the case of the Baptist Church the attacks were more fierce and torture of priests in remote areas was alleged Yet that Church remained the strongest of the so-called sects and during the persecution, which it apparently welcomed for reasons of martydom, even spread into new areas: every deportee became a missionary.

Methods used varied according to the scruples and cunning of local Party activists. A national change which helped the anti-Church movement was in 1961, when the Russian Orthodox priest became the employee of his local parish church council. By various means (such as threatening the jobs of council members or their families) the Party could often persuade a majority of the council members to dismiss the priest. Deliberately long-winded bureaucratic procedures (for example, the age-old Russian device of sending an applicant to office A, which sends him to office B and so on, thus neither refusing nor granting his request) might then ensure that a new priest was not appointed, or the church council could vote to close the church (a decision which would be published as '. . . at the request of the believers themselves'). Some thuggery and corruption also appeared in places: at one pilgrimage centre arriving pilgrims were threatened with arrest or beating-up unless they produced a bribe. It almost seemed that those of Gestapo mentality who had thrived under Stalin's regime, and had lost their opportunities with the post-Stalin emphasis on 'socialist legality', had found a last refuge in anti-religious work.

Moslem belief remained strong, but not Moslem institutions. Although the violent persecutions of Moslem priests had ceased around 1938, the war did not bring quite the same benefits as were enjoyed by the Orthodox Church. So-called 'Red Muftis', who tried to combine support of Soviet policies with traditional beliefs, were cultivated by the government. Although in the post-war period these puppet mullahs made excursions abroad to represent Soviet Moslems, and received Moslem statesmen visiting the USSR, they did not appear to gain the confidence of local believers. This failure was demonstrated by the growing number of unofficial priests and holy men, and of illegal (unregistered) places of worship.

The situation of the Jews did not improve under Khrushchev and it may well be true that the latter's prejudices included a measure of anti-semitism. As before, while the Jews' position was happier than under the tsars, they had difficulty in preserving themselves as a cultural group and (unlike tsarist times) could not emigrate.

The Relegation of Khrushchev

In October 1964 Khrushchev was on holiday by the Black Sea and two of his supporters controlling the news services—the editor of *Pravda*, and the head of the State Radio—were out of Moscow. The Party Presidium, meeting in his absence, decided that the time had come for a change of leadership. A meeting of the Central Committee was called and Khrushchev was summoned to appear before it. Here he was criticised, and resolutions were passed by which Brezhnev became First Secretary and Kosygin Premier. Mikoyan, who in July had replaced Brezhnev in the relatively unimportant office of President, remained in that office. After these arrangements had been made, a public announcement was made according to which Khrushchev had resigned because of old age and declining health. That day's edition of *Izvestia* (edited by Khrushchev's son-in-law) was suppressed, while *Pravda* and the radio announced the retirement of the former leader. The latter had thus little chance of reasserting himself and went into a mute retirement.

Pravda later published an article mentioning a new personality cult, and 'hair-brained schemes, half-baked conclusions, hasty decisions, unrealistic actions, bragging, phrase-mongering and bossiness'. Thus it was Khrushchev's flamboyance, his unbridled behaviour in public (like hammering the table with his shoe at a UN session), his humiliation over Cuba, the harvest failures, his alleged personalisation of the dispute with China, his nepotism (in particular the despatch of his son-in-law in 1964 to arrange his own visit to Western Germany), his dismissal of officials as scapegoats for his failures, and his bestowal on President Nasser of the Order of the Hero of the Soviet Union, which all culminated in this bloodless coup by his dissatisfied colleagues.

Although many Communists outside the USSR were disappointed that the Soviet leaders were still incapable of changing their leaders openly, most accepted the reasons given, at least publicly, while making it clear that they liked Khrushchev and approved his policies.

The Khrushchev decade will be remembered for its break with the past, which was decisive even if partial. But while Khrushchev plainly exposed the fundamental problems and changes which had to be faced, he was less successful in finding the appropriate policies. His successors reversed several of his actions, while leaving no doubt that there could be no return to Stalinist methods. Kosygin and Brezhnev were more serious in their approach and less reckless and flamboyant than Khrushchev. In their first year of office it seemed that the better life for the Soviet citizen which had dawned in 1953 would get better still, and that Stalin's slogan of the thirties was at last being realised: 'Life is getting better, Comrades, life is getting better!'

VIII

The Brezhnev Years

The Internal Situation

It was not long after the departure of Khrushchev that Brezhnev
began to emerge clearly as the new Soviet leader. Kosygin continued
to head the government, but Brezhnev as Party Secretary was dominant. After the mid-1970s his health was obviously in decline; there
were occasions when, in meetings with foreign leaders, he seemed
unable to stand without assistance and meaningful discussion was
impossible, since he limited himself to reading prepared statements.
But as his physical health declined, his political health seemed to
flourish.

The memory of the Second World War, like that of the Napoleonic
War a century earlier, was long cultivated in the USSR as representation of a time when all citizens stood together and triumphed against
the too-clever-by-half foreigner. By 1975, when the thirtieth anniver-
sary of the defeat of Nazi Germany was being heavily celebrated in
the USSR, a modern *War and Peace* had still not appeared from the
pen of any member of the Writers' Union, but the Soviet Union was
favoured with the appearance of a new war hero, Leonid Brezhnev.
Brezhnev, who had been a military commissar in the war, was
portrayed as quite a key figure in the defeat of Germany. Hitherto his
role in the war had been little noticed, and perhaps to compensate for
this neglect he assumed the rank of Marshal of the Soviet Union in
1976. He also received the Order of Lenin for the fifth time and became Hero of the Soviet Union for a second time. Soon, in public
places, portraits appeared of the new hero, festooned with orders in
his marshal's uniform and looking a full quarter-century younger

than he really was. While thus asserting his youth and his martial qualities, Brezhnev continued to buttress his position within the Party. Podgorny, chairman of the Presidium since 1965, was ousted and replaced in this position of Soviet 'president' by Brezhnev himself, who also retained his position as Party Secretary. Meanwhile, from time to time changes in the Politburo elevated Brezhnev's friends and demoted his possible rivals. Soon there was no outstanding individual in the Politburo who could be regarded as a natural successor to the Party Secretary. By the late 1970s key decisions were being made by a Politburo of septuagenarians whose grim ambition, it seemed, was to become in the proper fulness of time a Politburo of octogenarians. This was not a leadership where the bright young man, still less the bright young woman, was welcome.

Meanwhile, encouraged by the relaxations of the Khrushchev period, and alarmed by a perceptible tightening of authoritarian rule which occurred under his successor, a handful of so-called dissidents used whatever means were available to them to question some of the Party's policies and intentions. A relatively unprovocative move was a letter sent to the leadership in protest against what seemed to be a trend towards the re-establishment of Stalin as a figure to be revered. The effect of this letter cannot be measured, but there was no re-elevation of Stalin; the latter continued to be officially regarded as an important figure in the early decades of Soviet power who allowed certain malpractices to occur in his later years. When in 1976 the new edition of the *Great Soviet Encyclopedia* appeared, Stalin's entry was down to four columns. Meanwhile, Stalin's daughter Svetlana, who found Soviet life distasteful, was allowed to emigrate to the west.

Dissidents who sought to evade restrictions on the publication of their opinions used several techniques. One was the time-honoured device of publishing their work abroad, hoping that news of it would soon reach the USSR through foreign broadcasts. Another was the development of *Samizdat* (self-publication); this was the duplication by hand or by machine of works which could not be published through the usual state channels; the copies were then surreptitiously circulated from reader to reader. Best-known of these publications was *The Journal of Current Events*, which appeared fairly regularly and gave its readers news of what was really happening in the USSR, as opposed to what the official press said was happening. Penalties for writing, reproducing or possessing these documents could be severe. Finally, a technique especially disliked by the authorities was adopted by some of the bolder spirits; this was the calling of press conferences, attended by non-Soviet journalists living in the USSR, at which the dissidents' views could be expressed and gain worldwide publicity.

The government responded by harassing known dissidents and their friends and families, by prosecuting others on the charge of anti-Soviet agitation, and by placing others in psychiatric institutions specially equipped to restore them to 'sanity', sometimes with the forcible injection of mind-bending drugs but usually with more mundane techniques. In some cases permission to live abroad was granted to troublesome and well-known dissidents. In other cases the same effect was obtained by depriving a person of his Soviet citizenship and sending him out of the country. By the late 1970s much of the dissidents' output of protest was directed not so much at their initial targets but at the authorities' repression of themselves: the court cases where defence witnesses were not allowed to speak and where the 'public' attendance was limited to a specially selected hostile audience; the committal of dissidents to mental institutions on the strength of certificates signed by compliant psychiatrists; the anonymous threats whose origin was well-known; the demotion or dismissal from work of dissidents' friends and families.

Among the best known dissidents was Sakharov, a gifted scientist who had done much to develop the nuclear bomb and whose scientific prestige was so great that the authorities limited their counteraction to harassment. Sakharov wrote several perceptive works, warning that repression and lack of free discussion was leading the USSR to disaster. When he was awarded a Nobel Peace Prize he was not allowed to visit Stockholm to collect it, but his undelivered speech of acceptance soon appeared as a *Samizdat* publication. Although deprived of employment, Sakharov continued to be a member of the prestigious Academy of Sciences, suggesting either that that body itself enjoyed a limited independence from government interference, or that enough of its members sympathised with Sakharov to make his expulsion something more than the swift rubber-stamp operation preferred by the authorities. Another dissident was Orlov, one of a group of Soviet citizens who set up a committee to monitor how far the human rights enshrined in the Helsinki Agreement, signed by the USSR in 1975, were being observed in reality.

But it should be remembered that in the course of Russian history it has been times of relaxation which have brought forth the loudest protests against repression. Under Brezhnev repression certainly existed, but it seemed mild when compared to the paranoid cruelty of the Stalin period or even the steely unyielding coercion of Tsar Nicholas I; a hypodermic in the buttock was a step forward from a bullet in the head. It seemed that the Brezhnev regime, while determined to suppress any person or movement which threatened its credibility, was anxious to avoid measures which would exceed that object. This was said to be because the regime was sensitive to foreign opinion, both communist and non-communist. This might well be an accurate assessment, for Moscow's friends abroad were becoming less tolerant; several western communist parties made public protests when Orlov was sentenced to seven years hard labour after a particularly shabby trial.

Even though the dissident movement was small, and probably had negligible influence on the mass of the population, it evidently had an unnerving effect on the government. Possibly this was due to the basic lack of confidence which might be expected to undermine the spirits of a leadership still dependent on suppression of unwanted opinions to maintain its authority.

Meanwhile, the government was facing other problems which seemed no less threatening. Notable among these was the population problem. Briefly, this consisted of the following elements. There was a drop in the number of young people reaching working age, which meant that an economy hitherto based on abundant labour was faced with a labour shortage. There was a high death rate, especially for males, whose life expectancy had declined to 63 years (compared to 69 in the USA). There was a rising rate of infant mortality, accompanied by one of the world's highest rates of legal abortions (calculated by one source as an average of six abortions per woman-lifetime). The size of families in European Russia, and especially of Russian families, was hardly large enough to maintain the existing population, whereas in Central Asia the different peoples were reproducing at such a fast rate that they were expected to outnumber the Russians within a decade or so.

One cause of the high death rate was alcoholism, an evil that the government had once regarded as a survival of capitalism. In 1972 a cut was ordered in vodka output. Fines for drunkenness were increased, and supplemented by deprivation of social benefits for offenders. At the same time, the Party urged that more sporting and amusement facilities be provided; sorrows henceforth should be drowned in swimming pools, not drink. However, the drink problem persisted, and was regarded by some outside observers as a natural consequence of social tensions engendered by repressive 'puritanical' and 'Victorian' official attitudes.

The birthrate problem was also difficult to treat. The growth of the Central Asian population was not publicly regarded as any kind of threat although this phenomenon, combined with the difficulties with China, was obviously in the back of many minds and revealed itself by popular race-orientated jokes and remarks (like, for example, the one about the yellowing of the Red Army). The government would have liked an increase in the birthrate among the Slavic populations and a reduction among the Moslem peoples. This was probably why contraceptives imported from Hungary were virtually unobtainable in European Russia, but easily obtainable in Central Asia; easily obtainable by Russians, that is, for the local doctors, Moslems, did not prescribe them to Moslem women.

Not only Central Asian doctors, but also local Party leaders, seemed unwilling to come into conflict with the local priesthood on this issue. In this respect, at least, the control once exercised by Moscow over republican Party leaders seemed on the wane. This must have been another worrying thought for the Politburo. The situation in Georgia was particularly disquieting in the mid-1970s. The Georgians, a fiercely independent people, were not the sort to enjoy the Russian concept of the socialist state. But in Stalin's time they had been kept happy by special privileges and by the thought that Stalin was, after all, a Georgian himself. Subsequently the Georgian Party began to acquire Mafia-like characteristics. Georgians, thanks to natural and cultural endowments, had become one of the most prosperous nations of the USSR and the local Party leaders, by means of the excellent opportunities for corruption offered by the one-party state, enriched themselves so openly that they could hardly escape prosecution. This prosecution duly took place, preceded by the dismissal of the main figure, the Secretary of the Georgian Communist Party. However, his successor was not entirely satisfactory, for there was hardly a Party official, it seemed, who was not involved in one way or another with bribery or misappropriation of funds.

In 1977 a new State Constitution was adopted for the USSR. This was based very closely on the 1936 Constitution, with the notable innovation that the leading role of the Party was acknowledged. In 1978 there followed corresponding new constitutions for the republics of the USSR. In the initial drafts of these it seemed that the Georgian, Armenian, and Azerbaijani languages were no longer to appear as the official languages in their respective republics. This feature brought forth demonstrations in the Georgian capital which could be interpreted as nationalist and anti-Russian. But instead of suppressing the demonstrations, the local leadership promised to have the Georgian language restored to its former status in the final draft. Towards the end of the 1970s it remained to be seen, therefore, how far Moscow would be able to reassert its once-complete control over the Georgian Party. The expectation was that the Politburo would follow its usual approach and seek to regain its position stage by stage, without risking an open conflict. Elsewhere in the USSR, nationalism could be handled differently. In the Ukraine, for example, arrest and imprisonment was the fate of several of those accused of advocating the 'Ukrainianization' of the Ukraine.

One safety valve for internal dissent was emigration. In this the Jews became, for once, a privileged section of the USSR, for many thousands were allowed to emigrate in the 1970s. Ethnic Germans were also allowed, sometimes, to leave. In 1974 some of them created disturbances in the Baltic republics in protest at the tendency of officials to delay their departure. Would-be Jewish emigrants also suffered from official harassment; some were refused permission to emigrate, some had to pay large sums for this privilege, and some were dismissed from their jobs simply for requesting permission to emigrate.

The Economy

After the departure of Khrushchev economic growth continued, but the average rate of growth was disconcertingly lower than expected, being about 7 per cent annually in the Eighth Five Year Plan (1966–70) and about 4½ per cent in the Ninth (1971–75). Average growth in the Tenth Five Year Plan (1976–80) was expected to be around 5 per cent annually. Moreover, problems experienced in earlier periods remained unsolved; first among these was the difficulty of ensuring efficient and good quality production under the centralised planning system.

Wastefulness in the use of raw materials and of man-hours, and failure to utilise expensive plant as fully as its high cost required, were among the signs of managerial weakness. The question of management was discussed endlessly, and many experiments in restructuring the managerial system were introduced. It seemed, though, that all experiments, however successful, were destined to remain as experiments only. Evidently there was enough entrenched opposition to change to stop any large-scale reform. Khrushchev's system of regional economic councils was dismantled immediately after his departure, and industrial ministries in Moscow regained most of their centralised administrative powers. This meant the return of old problems associated with a system in which quite small decisions were taken by administrators sitting thousands of miles away from the enterprises with which they were dealing. Interestingly, centralisation did not foster the coordination between industries so important in the modern economy. This was because ministries were as reluctant to establish give-and-take relationships with other ministries as they were to regard the managers of their own enterprises as anything other than executors of their instructions. An everyday consequence was that factory managers were frustrated by non-delivery of raw materials by industries subordinate to other ministries. Also, the sheer impossibility at the centre of collecting all relevant data from the scattered enterprises and incorporating it in a rational decision-making process became painfully obvious as the economy grew more complex. It might have been expected that the introduction of computers would have solved this problem, but it did not. While computers could certainly save manpower and make possible a wider range of statistical analyses, they did not increase flexibility. As in other countries, the computer was no more willing than a bureaucrat to change its mind.

Possible solutions to the management problem centred around two concepts. These alternatives were a greater role for the 'market mechanism', and a slimming of the centralised system so that only the very basic questions would be decided in Moscow. The market mechanism, which above all would have brought prices closer to costs, and given to profits much more real meaning as incentives for managerial efficiency, was accepted to only a limited degree. There were not only ideological objections, but the existing system was well-liked by powerful interests inside the USSR. For example, the accepted practice of fixing prices well below production costs meant that many items (meat was one such item) were extremely cheap but very difficult to obtain. But the existence of special shops only open to Party officials, government administrators, and a few other privileged classes, in which 'unobtainable' goods were sold freely at the low official prices, meant that for a lucky few low prices did bring enhancement of the standard of living. (The natural consequence of such a situation, the development of a black market where the unprivileged might buy, expensively, goods obtained, cheaply, by the privileged, did slowly develop despite the occasional execution of black market middlemen). Another group that favoured the centralised planning system was that engaged in high-priority sectors of the economy (the defence industries, for example), for whom it was far easier to obtain resources in the existing centralised structure.

Slimming the centralised system by transferring decision-making to those on the spot seemed to threaten fewer interests, and in fact a considerable move in this direction was made with the establishment of 'productive associations', in which enterprises engaged in the production of an identical or related end-product were grouped together in an association. Many decision-making functions were transferred to these associations. But here again there was some resistance; the establishment of these associations fell well behind schedule, many associations were smaller than they should have been, and the association managers had salaries no higher than ordinary enterprise managers. The introduction of these associations signified the end of an earlier experiment, regarded as Kosygin's pet reform and starting in 1965. This had been intended to give greater independence to managers. But, having lived so long under the old system, most managers did not appreciate their greater powers. They made as few changes as possible and, as Brezhnev expressed it, they feared innovation 'like the devil fears incense'.

In some fields, Soviet technological and entrepreneurial backwardness could be alleviated by the import of western technology. Thus a new vehicle plant was built by the Italian Fiat company, and eventually Russian versions of Fiat models were produced in the USSR. A step towards increasing the very small share of the highways in Soviet transport was taken when American, West German, French and British companies were engaged to build the new Kama motor truck plant. This was intended to be the world's biggest truck plant, but in 1974 its construction was already two years behind schedule and it was still only partly in use in 1979. Western managers, working in the USSR on projects such as these, had a very compliant labour force at their service, but still faced the familiar burdens of the Soviet manager, especially the problem of delayed or poor-quality materials and components. Many other industries benefited from western assistance. Some agreements were of the 'turnkey' type, in which the western entrepreneurs built a plant of their own design and then handed over the keys (that is, transferred it to the appropriate ministry for operation). In the 1970s the 'compensation' agreement became common. In this, western capital and technology were used to exploit a Soviet resource, and payment took the form of an agreed proportion of the new plant's output.

The world oil crisis of the mid-1970s coincided with discoveries of oil in Western Siberia, and a start was made at exploiting these massive reserves with the assistance of western technology. To facilitate the export of this oil to Japan, thousands of miles distant, the new Baikal-Amur Railway was started. This west to east line, north of the Trans-Siberian Railway, was to connect with coal and metal deposits also. Scheduled for completion in 1983, running through mountainous, seismic, and sometimes permanently frozen terrain, this railway (BAM) was one of the world's greatest railway undertakings. But it was felt that much more investment in transport would be required to avoid an oil shortage, since so many of the reserves were located in remote regions.

Several sectors of industry continued to be specially favoured. Defence industries were a notable case. In these, priorities in the supply of materials and capital, and a relaxation of ideological pressures, ensured that products intended for military use would be of far greater quality than the normal Soviet product. The space effort was another such field. Soviet successes in space included unmanned landings on Venus and, in 1975, a joint mission in which American and Soviet space crews were linked up for two days; this was the first occasion that Soviet television broadcast 'live' coverage of Soviet space missions. In another high-technology field, supersonic passenger aircraft, the USSR was less successful. A prototype of the TU-144 crashed at the Paris Air Show in 1973, but nevertheless Aeroflot was able to claim in 1976 that it was the TU-144, not the Concorde, that had made the first regular commercial supersonic flights. This was achieved by scheduling it on freight-only services. Subsequently it was placed in passenger service between Moscow and Central Asia, but its huge fuel consumption, excessive noise, and perhaps other faults soon took it out of service.

Although it was not excessive noise that was the deciding factor in the TU-144's withdrawal, the Soviet government, contrary to some western accounts, was interested in environmental questions. It is true that there was no legislation like that of the USA, in which legal and enforceable constraints were placed on industrial pollution. On the other hand, pollution problems were widely discussed in the USSR and there were occasions when the start-up of new plants was delayed until purification measures were guaranteed. In 1974 a decision was made that all industries polluting the Volga/Urals river systems should cease to do so by 1980.

As always, the weakest sector of the economy was agriculture. Grain production was the key index. Year-by-year variations in production were influenced by the weather above all else, but a bad harvest frequently resulted in disgrace for the Party officials involved, from the Party secretaries of agricultural districts up to the Minister of Agriculture. However, taking five-year averages, grain production did increase, although it did not increase fast enough to meet the population growth in Central Asia as well as the need for a more healthy diet. Protein production was low, mainly because not enough grain could be allocated as animal feed. Hence grain imports from North America continued. Despite increased production of fertilizers, better conditions for collective-farm peasants, and more infrastructural services like electricity supply and roads, productivity on the collective farms remained low. However, the peasants' lives were improved by the guarantee of a small wage, and the issue of internal passports (making it no longer necessary to obtain special permission to leave the district). At the same time, productivity on the peasants' private plots was very high, and these plots played a surprisingly important role in keeping the towns supplied with food. For this reason, putting ideology aside yet once more, the Soviet government again began to encourage private plot husbandry. In 1978 one third of Soviet cows were privately owned, and this was the healthiest and most productive third.

Foreign Affairs

In the 1970s western commentators were emphasising Soviet expansionism, as demonstrated by support for successful revolutionary movements in Africa and the Middle East and by the growth of the Red Navy. In Moscow, however, the perspective was very different, for it seemed that the USSR had few friends in the world and was virtually beleaguered. True, there were countries that were willing to sign treaties of friendship in return for military or economic assistance, but such countries could be expected, in due course, to bite the hand that had fed them. Moreover, foreign affairs no longer centred simply around the confrontation between the capitalist and communist 'camps', for the western nations were willing to moderate their differences with the USSR. It was communist parties outside the Soviet Union which were particularly worrying, for they had begun to indulge in damaging criticism of the state which since 1917 had been regarded as the leader and nucleus of the world communist movement.

The western powers were willing to sign agreements on strategic arms limitation (the SALT agreements) which, although less effective than was claimed in limiting arms production, at least showed that negotiations on such a mortal issue could take place in a reasonably friendly atmosphere. In the Helsinki Final Agreement (1975) the western powers also agreed to regard as permanent the European frontiers established in 1945. This was a valuable concession, and especially helpful in consolidating the communist regimes in the German Democratic Republic and Poland. In the west it was soon said, by some critics, that the Helsinki Agreement was a 'sell-out', since the concessions made by the USSR in return were never translated from paper to reality. Such concessions involved a Soviet undertaking to relax restrictions of various personal freedoms like freedom of movement and freedom of expression. But the advantages gained by Poland and the German Democratic Republic meant that those nations were henceforth a little less dependent on the USSR, for the latter's role as defenders of their frontiers no longer seemed quite so important.

The relationship of the USSR with other communist countries was increasingly strained. Although from time to time conciliatory gestures were extended towards Peking, China remained implacably hostile. However, a new trade agreement reached in mid-1979 promised at least a breathing space in the hostilities, and possibly a change of direction. In 1969 there had been armed clashes on the Soviet-Chinese frontier, and the Soviet press for a time carried articles in which the concept of the 'Yellow Peril' was strongly implied. The death of Mao Tse-tung only seemed to make relationships worse, although Mao's aptitude in making scathing comments about Soviet policies was perhaps irreplaceable (for example, Mao on Stalin's collectivisation of agriculture: 'They drained the pond to catch the fish'.)

The existence of China, communist but estranged from the USSR, gave some of the smaller communist parties an alternative patron. They were no longer so dependent on Moscow. In Eastern and Central Europe, however, this new independence had its limits because China was not powerful enough to be regarded as protector of last resort. Leaders of ruling European communist parties had to construct and present their policies in such a way as not to antagonise the USSR beyond a certain point, while simultaneously convincing their peoples that they were willing to withstand Soviet pressures. Each in their own way, they achieved this. The most openly un-friendly communist regime, after Albania, was that of Rumania. In the late 1970s, after the admission of Vietnam to the Comecon economic block, the Soviet government wished to extend the Warsaw Pact to the Far East; this would have involved Eastern European forces in the USSR's quarrel with China, and the Rumanians led the way in rejecting the idea. But there were limits to such manoeuvres; not only did the USSR supply oil to these countries, but in 1968 it demonstrated its willingness to use armed force against them. This occurred when a rejuvenated communist regime in Czechoslovakia attempted to introduce 'socialism with a human face'. The Czech relaxation on freedom of expression might well have created demands for similar rights in other communist countries, and eventually even in the USSR. Such a freedom, the right to express and listen to alternative opinions and concepts, is the most threatening kind of freedom for a Soviet-type regime, so the Red Army invaded Czecho-slovakia and installed a leadership more palatable to Moscow. The overthrow of a genuinely popular communist government was perhaps the crucial event that settled the relationship of the various communist parties towards Moscow. The powerful parties of France and Italy were particularly outspoken, and it seemed that henceforth the Soviet regime would be regarded less as an example of Marxism in action than as simple old-style Russianism. The new realities became especially evident in the mid-1970s, when the USSR was trying to organise a 'summit' meeting of heads of the European communist parties. The latter showed no enthusiasm, anticipating that such a meeting could be expected to endorse a statement re-asserting the USSR's leading role in the communist movement. Nevertheless, the meeting was eventually held in 1976, and the Italian, French and Spanish parties were especially unsympathetic to the Soviet Union. 'Eurocommunism', the very un-Soviet line followed by the Italian and Spanish parties in particular, was attacked by the Soviet spokesman, but the final declaration did omit any mention of the Soviet leading role. Several of the keynote speeches of non-Soviet leaders were not reported in the Soviet press, since they were quite at variance with the picture habitually presented to Soviet citizens.

In the non-communist world, Soviet military missions were invited to leave Egypt in 1972, and the Sudan subsequently. In East Africa the USSR openly supported the regime of General Amin in Uganda, and was especially interested in the Horn of Africa. A treaty of friendship with Somalia, enabling among other things Soviet warships to use Somalian ports, came to a bad end in 1977 when the USSR decided to switch its support to Somalia's foe, the self-proclaimed Marxist government of Ethiopia. Soviet military help played a key role in enabling the Ethiopians to stem a Somalian onslaught. In the South Yemen, a Marxist regime offered naval facilities and airports. In 1978 a government friendly to the USSR was established in Afghanistan, and promptly called on Soviet help to maintain itself in power. All these moves were regarded with some alarm in the west, although it seemed doubtful whether any long-term benefit would result for the USSR. As so often previously, it was probable that the various regimes would use Soviet help and then, when they felt strong enough, reject it. Whether this would happen in the case of Cuba seemed doubtful, despite a relaxation of tension between that island and the USA. Cuba was heavily dependent on Soviet aid and seemed unlikely to attain economic independence. For this reason Cuba continued to be one of Moscow's staunchest allies. Another staunch ally was Vietnam, which took the Soviet side in the Russo-Chinese argument. However, when Chinese troops made a temporary but threatening excursion into Vietnam in 1979, Soviet support was confined to supplies and stirring declarations.

The Arts

In the arts, the Brezhnev regime was characterised by a relentless sterility, steadfastly preventing those who had most to say from saying it. But if the aim of the regime was to prevent the exuberance of the Krushchev years degenerating into anarchy, then the wavering between low-key repression and occasional relaxation is understandable. Walking the tightrope between gradual relaxation and uncontrollable release of pent-up tension is never easy, and is always likely to produce decisions and actions that are easy to criticise or ridicule.

One such occasion was the attempt to hold a public exhibition by 'unofficial' artists (that is, those who painted even though they were not members of the Artists' Union, and who tended to go beyond the boundaries of officially approved Socialist Realism). This open-air display of art in Moscow was attacked by the same kind of officially-recruited hooligans in the guise of 'an enraged public' as had been employed by the officials of Tsar Nicholas II in anti-semitic outrages. To make absolutely sure of wrecking the whole show, bulldozers were brought in, a technological triumph beyond the resources of the tsarist regime. All this was witnessed by foreign journalists, so it was not surprising that the image of the Soviet Union as some kind of relic from the Dark Ages was reinforced. But afterwards the local Party secretary was transferred, and approval was given to the artists to stage another exhibition.

In literature a degree of liberalisation was exemplified in the decision to publish in the Soviet Union, 36 years after it was written, Bulgakov's great novel *The Master and Margarita*. But several highly talented writers could achieve publication only in the west, not in the USSR. The censorship's yardstick seemed to be that books attacking certain sections of Soviet society might be permissible, but those which directly or indirectly questioned the whole structure or ideology of the Soviet system were to be banned.

The outstanding writer was Solzhenitsyn. Khrushchev had allowed publication of his *One Day in the Life of Ivan Denisovich*, but his subsequent and outstanding *Cancer Ward* was refused publication. Subsequently Solzhenitsyn published abroad other outstanding work, and became a sort of latter-day Tolstoy, using his reputation as one of the greatest of novelists to disseminate his uncompromising moral views. A Nobel Prize winner, he was deprived of his Soviet citizenship in 1974 and sent abroad. His multi-volume account of the inane cruelties of the Stalinist labour camp system, *The Gulag Archipelago*, was described in the Soviet press as unfounded slander, even though it simply put flesh on bare truths openly acknowledged in Khrushchev's time.

The Soviet leadership was ill-equipped, through lack of practice, to defend itself in open argument both against intelligent critics like Solzhenitsyn and the attacks by foreign political spokesmen. Such attacks came not only from populous China, bordering underpopulated Siberia, but also from communist parties from many parts of the world and from once-revolutionary regimes in the Third World, not to speak of the traditional enemies of the Soviet state. It was hardly surprising that the USSR felt beleaguered, and it stands to the credit of Brezhnev and his colleagues that this unease did not degenerate into Stalinist paranoia. It was this steadfastness in the face of problems not always obvious to outside observers that would probably be regarded as the unexciting, but real, achievement of the Brezhnev years.

Bibliography

The following titles, having been chosen primarily on the basis of their suitability for readers of this book, form a very selective list. S. Utechin's *Concise Encyclopedia of Russia* (1961) contains many suggestions for reading, and is itself a valuable source of reference. J. N. Westwood's *Endurance and Endeavour; Russian History 1812-1971* (1973), apart from providing a fairly detailed survey of 160 years of Russian history also contains a 20-page annotated bibliography. In addition, scholarly journals (*Slavic Review, Slavonic and East European Review, Russian Review, Soviet Studies, Canadian Slavonic Papers, Canadian-American Slavic Studies*) devote much of their space to reviews of new books in the field of modern Russian history.

Revolution

Chamberlin, W. *The Russian Revolution 1917-1921* (Vol. 1), 1954
Footman, D. *The Russian Revolutions*, 1962
Katkov, G. *Russia 1917*, 1967

Eye-witness anthologies

Mohrenschildt, D. von *The Russian Revolution of 1917*, 1971
Pethybridge, R. *Witnesses to the Russian Revolution*, 1964

Civil War

Chamberlin, W. *The Russian Revolution 1917-1921* (Vol. 2), 1954
Footman, D. *Civil War in Russia*, 1961

Biography

Cohen, S. *Bukharin and the Bolshevik Revolution*, 1973
Crankshaw, E. *Khrushchev; A Career*, 1966
Deutscher, I. *The Prophet Armed; Trotsky 1879-1921*, 1954
Deutscher, I. *The Prophet Unarmed; Trotsky 1921-1929*, 1954
Deutscher, I. *Stalin*, 1961
Fischer, L. *The Life of Lenin*, 1965
Reddaway, P. and Shapiro, L. *Lenin: The Man, The Theorist, The Leader*, 1967
Shukman, H. *Lenin and the Russian Revolution*, 1966

Stalinism

Conquest, R. *The Great Terror*, 1968
Lewin, M. *Lenin's Last Struggle*, 1968
Medvedev, R. *Let History Judge*, 1972
Nove, E. *Was Stalin Really Necessary?*, 1964
Rigby, T. *Stalin*, 1966
Solzhenitsyn, A. *The Gulag Archipelago 1918–1956*, 1974

Economics

Dobb, M. *Soviet Economic Development since 1917*, 1960
Nove, A. *An Economic History of the USSR*, 1969

Party and Government

McAuley, M. *Politics and the Soviet Union*, 1977

Foreign Relations

Kennan, G. *Russia and the West under Lenin and Stalin*, 1961
Ulam, A. *Expansion and Coexistence 1917–1967*, 1968

Second World War

Bialer, S. *Stalin and his Generals*, 1969
Clark, A. *Barbarossa*, 1965
Petrov, V. *June 22 1941*, 1968
Werth, A. *Russia at War 1941–1945*, 1964

Literature

Alexandrova, V. *A History of Soviet Literature 1917–1964*, 1964
Brown, E. *Russian Literature since the Revolution*, 1963
Hayward, M. *Soviet Literature in the Sixties*, 1965

Memoirs

Ginsberg, E. *Into the Whirlwind*, 1967
Khrushchev, N. *Khrushchev Remembers*, 1971

The Contemporary USSR

Brown, A., Kaser, M. *The Soviet Union since the Fall of Khrushchev*, 1975
Davies, R. et al *The Soviet Union*, 1977
Miller, J. *Life in Russia Today*, 1969
Soloukhin, V. *A Walk in Rural Russia*, 1966

INDEX

Timoshenko, Marshal, 128
Tito, President, 148, 152, 155, 173
Togliatti, P., 175
Tomsky, M., 68, 94, 96–99
Tourism, 170, 177
Trade, *see* Foreign trade, Retail trade
Trade unions, 52, 94; *see also* Working conditions
Transcaucasia, 61, 62, 201–202
Trans-Siberian Railway, 11, 38, 39, 45
Trials, show, 76, 94, 97
Trotsky, L.:
　pseudonym, 19
　in Revolution, 23
　in Civil War, 28
　recommends elections, 31
　negotiates peace with Germany, 37
　reorganises Red Army, 39–40, 41, 42
　defeats Denikin, 46, 47
　opposes attack on Warsaw, 48
　off-duty activity, 50
　Jewish origin, 51
　contempt for Stalin, 65
　political tactics, 65
　fails to reveal Lenin's notes criticising Stalin, 66
　attacks collective leadership, 67–68
　removed from War Commissariat, 68
　expelled from Politburo and Party, 68
　exile and murder, 69
　concept of world revolution, 72
　opinion on China policy, 77
　trade union policy, 94
Truman, President, 142, 144, 145
Tsars, 11, 13; *see also* Nicholas II
Tsushima, Battle of, 11
Tukhachevsky, Marshal, 48, 57, 100
Turkey, 78, 116, 146, 186
Twentieth Party Congress, 170

Ukraine, 25, 37, 44, 48, 61, 67, 110, 114, 135, 142, 192, 202
Ulbricht, W., 117, 176
United Nations, 141, 154, 194
United States of America:
　opposes Allied intervention, 37
　intervenes, 38, 46
　persuades Japan to evacuate, 39
　gives famine relief, 59
　recognises Soviet government, 76
　Lend-Lease, 137, 138, 145
　attitude towards USSR, 147, 149
　propaganda attacks on, 159
　post-war relationship, 175, 178–179

　in Cuban crisis, 177–178
　in Suez crisis, 180
　espionage activity, 186
　in arms race, 186
Urals-Kuzbass Combine, 89
U2 incident, 177, 180, 186

Varga, E., 159
Vernadsky, Professor, 143
Vietnam, 209
Virgin lands, 187–189
Vlasov movement, 135
Volga-Don Canal, 156, 170
Volga Germans, 137
Vorkuta mines, 96
Voroshilov, Marshal, 42, 45, 96, 121, 124, 172
Voznesensky, N., 124, 162–163
Vyshinsky, A., 97, 98, 99, 100, 140, 155

War Communism, 25, 55
Weygand, General, 48
White army, 25, 27, 43, 44
White Sea Canal, 96
Workers' Control, 52
Workers Opposition, 30
Working conditions, 49, 53, 94, 156, 192
World Peace Council, 153
World Revolution, 72, 77; *see also* Comintern
Wrangel, General, 43, 47

Yagoda, G., 65, 99, 100
Yalta Conference, 139, 141, 142
Yemen, South, 209
Yenukidze, A., 101
Yevtushenko, E., 191
Yezhov, N., 98, 99, 102
Yudenich, General, 46
Yugoslavia, 123, 148, 152, 173, 177

Zhdanov, A., 99, 126, 149, 155, 158, 162–163, 164
Zhukov, Marshal, 124, 129, 131, 132, 164, 167–169
Zinoviev, G.:
　Lenin's colleague, 28–29
　resigns, 31
　in collective leadership, 66
　attacked by Trotsky, 67–68
　loses posts, 68
　as Comintern head, 73
　economic views, 84
　liquidated, 96–99
'Zinoviev Letter', 76
Zoshchenko, M., 158

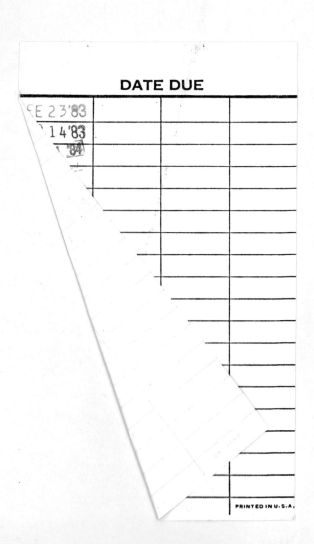

DATE DUE

FE 23'83			
14'83			
'84			